NEWS OF THE BLACK FEAST

Borgo Press Books by BRIAN STABLEFORD

Algebraic Fantasies and Realistic Romances: More Masters of Science Fiction
Beyond the Colors of Darkness and Other Exotica
Changelings and Other Metamorphic Tales
A Clash of Symbols: The Triumph of James Blish
The Cosmic Perspective and Other Black Comedies
The Cure for Love and Other Tales of the Biotech Revolution
The Devil's Party: A Brief History of Satanic Abuse
The Dragon Man: A Novel of the Future
Firefly: A Novel of the Far Future
The Gardens of Tantalus and Other Delusions
Glorious Perversity: The Decline and Fall of Literary Decadence
Gothic Grotesques: Essays on Fantastic Literature
The Haunted Bookshop and Other Apparitions
Heterocosms: Science Fiction in Context and Practice
In the Flesh and Other Tales of the Biotech Revolution
The Innsmouth Heritage and Other Sequels
Jaunting on the Scoriac Tempests and Other Essays on Fantastic Literature
The Moment of Truth: A Novel of the Future
News of the Black Feast and Other Random Reviews
An Oasis of Horror: Decadent Tales and Contes Cruels
Opening Minds: Essays on Fantastic Literature
Outside the Human Aquarium: Masters of Science Fiction, Second Edition
The Path of Progress and Other Black Melodramas
Slaves of the Death Spiders and Other Essays on Fantastic Literature
The Sociology of Science Fiction
Space, Time, and Infinity: Essays on Fantastic Literature
The Tree of Life and Other Tales of the Biotech Revolution
Yesterday's Bestsellers: A Voyage Through Literary History

NEWS OF THE BLACK FEAST

AND OTHER RANDOM REVIEWS

by

Brian Stableford

THE BORGO PRESS

An Imprint of Wildside Press LLC

MMIX

*I.O. Evans Studies in the Philosophy
and Criticism of Literature*
ISSN 0271-9061

Number Forty-Three

www.wildsidepress.com

FIRST EDITION

CONTENTS & ACKNOWLEDGMENTS

Introduction 9

Part One: News of the Black Feast

First Series

1 (*Screem* Winter 1995) 15
2 (*Screem* Fall 1995) 17
3 (Submitted to *Screem* on 2 December 1995) 20

Second Series

1 (*Bats and Red Velvet* 21; May 1997) 23
2 (*BRV Magazine* 22; September 1997) 26
3 (*BRV Magazine* 23; February 1998) 29
4 (*BRV Magazine* 24; June 1998) 32
5 (Submitted to *BRV Magazine* on 2 July 1998) 34

Part Two: Hollywood Novel Reviews

(Submitted to *Hollywood: The 100 Best Novels* on 13
   February 1995) 37

Part Three: Reviews from *Necrofile*

"Return of the Dark Angel": *The Angel of the West Window*
   (Gustav Meyrink). #3 (Winter 1992) 57
"Wales of Terror": *Candlenight* (Phil Rickman). #4 (Spring
   1992) 60
"The Devil Made Them Do It": *Satanskin* (James Havoc)
   & *Red Stains* ed. Jack Hunter. #6 (Fall 1992) 63

"How Modern Horror was Born": *Tales of the Dead: The Ghost Stories of the Villa Deodati* (ed. Terry Hale) & *Fantastic Tales* (I. U. Tarchetti). #7 (Winter 1993) 67

"Somme Enchanted Evening": *Lovedeath* (Dan Simmons). #11 (Winter 1994) 72

"Double, Double, Toil and Trouble": *The Dark Domain* (Stefan Grabinski). #12 (Spring 1994) 79

"Life's a Bitch, and Then...": *Strange Angels* (Kathe Koja). #13 (Summer 1994) 82

"In the Prison of the Past": *Nevermore* (William Hjortsberg). #15 (Winter 1995) 84

"Lust in Vain": *Love in Vein* (ed. Poppy Z. Brite), *Love Bites* (ed. Amarantha Knight) & *Blood Kiss* (ed. Cecilia Tan). #16 (Spring 1995) 88

"Mazy Modern Monsters: *The 37th Mandala* (Marc Laidlaw). #20 (Spring 1996) 93

"Our Critics, Our Vampires: *Our Vampires, Ourselves* (Nina Auerbach). #21 (Summer 1996) 95

"As in Ancient Days": *Tales of Zothique* & *The Book of Hyperborea* (Clark Ashton Smith). #22 (Fall 1996) 99

"The Body (and Mind) Fantastic": *Writing Horror and the Body* (Linda Badley), *Sacrament* (Clive Barker) & *Servant of the Bones* (Anne Rice). #23 (Winter 1997) 102

"Brutal Judgment": *The Panic Hand* (Jonathan Carroll). #24 (Spring 1997) 107

"Love-Sickness and its Consequences: *The Dealings of Daniel Kesserich* (Fritz Leiber) & *Asylum* (Patrick McGrath). #25 (Summer 1997) 110

"When the Chill Sets In": *Night Relics* & *Winter Tides* (James P. Blaylock). #27 (Winter 1998) 113

"Ghosts and Scholars": *A Night with Mephistopheles* (Henry Ferris) & *The Haunted Chair and Other Stories* (Richard Marsh). #29 (Summer 1998) 118

"Graves and Zombis": *Darker Angels* (S. P. Somtow) #30 (Fall 1998) 123

"Roma Mater": *Judgment of Tears* (Kim Newman). #31 (Winter 1999) 127

"Blood Brothers": *The Cleft and Other Odd Tales* (Gahan Wilson) & *The Barrens and Others* (F. Paul Wilson). #31 (Winter 1999) 131

"Burdens of the Past": *Fog Heart* (Thomas Tessier) & *Head Injuries* (Conrad Williams). #32 (Spring 1999) 135

"NOW is the Winter of our Discontent": *Satan Wants Me* (Robert Irwin). #32 (Spring 1999) 138

Part Four: Reviews from *The New York Review of Science Fiction*

King of Morning, Queen of Day (Ian McDonald). #41 (January 1992).. 142
The Norton Book of Science Fiction: North American Science Fiction 1960-1990 (ed. Ursula K. Le Guin & Brian Attebery). #62 (October 1993) 145
The Breath of Suspension (Alexander Jablokov). #76 (December 1994)... 158
Days of Cain (J. R. Dunn). #113 (January 1998)........................ 161
The Fantasy Hall of Fame (ed. Robert Silverberg). #121 (September 1998) 164
King Rat & Perdido Street Station (China Miéville). #140 (April 2000)... 176

Index.. 181
About the Author 201

INTRODUCTION

My publication log records a total of 387,000 words of reviews published between 1968 and the present day (21 August 2006). The record is not complete, because there are undoubtedly some published reviews of which I never received copies, and which were therefore never entered into the log. Nor does that total include reviews that were written but failed to achieve publication for one reason or another. The present selection is, therefore, a relatively small sample of my output. It is heavily biased towards recent years, in the interests of maintaining some slight semblance of contemporary relevance. This may, of course, be a futile gesture, given that many newly-issued books nowadays disappear from the shelves virtually overnight and the returns are often pulped. As all habitual readers will have observed (if that species is not yet extinct), it is far from uncommon for books published in the late 1990s to have vanished from human ken, while large numbers of copies of books published in the early 1970s—in much larger print-runs, which sat around in bookshops for months rather than minutes—are available from ABEbooks for little more than the cost of the postage.

When I first started reviewing books—in 1968—for Peter Weston's fanzine *Speculation*, I had no income and was so strapped for cash that I was delighted to discover that one could get books for free simply by volunteering to write about them. Nowadays, although I am once again in a situation where I have no significant income, that arrangement doesn't seem like much of a bargain, although I still write to *Foundation*'s reviews editor now and again to volunteer my services if and when a book is published that I am desperate to acquire but too parsimonious to buy.

In 1968 reviewing was an occasional self-indulgence; I worked exclusively for *Speculation* until 1971, when that magazine died, and did no more until I was recruited to *Foundation*'s extensive panel of reviewers by Christopher Priest in 1974. Chris did try to explain to me what Peter Weston never had, which is that book reviewing is essentially a form of advertising carried out—unlike most forms of advertising—in a spirit of reciprocal altruism, but I was too stupid to get my head around the idea. I persisted in saying what I actually thought of the books I reviewed (sometimes on the basis of ill-considered knee-jerk responses of which I later repented) instead of restricting myself diplomatically to carefully-measured praise. Chris was kind enough to bin most of my negative reviews, but I was never grateful for his educational efforts and persisted in my evil ways. It was a foolish thing to do, and I regret it now, but the habit became ingrained and I never contrived to shake it off.

I began reviewing books on a wholesale basis in 1976, when I chanced to find myself living in the same town as Christopher Fowler (not the author and film-maker of that name but the man who subsequently married Pat Cadigan), who was then editing the British Science Fiction Association journal *Vector*. In order to save postage, Chris rarely remailed the review copies he received, but let them mount up in huge piles in his bedroom until opportunities arose to redistribute them by hand. Anyone who called at his home could exit with a pile of books, the only condition being that for every desirable title one seized upon with glee one had to "take some of the rubbish", thus preventing the titles no one actually wanted to review from creating a permanent log-jam. This did not help me to break my habit of saying rude things about what I considered to be bad books.

I was *Vector*'s most prolific reviewer for some years, but the link was abruptly broken in 1980, when the journal was delivered into new editorial hands. By then I had diversified into several other outlets, and was able to maintain production on a wholesale basis. For much of the early 1980s I attempted single-handedly to cover all native British sf and fantasy for Bob Collins' critical journal *Fantasy Review*. None of that early work is sampled here, however—or ever will be sampled in any similar volume—because it was all done before I acquired a word-processor, and no electronic copies are available for cutting and pasting.

I have always been a painfully slow learner, but my early exploits in *Speculation* and *Foundation* apprised me soon enough of the then-seemingly-amazing fact that the writers I was reviewing actually read the reviews I wrote. It took a few years longer for me to cotton on to the fact that they were almost certainly the only people who ever did—or were, at least, the only people who actually cared what I wrote. This discovery brought a certain strange sense of freedom, in that I began to figure that if the damn things were, in essence, mere space fillers of no real interest to anyone (unless they happened to provide quotable advertising copy) then there was no reason why I should not express myself therein more openly and more honestly than I ever felt free to do in work that had to be more carefully tailored to potential editorial requirements. For this reason, many of the book reviews I did in the 1990s were far more exemplary of my natural rhetorical style than anything else I wrote in that or any other period.

I say that the reviews I produced in the 1990s are more typical of my *style* because they are, for the most part, exercises in mannerism, even though they also reflect my actual attitudes to the genres in which I work and my honest opinions of the specific works under consideration. As with all attempts to be witty—and the most ambitious of them do attempt to be witty, in my own admittedly-bizarre fashion—they are mostly conspicuously artificial in their rhetorical method. I rarely found so little of interest in an item under review as to persuade me to express my views in a colorless tone of dismal banality.

Authors occasionally took great exception to my rhetorical methods—one review not included here drew a particularly eloquent and heartfelt response from John Kessel, to the effect that, although I was entitled to my opinion of his work, he objected in the strongest possible terms to the manner in which I had expressed it—but years passed before the realization eventually hit home that I really had no reason or excuse for inflicting such pain and gave up reviewing altogether, except in rare cases of avid book-hunger or in even rarer cases in which authors actually asked me to review their works. These days, I rarely insult a book unless the person responsible for it has previously insulted me, or specifically requests me to write a review of the work in the full knowledge that I will hate it—something that, surprisingly enough, does occasionally happen.

In essence, therefore, this collection is mostly a record of adventures in perversity, much of it (including all my favorite bits) being illustrative of a sick taste for weird comedy that I find few other opportunities to indulge. One of the more extreme examples of work in this vein gives the collection its title, which I employed on two series of review columns written for the Gothic music fanzines *Screem* and *Bats and Red Velvet* (shortened in later issues to *BRV*). Gothic fanzines are, of course, the perfect medium in which to indulge in flamboyantly perverse comedy. The last column in each series was written for an issue of the magazine that never appeared. There is some repetition in the introductions to the two series, and

11

some slight overlap with other reviews reprinted later in this volume, but the duplicated material could not be deleted without injuring the flow; I apologize for any irritation this may cause.

In the interests of contrast, I have followed "News From the Black Feast" in these pages with a group of reviews I did for an ill-fated book of essays on *The 100 Best Hollywood Novels*—one of an extensive series of volumes launched by said Pringle's account of *The 100 Best Science Fiction Novels* and Michael Moorcock's *The 100 Best Fantasy Novels*. I had previously contributed to *The 100 Best Horror Novels*, which editors Steve Jones and Kim Newman distributed to 100 different authors, and *The 100 Best Detectives*, edited by Max Jakubowski. The publisher of most of these works, Xanadu, never got around to printing *The 100 Best Hollywood Novels*, although a complete text was delivered by editor David Pringle, so this is the first time these reviews have appeared in print. They represent a more orthodox style of review-article writing, in which one is bound to accentuate every positive in order to justify the inclusion of the text under consideration in what is supposedly a highly selective list, and one has to work to a very specific word-limit.

The next set of items comes from a critical journal published by Marc Michaud's Necronomicon Press from 1992-99, edited by Stefan Dziemianowicz. I always held the publisher and editor in the highest regard, and some of the work I did for *Necrofile* was the most pleasurable and zestful reviewing I ever did. Two of my favorite exemplars were reprinted in an earlier Borgo Press volume, *Slaves of the Death Spiders*, and I have omitted some of the less interesting examples from what remained, but the sampler provided here represents the bulk of my endeavors, and the chronological arrangement probably offers the most revealing account of the evolution of my reviewing style in the relevant period. I did not notice at first that the editor was adding supposedly-apposite titles to my reviews, but as soon as I did I started providing my own. The contents page gives the titles used in the magazine, but I have omitted titles that were not mine from the reviews in the text, and retained my own title in one case where it was changed by the editor.

The final batch of reviews is a selection from my contributions to David Hartwell's *New York Review of Science Fiction*. Although *Foundation* was founded may years earlier, the *NYRSF*'s more frequent publishing schedule—which it has now maintained with amazing assiduousness for the best part of twenty years—means that it soon overtook it in terms of the number of issues it had produced.

It therefore published far more of my non-fiction during the 1990s, including reviews, than any other periodical. David and his various associate editors were very flexible in allowing me to review eccentric works that happened to take my fancy as well as books they sent me, and were always prepared to let me ramble on at ludicrously excessive length if and when the mood took me. Lots of NYRSF reviews remain to provide the bedrock of a second collection of this sort should I ever have cause to produce one but the ones featured here provide a typically quirky set of samples.

—Brian Stableford
August 2006

NEWS OF THE BLACK FEAST, BY BRIAN STABLEFORD

PART ONE

NEWS OF THE BLACK FEAST

First Series

i.

We are partway through the 1990s; it is *fin-de-siècle* time again. One era slouches into senile decrepitude while another burns, phoenix-like, in the expectation of its birth. Since the pace of progress first accelerated to become perceptible within the span of a human life such periods have been marked by a sense of terminus, if not actual apocalypse. This sense of living in the Last Days inevitably brings forth in civilized persons a capacity to take suave and somber delight in all that is dark, morbid, cruel, perverse and extreme. The end of the eighteenth century produced Blake's "prophetic books", Matthew Gregory Lewis's Gothic extravaganza *The Monk* and the Marquis de Sade's *Justine* and *Juliette*. The end of the nineteenth produced the Decadent Movements of Europe, which were provided with a scathingly sarcastic and magnificently bizarre philosophy by Joris-Karl Huysmans' *À rebours*: the "yellow book" that corrupted Dorian Gray.

Jean Des Esseintes, the hero of *À rebours*, took the utmost care in preparing a cultural menu for the "black feast" of nineteenth-century Decadence. We have had a hundred years of progress since then, and much has been added to the darker stock of the human imagination; Bram Stoker's *Dracula*—a product of the 1890s—has been a thousand times reborn, emerging at last as the Byronic hero he was always meant to be; Gothic imagery is back in fashion yet again, in yet another new form. We are telling the old tales again, but we are telling them in our own way. We are deepening the darkness, reaching towards limits we have never reached before.

15

Decadent fiction has many forms and many faces. It is respectful of the past, sometimes to the point of antiquarian eccentricity, but its primary concern has always been the future—not the public aspect that is future history, but the private aspect that is personal oblivion. Thus, we may note, on the one hand, the hesitant emergence of Thomas Ligotti, a gentleman Decadent of the Old School, punctiliously mannered in matters of style and relentlessly downbeat in matters of substance, while we observe, on the other hand, the meteoric rise of Poppy Z. Brite, who is to contemporary horror fiction what Rachilde was to the French Decadents, writing with all the bold, aggressive intensity of vivid youth.

Ligotti's *Noctuary* (Robinson 1994) is his third collection, bringing together a handful of recent stories—including the brilliant novella "The Tsalal", in which a whole town becomes possessed by a lone demonic inhabitant, and a marvelously nasty-minded account of "Mrs Rinaldi's Angel"—with those of his contributions to small press magazines that had hitherto been considered too slight for collection. It is good to have the latter items preserved; Des Esseintes was of the opinion that the prose-poem is the most perfect form of Decadent Art, and it would be a tragedy were the theories of crass editors to deny modern writers any opportunity to employ the form.

Brite's second novel, *Drawing Blood* (Roc, 1994), is slightly disappointing; although much more tightly-focused than her first it lacks the jagged cutting edge that gave *Lost Souls* its power. By the time the haunted house that is the plot's true protagonist finally rouses itself to show what it can *really* do, the reader has been becalmed for 200 pages in a homosexual love story that is only mildly disturbed by absent-minded twitches of supernatural malevolence. By far the best of Brite, to date at least, is to be found in *Swamp Fetus* (Borderlands Press, 1993), which runs a remarkably elastic gamut from the self-consciously sardonic "His Mouth Will Taste of Wormwood" to the disturbingly earnest "Calcutta, Lord of Nerves" and the deftly surreal "The Ash of Memory, the Dust of Desire". Whether or not Des Esseintes was right about prose-poetry there is no doubt that the Decadent sensibility cannot readily be extended to take in the pedestrian kinds of character-development and dialogue that novels demand, and it is earnestly to be hoped that Brite will continue to produce short work of this fabulous quality, for art's sake, alongside the novels she will be required to produce for her bank account's sake.

Swamp Fetus is published by one of the many small presses now springing up in rebellion against the ossification that has overtaken mass-market publishing as its accountants embark on the simple-minded (and futile) quest for the lowest common denominator of public taste. It is to the small presses that we must look for the true cultural heart and soul of the present day. One that does sterling, if mostly backward-looking, work is Dedalus, whose books are marketed in the US by Hippocrene. The latest in its long-running series of "Decadence from Dedalus" is *The Dedalus Book of German Decadence: Voices of the Abyss* (Dedalus, 1994), whose contents serve to remind us that much of the produce of the last *fin de siècle* still remains hidden because it was considered too obscene to be translated into English at the time. This collection includes Thomas Mann's Wagner-inspired tale of brother/sister incest "The Blood of the Wälsungs" (which could not be published at all when it was first written because of objections from the author's family) and George Trakl's fine prose-poem "Desolation" (whose author cemented his Decadent credentials by committing suicide in a lunatic asylum at the age of 27); its brightest star is, however, the dream-fantasy novella "Androgyne" by the Polish writer Stanislaus Przybyszewski, which features an altogether more extraordinary kind of incest.

Also from a specialist small press is *Daughters of Darkness: Lesbian Vampire Stories* (Cleis, 1993). Apart from J. Sheridan Le Fanu's ground-breaking "Carmilla" all the works included are contemporary, and all are written by women—an editorial policy that has the unfortunate effect of omitting Jean Lorrain's classic tale of lesbian vampiric pedophilia "The Glass of Blood" but which otherwise works well. Jody Scott's *I, Vampire* and Elaine Bergstrom's *Daughter of the Night* are among the novel-length works tantalizingly sampled, but the story that outdoes all the others in terms of its calculated Decadence and its striking originality is Pat Califia's "The Vampire", which applies the logic of natural selection with exactly the kind of skilful perversity the 1990s require.

Further reports on the catering for today's black feast will follow in due course....

ii.

One of the fascinations that inevitably increase along with *fin-de-siècle* consciousness is literary Satanism: the attempt to make apologetic cases for fallen angels, by means of which they become heroic rebels and Promethean helpers of mankind rather than agents of damnation. William Blake kicked the whole thing off in the 1790s by observing that Milton had been of the Devil's party without knowing it; Anatole France graced the 1890s with his account of "The Human Tragedy" (in *The Well of Saint Clare*, 1895), in which an honest priest finds that his only friend on earth is Satan. The present *fin-de-siècle* offers us *Metal Angel* (Roc 1994) by Nancy Springer, in which Volos, a dropout from the divine choir, dons frail flesh in order to become an exponent of the devil's music—rock music that is (the text assures us) nearly but not quite heavy metal.

God's agents punish Volos according to their horrible habit, damning him for his innocence as well as his temerity, but, like the hero he is, he keeps right on rocking. While *en route* to his crucifixion and resurrection, he contrives to save the soul of his lyric-writer and her pious husband from the awful sink of iniquity that is modern Fundamentalism. (Nancy Springer married a Lutheran minister, but was able to liberate him with the money she made from her writing.)

Demons of other kinds continue to haunt and harry us, of course, but as the countdown to the Millennium eases through single figures it is the irony of that predicament that comes gleefully to the fore in cautionary tales like Christopher Fowler's *Spanky* (Warner 1994). The reader knows all along that the obligingly demonic Spanky is not directing the narrator's make-over without an ulterior motive, and is not in the least surprised when seduction turns to blackmail and the yuppie dream to splatterpunk nightmare, but the whole point is that there can be no real surprises in a parable like this. The better the build-up—and Spanky's deft resolution of the protagonist's attitude problem is beautifully stylish in its cynicism—the more graceful the fall becomes. The plot pretends that the narrator is the hero, or at least the victim, but this is the 1990s and connoisseurs of black revelry know that it is Spanky we ought to be cheering for, and Spanky we ought to mourn when the narrator wins his Pyrrhic victory.

Most literary Satanists modestly confine their analyses to scrupulous consideration of the petty Satanism of human beings. The Marquis de Sade was one of the key figures of the eighteenth *fin-de-siècle* in this respect, and the fabulous Rachilde was one of the stars of the nineteenth. Now, at long last, more of Rachilde's works are becoming available in English, including *The Marquise de Sade* (Dedalus 1994), translated by Liz Heron. The story chronicles with minute and loving care the psychological evolution and sentimental education of a cruel and calculating *femme fatale*. It is well enough done to leave one wondering why all women weren't that way in 1887—and why so precious few of them are even in 1995.

Some literary Satanists, on the other hand, have always been prepared to go the Whole Hog. On the evidence of previous "Vampire Chronicles"—which seemed to have accepted the irrelevance of God and the Devil to the vampire condition—one would not have expected Anne Rice to be one of them, but she is nothing if not surprising. In *Memnoch the Devil* (Chatto & Windus, 1995) the eponymous Adversary wants Lestat to play for his team and tilt the balance of the ongoing conflict in his favor. Once Lestat has gone to Heaven and had a quiet word with God, though, he seems to forget that he too was once a petty Satan, proud to be beyond the scope of human notions of Good and Evil. This is not entirely surprising, given that Memnoch (who just *hates* being called Satan) is also on God's side, the War in Heaven lovingly detailed in the *Book of Enoch* here being reduced to a Slight Difference of Opinion in Heaven.

Anne Rice seems to think that once Memnoch has explained to Lestat and the reader exactly what Hell is really *for*, even the reader will be on God's side. Those of us who have read *Metal Angel*, however, know far better; Volos has already assured and convinced us that spending all eternity in God's muzak-filled Heaven, utterly committed to never-ending loyalty, gratitude and love, would be Absolute Hell for any right-minded rock fan. Even without such good advice, regular readers who have come to know and love Lestat rather better than his creator seems to do, will know perfectly well that anyone proud to be a vampire would not deign to look twice at this carefully-reinvented God's ridiculously old-fashioned Heaven; any vampire with taste would want music to make the blood sing, not music to trumpet the everlasting glory of the Divine Synthesizer and the servile labours of his Satanic Sampler.

If Lestat were half the vampire—or even half the man—he used to be, he would have found a much better use for the gift that Christ hands over to him at the crucifixion than the plot of *Memnoch the Devil* allows him. He might, perhaps, have used it to wipe his nose, or to mop up the spillage of his next few dozen victims. He would *not* have used it to revive the ailing fortunes of the Catholic faith. Even the most diehard Decadent has to admit, though, that some of its most eloquent spokesmen didn't quite stay the course. Like his most famous creation, Jean Des Esseintes, Joris-Karl Huysmans recommitted himself to the Catholic faith—hopefully for the same reason, which was that it was the most picturesque and the most absurd fantasy of them all—and if Anne Rice should choose to do likewise, she might still be reckoned to be following a noble tradition of sorts.

iii.

Apocalyptic fantasies are hardy perennials of the perfumed garden of Decadent literature, but the advent of a *fin-de-siècle* period tends to intensify their production, or at least their appreciation. Decadent fantasies of this kind are, of course, sharply distinguished from alarmist accounts of ecocatastrophe or nuclear war by virtue of their connoisseur's view of creeping disruption and their blithely fatalistic attitude to the delicious inevitability of doom.

One connoisseur's view of creeping disruption is elaborately worked out in Storm Constantine's *Stalking Tender Prey* (Creed/Signet 1995). This is the first volume of a trilogy whose culmination will presumably arrive in ample time for the Millennium, to which it looks forward with rapt anticipation. The story serves to introduce an extensive cast of characters, central among which are Peverel Othman and Lily Winter, who are reincarnations of Shemyaza—the leader of the fallen angels in the apocryphal *Book of Enoch*—and Istahar, the human woman with who he fell in love. The Grigori (also known as the Nephilim), who are the contemporary descendants of the progeny of the initial miscegenation of Shemyaza's rebel "angels", are still very much alive and active, and desperately uncertain as to the significance of Shemyaza's return. They are all sure that it portends some sweeping change, but none of them knows what, or how best to respond. Although this first volume ends—as first volumes of trilogies tend to do—with a frustrating anti-climax, there can be no doubt that the narrative groundwork has been laid for an eventual conclusion of cataclysmic dimensions, when Shemyaza will return in all his ambiguous glory.

The most blithely fatalistic of all attitudes to the inevitability of doom can be savored to the full (at last!) in a definitive collection of Clark Ashton Smith's *Tales of Zothique* (Necronomicon Press, 1995). This uses corrected texts wherever possible and provides a definitive chronology of the series, which examines with adamantine cynicism the death-throes of a dying Earth reclaimed by all the corruptions of sorcery and demonic possession. Although they were written during the 1930s the tales represent the last gasp of a particular chain of descent that led from the fantasists of the French Decadent Movement through the Bohemians of the West Coast of America to the calculated extreme of exoticism cultivated by a few members of the Lovecraft school; of these, Smith was by far the boldest, constructing fantasies gaudier and more remote from quotidian existence than any that had ever been imagined before. The production of this final version of his most Decadent tales is both timely and very welcome.

Another American who became entranced by and involved in the Decadent Movements of the 1890s was Vincent O'Sullivan, a friend of Ernest Dowson, Aubrey Beardsley and Oscar Wilde, who outlived them all, although he eventually died in miserable circumstances in Paris not long after it fell to the Nazis in World War II. *Master of Fallen Years: Complete Supernatural Stories of Vincent O'Sullivan* (Ghost Story Press, 1995) edited and introduced by Jessica Amanda Salmonson is an excellent collection, reproducing the relevant items from *A Book of Bargains* (1896), which was one of the key texts of the English Decadent Movement, and adding a series of pieces rescued from the obscurity of various magazines. The fifteen tales range from the classic *conte cruel* "The Monkey and Basil Holderness" to the marvelous neo-Gothic novella "Verschoyle's House". The fine extended prose-poem "Will" is one of several pieces savoring the aesthetics of decease, and most of the eight poems added as a bonus do likewise. The book is a godsend to collectors, whose chances of assembling a set of these tales has long been negligible, and it makes fascinating reading for everyone capable of appreciating what O'Sullivan (in a prefatory essay also reprinted here) called "the kind of fiction called morbid".

Our particular *fin-de-siècle* has, of course, succeeded in extrapolating the kind of morbidity that O'Sullivan could only extrapolate individually to a much broader generality. The cosmic apocalypticism of Clark Ashton Smith is an extreme that cannot stand overmuch repetition but its establishment as the further end of the spectrum has allowed easier access to fantasies that combine a secure anchorage in the familiar with imagery embracing awesome vistas of exotic possibility. Like Storm Constantine, Freda Warrington is fond of weaving the mythology of fallen angels and the iconography of vampirism into effective tales of erotic obsession, and *The Dark Blood of Poppies* (Macmillan, 1995) carries forward the series begun with *A Taste of Blood Wine* and *A Dance in Blood Velvet*. Here the dancer Violette Leduc—who might or might not be possessed by the spirit of Lilith in much the same way that Peverel Othman is possessed by that of Shemyaza—moves to centre stage, as would-be predator upon the blood of the mortal Robyn and potential victim of a conspiracy of vampires who believe that they are God's appointed scourge for the destruction of Lilith. Here the looming apocalypse threatens the Crystal Ring—the parallel world created by the collective unconscious of humankind—rather than the mundane world in which the characters also live (which is guaranteed at least a further threescore-years-and-ten by virtue of the tale being set in the roaring twenties) but that does not detract at all from the novel's dark sensibility.

Only time will tell, of course, whether the world we know and try to love will actually end—and, if so, whether it makes its exit with a bang or a whimper—but that is not the point of Decadent apocalyptic fantasy. True Decadents have no interest in vulgar prophecy, which is best left to charlatans; they know full well that nothing in fiction is devalued by virtue of being a lie, provided only that it be a lie of grandiose proportions. In a way, a world that never actually ended but nevertheless contrived to preserve an urgent sense that it was forever *about to end* might qualify as the best of all possible worlds for the connoisseur of literary morbidity. Given this, there is surely much in the history of our own century for which we ought to be truly thankful, as we lurch towards its end.

NEWS OF THE BLACK FEAST

Second Series

i.

We are within four years of the century's end. Since the pace of progress first became conspicuous, the end of every century has been marked by a sense of terminus: a *fin-de-siècle* sensibility that leads particularly sensitive individuals to take somber delight in the contemplation of darkness and degeneration. Although such individuals know full well that history must and will continue, they mask that awareness with the conviction that the new can only arise, phoenix-like, from the burnt-out ashes of the old.

The closing years of the eighteenth and nineteenth centuries both saw a remarkable upsurge in works of art that celebrated the morbid, the extreme, the visionary and the frankly bizarre. One produced the Marquis de Sade's *Justine* and *Juliette*, Goya's *Caprichos*, William Blake's "prophetic writings", T. R. Malthus' *Essay on Population* and a host of Gothic novels, including Matthew Gregory Lewis's *The Monk*; the other produced Oscar Wilde, Tchaikovsky's *Pathétique*, Bram Stoker's *Dracula*, Havelock Ellis's *Studies in the Psychology of Sex* and a wholesale Decadent Movement in France whose ideas and ideals—crystallized out by Joris-Karl Huysmans' *À rebours*—were exported throughout the Western world.

Now it is our turn.

Modern fantasy fiction has, of course, taken aboard *fin-de-siècle* consciousness with an enthusiasm of which no earlier century was capable. Its products are amazingly prolific, sprawling across a spectrum that extends from the works of such defiant amateurs as Thomas Ligotti and D. F. Lewis to the best-selling novels of Clive Barker and Anne Rice. Modern art is replete with flagrant images of death and decay, whether one considers comic books or the candidates for the annual Turner prize.

In the eighteenth century a Decadent lifestyle was the prerogative of rich aristocrats like William Beckford of Fonthill Abbey (author of *Vathek*) and Horace Walpole of Strawberry Hill (author of *The Castle of Otranto*). A century later, aristocrats like Count Stanislaus Eric Stenbock found their fortunes evaporating, while *nouveau riche* aesthetes like Oscar Wilde found the ones they made impossible to hang on to, as the last noxious gasp of Victorian morality blew them away. In our democratic era, however, a Decadent lifestyle is accessible at street level, available to any and all dissenters from middle-class notions of respectability. Its most blatant contemporary manifestation is, of course, the Goth subculture, whose name pays due but ironic homage to the architectural and literary ambitions of Beckford and Walpole. In 1992 Mick Mercer's *Gothic Rock* was able to describe the Goth subculture purely in terms of music and costume but his new guide-book, *The Hex Files: The Goth Bible* (B. T. Batsford) dutifully records the manner in which its fringes have begun to overlap and fuse with vampire fandom, neo-paganism and the S/M fetish scene.

The annotated snapshot of the Goth scene offered by *The Hex Files* is likely to be controversial, especially for its insistence that one-time core bands like The Sisters of Mercy, The Mission and Fields of the Nephilim are now so passé that even bands that appear to be continuing their work—*e.g.*, The Merry Thoughts and The Garden of Delight—can be casually dismissed as purveyors of worn out goods. The book makes a conscientious attempt to give credit where it is due within the British scene—which is, of course, its core concern—but the author makes it abundantly clear that such progress as the genre is making is led from elsewhere. The bands he regards as the cutting-edge of Goth/Dark Wave music include Italy's Ataraxia, France's Corpus Delicti, Germany's Sopor Aeternus and the Ensemble of Shadows and the USA's London After Midnight.

It is worth noting that all these bands share certain characteristics, which link them as securely to the typical concerns of *fin-de-siècle* culture as to the Goth subculture of the 1980s. Their writers give every indication of being widely-read, poetically ambitious and familiar with a wide range of musical styles—styles that they are attempting to combine in a quasi-alchemical fashion. Ataraxia and Sopor Aeternus, in particular, have combined very disparate influences in such a way that their work fuses ancient and modern musical forms in a calculatedly grotesque but highly effective fashion—a chimerical ambition that is carried over into their exotic and multi-lingual lyrics. Corpus Delicti and London After Midnight are more conventional, but they too have cultivated distinctive musical mannerisms that are conscientiously echoed in their self-presentation and their lyrics.

Given this, it is hardly surprising that the fan base mapped out in *The Hex Files* includes numerous periodicals and societies whose interests are literary and philosophical as well as musical and imagistic. The common concerns of the subcultures mapped in *The Hex Files* echo common concerns of the countercultures of the 1790s and 1890s; in Mick Mercer's eyes, at least, Goth subculture is expanding to embrace many, if not all, of the issues addressed by Huysmans in *À rebours*: a book that laid before its readers an entire "black feast" of blithe perversities.

In literary terms, as in musical terms, the black feast has several courses. For starters, it offers new editions of the classics of the last *fin-de-siècle*. A number of small publishers—most notably Dedalus, Creation (the publishing arm of Creation Records) and Atlas—are heavily committed to such rescue work, and they are now joined by a newcomer, whose debut publication is Count Stenbock's *Studies of Death* (Durtro Press, 1996). Stenbock made up for his slender literary productivity with his lifestyle, which Arthur Symons described as "bizarre, fantastic, feverish, eccentric, extravagant, morbid and perverse", although it is possible that he exaggerated slightly. To the contents of the 1894 collection *Studies of Death*—which include the excellent *conte cruel* "Viol d'Amor" and the pre-Stokerian "The True Story of a Vampire"—editor David Tibet has added the fine allegorical werewolf story "The Other Side" and two translations from Balzac. In its mannered tone and flippantly scandalous content, Stenbock's work is typical of the effete variety of Decadent consciousness.

The main course of modern Decadence is, of course, provided by contemporary writers dealing with twentieth century settings. These include a self-appointed "Unholy Trinity of Dark Wave authors" who all receive due notice in *The Hex Files*: Cleo Cordell, Storm Constantine and Freda Warrington. Storm Constantine's *Scenting Hallowed Blood* (Signet, 1996) is the centerpiece of a trilogy begun in *Stalking Tender Prey*, which features the miraculous re-emergence of the Biblical fallen angels whose progeny were the Nephilim of *Genesis*. Here the reincarnate Shemyaza prepares to liberate the magical power that has locked up like a slumbering ser-

25

pent within the Earth's crust, ending the old world and preparing for a braver-than-brave new one, whose nature will become clear in the third volume (due in the Autumn). The zestful climax of the present volume offers a tantalizing hint of the grandeur to come.

For dessert, there are the contemporary novelists who delight in sweet reminiscences of *fins-de-siècles* past. Dracula has been more active in the 1990s than ever before, and will doubtless become more active still in this, his centenary year. A sweeping celebration of 1890s Gothicism is provided by Tom Holland's *Supping with Panthers* (Little Brown, 1996), in which Lord Byron, hero of Holland's *The Vampyre*, rubs shoulders with Bram Stoker while Dr. John Eliot (a Sherlock Holmes clone) becomes ever-more-intimately involved with a marvelously sinister *femme fatale* who is an avatar of Lilith, earth-mother of all vampires—an involvement that ultimately leads to a series of gruesome murders in Whitechapel. This series too will continue in 1997, in a volume that reaches further back in history to a year which, although not at a century's end, seemed nevertheless to many Bible-readers to be pregnant with the apocalypse: 1666. Holland's work seals the continuity that connects our sense of terminus with that of previous eras, reminding us that the decline and fall of Decadence is something that never actually ends, but is paradoxically eternal

1997 will undoubtedly bring many more enrichments and embellishments to the black feast of our *fin-de-siècle*. Literary, cinematic and musical elements will all be featured, and will be available for quasi-alchemical combination by sensitive gourmets. Further reports on the menu will be offered in these pages.

In the meantime, dance, drink and be merry, for tomorrow....

ii.

It was during the last *fin-de-siècle* that Nietzsche made his famous observation that "God is dead"—by which he meant, of course, that the idea of God had ceased to be a significant force in human affairs. Unlike Joris-Karl Huysmans—who argued at the end of the Decadent Bible that the sheer impossibility of believing might, in a spirit of healthy perversity, make faith worthwhile—Nietzsche thought the death of the deity a thoroughly good thing, but he was over-optimistic. Dead though He undoubtedly is, God's corpse continues to manifest signs of cultural activity as our own century limps ignominiously to its end.

In his last novel, *Towing Jehovah* (1995), James Morrow addressed the thorny question of exactly what we ought do with God's corpse—which, for the sake of the narrative, was imagined to be floating somewhere in the Atlantic. He concluded that the Vatican would probably want to provide a suitable secret resting-place, and proceeded to examine the predicament of the tanker-captain commissioned to tow the rotting mass to a rough-and-ready cryonic chamber hollowed from the Arctic ice. Morrow's new novel, *Blameless in Abaddon* (Harcourt Brace) admits that, in the modern world, the Vatican would be unlikely to have its way, and opens with the divine corpse enshrined as the central exhibit of a Florida theme-park operated in typically businesslike fashion by American Fundamentalists. The discovery that fugitive life-signs are, indeed, still detectable in the remoter depths of the gigantic cadaver, inspires cancer victim Martin Candle to summon God to appear at the World Court in the Hague, to answer the charge that, as creator of the universe, He is guilty—at least by neglect—of all the suffering it contains.

God is defended in court by the zealous millionaire G. F. Lovett, who has the advantage of two thousand years of theodicy (attempts by various devout philosophers to solve "the problem of evil", which asks how evil can possibly exist in a world ruled by an omnipotent and omnibenevolent God). Martin, for his part, is supported by many of the people he encounters during a preparatory odyssey through God's decaying mind, including Adam and Eve, Abraham and Isaac, and the much afflicted Job, whose predicament Martin and all his fellow sufferers are recapitulating. The court's eventual decision and the author's final judgment are strikingly different—but that is only to be expected, given that Morrow appoints the Devil to provide a cynical commentary on the proceedings. Literary Satanism has, of course, played a central role in Decadent philosophical discourse since the days of Blake and Shelley, and Morrow's contribution to its propagation represents a further giant stride in its progress.

It is, of course, the duty of the true Decadent to oppose all forms of orthodoxy and to react against criticism by moving to further extremes. Few writers in these liberal days suffer actual persecution but one notable exception is David Britton, who was unlucky enough in the 1980s to attract the attention of "God's cop", James Anderton, who was then Chief Constable of Manchester. Although Anderton has retired, the Obscene Publication Squad he founded lives on, and continues to wage war on Britton; a seizure order against his novel *Lord Horror* was eventually thrown out on appeal but the court ordered that copies of the comic *Meng & Ecker* seized at the same time were to be destroyed.

Widely featured in comic books as well as in the novel named for him, Lord Horror fit appeared on a twelve-inch single released by Savoy Records in 1986, where he featured as lead vocalist for the "The Savoy-Hitler Youth Band" on a stirring rendition of Bruce Springsteen's "Cadillac Ranch", whose lyrics were superimposed on the backing of New Order's "Blue Monday" (Lord Horror's voice was supplied by P. J. Proby, who also "played" him on most of the other singles that were eventually collected on the *Savoy Wars* CD) The record's sleeve—which resulted in a near-total ban—featured a caricature of Anderton, his head exploding amid a tattered halo of hateful obscenities. The characterization of Lord Horror—who proudly wears the glamour of Fascism, and exhibits the prejudices and aspirations fundamental to Nazism—is calculated to excite revulsion, and all his manifestations employ grotesque shock tactics to put such attitudes in the pillory. The continuation of Britton's court battles helped shift the main focus of his attention to Lord Horror's two "creep boys", Meng and Ecker, who took the leading roles in the novel *Motherfuckers*, in which the spirit of the Holocaust is incarnate in Dr. Mengele, who separated Siamese twins Meng and Ecker in the course of his experiments in Auschwitz. Lord Horror, this text explains, is "Auschwitz made myth."

Issues of *Meng & Ecker* subsequent to the one that was destroyed have followed the same unrepentantly gross formula as the first, and the full set is reprinted, with much new material, in *The Adventures of Meng & Ecker* (Savoy), with vivid artwork by Kris Guidio (who used to draw the Cramps comic strip in the '80s). James Anderton makes the expected appearances as *bête-noire-in-chief*, while Britton's fellow jailbird (although he was not, of course, imprisoned at the same time) Oscar Wilde is featured more than once, as special guest and presiding genius. *The Adventures of Meng & Ecker* is not pornographic in the sense that it could be employed for titillation, but it *is* calculatedly obscene, in a seriously discomfiting fashion. Its humor is scabrous, but occasionally brilliant; its grossness is repulsive, but always flamboyant. The narrative links that all Britton's work forges between the politics of hate, cute cartoon characters, academic philosophy, Decadent literature, the streets of Manchester and domestic untidiness are intended to taunt readers with the suggestion that the veneer of politeness that masks civil society is both thin and brittle. As the back cover observes,

Judge Gerard Humphries' condemned the first *Meng & Ecker* comic by saying that "this comic contains pictures that will be repulsive to right-thinking people"—neglecting, of course, to realize that that was their purpose and point.

Nietzsche's announcement that God is dead was an element of his argument that the time had come to move away from traditional ideas of good and evil. In the past, he pointed out, "good" had been characterized simply by the amelioration of manifest evils—pain, disease, hunger and misery—but, in a world where science and society have the power to free us from these evils, we are required to come up with a more positive and constructive notion of good. To this end, we must decide how we might best seek to *use* our freedom. Alas, while God's rotting corpse still harbors life beneath the noisome reek of its decay, there are many of His disciples who insist that freedom itself is an evil that must be opposed.

iii.

Given that this is *Dracula*'s centenary year, it was inevitable that someone would be invited to produce a sequel. It was equally inevitable that whoever was offered the job would think for a few minutes about the utter impossibility of the task, and then accept it; there is, after all, a special heroism in suicide missions.

Great bad books, even more than great good books, are quintessential products of their time, and *Dracula* is perhaps the greatest bad book ever penned. Most would-be sequel writers would be able to find some means of coping with the fact that the original text never comes remotely close to making sense, or achieving internal consistency, but no man or woman alive could duplicate or extrapolate its pig-headed Victorianism. Too much water of thought has passed under the bridge of understanding. A hundred years of liberalism, Freudianism, cinema, modern medicine and tourism have put a conclusive end to Bram Stoker's special brand of kinky naivety; it has been beheaded, staked through the heart and burnt, forever consigned to the graveyard of extinct ideas.

Stoker's nightmares were, of course, thoroughly masculine; his Dracula functions, most of the time, as an irresistible force of sexuality that threatens to turn chaste maidens and good wives into helpless instruments of desire. It might have been possible even today for Penguin to find a male author possessed of some such similar anxieties but they were wise not to try. Freda Warrington's *Dracula the Undead* (Penguin)—due for release on Halloween—has no alternative but to work within the ideative straitjacket of the original, all-but-choked by bonds of absurd ignorance, but it does make use of the only good card licensed by the rules of the belated-sequel game. Here, Mina Harker and her fellow diarist Elena Kovacs are figments of the female imagination rather than the male, and they see Dracula through very different eyes. The plot that they are forced to enact, involving the Scholomance (a school allegedly founded by the Devil) and the kidnapping of the Harkers' young son, is no better than Stoker's—although it is markedly truer to the spirit of the original than the plot of Hilary Bailey's direly unfortunate *Frankenstein's Bride* (1995)—but it does mask a subtext that is intelligently and interestingly related to the subtext of its model.

Given that *Dracula the Undead* could never have been anything more than a half-strangled echo, we must look elsewhere for the works that stand in a similar relation to this century's end as *Dracula* to the last. If we are to confine our attention to vampires by far the most outstanding work of 1997 is Tom Holland's *Deliver Us from Evil*, which uses the revised vampire mythology of *The Vampyre* (1995) and *Supping with Panthers* (1996) as background to a monumentally melodramatic tale of the seventeenth century. Holland has been exceedingly careful to fit his fantasies into the interstices of known history, but the secret history he has constructed behind that mask has grown increasingly ambitious in its bizarrerie as the series has progressed. Here we discover the "truth" about the Golem of Prague, the Wandering Jew, the great plague of 1665 and the Great Fire of London—and it is greatly to Holland's credit that his use of all these motifs is far more spectacular than anything previously done with any of them.

The horrific passages in *Deliver Us from Evil* are as gruesome as anything in modern fiction—a difficult feat given the gross triumphs of the last twenty years—and they are effectively contrasted by the Decadent sensuality that transforms the vampiric Kit Marlowe and the neo-vampiric Earl of Rochester into ultimate libertines more than matched by their female counterparts. As might be expected of a novel by a literary scholar, John Milton and John Aubrey also appear in cameo roles, but cast no shadow of dignified disapproval over the story's wild excesses. Holland is the best of all the writers of revisionist vampire fiction who have followed in the wake of Fred Saberhagen's *The Dracula Tape*, Pierre Kast's *The Vampires of Alfama* and Anne Rice's *Interview with the Vampire*, and not for lack of worthy competition. Given that each of his novels has so far outdone the last, it is even possible that he has further improvement still to come.

Holland has remade the Stokeresque vampire as comprehensively as Stoker remade Polidori's and le Fanu's, but, if one requires a more drastic reconstruction of myth, folklore and literary sensibility, the key novel of 1997 is *Earthquake Weather* by Tim Powers (Legend). Powers turned Lord Byron into a vampire-lover several years before Holland produced *The Vampyre*, in the excellent *The Stress of her Regard* (1989) but has since devoted his attentions to more refined forms of "psychic vampirism". *Last Call* (1992) explained how the young Scott Crane returned to Las Vegas to confront his monstrous father in the card game to end all card games, thus inheriting the spiritual kingship of the Western USA whose throne had been established there by Bugsy Siegel. *Expiration Date* (1996) built up an extraordinarily complicated and highly distinctive account of living people who cultivate power and immortality by feeding on the energy of ghosts. *Earthquake Weather* is a sequel to both these texts, adding a further layer of complexity to the already-Gordian knot that results from the entanglement of their once-separate metaphysical schemes. At the heart of this elaborated synthesis is a new conception of the Greek god of intoxication, Dionysus, and his role in human affairs.

Like *Deliver Us from Evil, Earthquake Weather* offers its readers a far-reaching reinterpretation of many events of known history—and, because Powers, like Holland, is a literary scholar, it also draws considerable inspiration from the imaginative labours of writers past. Powers' work has always been intoxicated, but usually in a fairly mellow sort of way. His dark and nasty villains have, until now, been countered by brave and vigorous heroes prone to mellow bonhomie and cavalier braggadocio, but in *Earthquake Weather* those heroes have to operate mob-handed, cursed all the while by horrible hangovers and extravagant deliria. The lead characters are not merely drunks, but problem drunks. Dionysus, their presiding deity, is no mere sot, subsidiary in his implication to Zeus the All-Father and promiscuously fecund Pan, but the very lynch-pin of the universal scheme that enfolds and defines human life and human endeavor. *Earthquake Weather* might be incomprehensible to readers who have not read *Last Call* and *Expiration Date,* but it is a masterpiece of sorts, awesome in its achievement as well as its complexity. It reaches imaginative parts that other books cannot reach, and it has the power to nourish those parts with intelligence and imagination of a rare vintage.

iv.

When Théophile Gautier identified Charles Baudelaire as the first master of "Decadent" literature he was, of course, being carefully immodest. The aspects of Baudelaire's work he praised most extravagantly were those that closely resembled a favorite aspect of his own, as exemplified by the classic erotic fantasies: "Clarimonde", "Arria Marcella", "One of Cleopatra's Nights" and *Mademoiselle de Maupin*. These works assisted such poems as Baudelaire's less prettified "Metamorphoses of the Vampire" to produce the idea and image of the *femme fatale,* which beguiled and obsessed the writers of the *fin-de-siècle,* and was given visual expression by such artists as Dante Gabriel Rossetti, Fernand Khnopff and Gustave Moreau.

The most explicitly erotic products of the *femme fatale* boom were, of course, driven underground. Although Pierre Louÿs was able to publish *Aphrodite* and *The Adventures of King Pausole* openly, the supplement to *Aphrodite* that carefully documented the full range of services available in the garden of temptation was issued clandestinely, as was *Trois filles et sa mère* (an adept and thoroughly readable translation of which was recently issued by Creation Books' "Velvet" series, under the inaptly-borrowed title *The She-Devils*).

One of the less fortunate aspects of our own *fin-de-siècle* is that the ongoing tradition of Decadent erotica was decisively interrupted by the demise of Maurice Girodias' Olympia Press, which left a huge gap that other publishers of ambitious erotica have struggled in vain to bridge. Creation Books has done some good work in this respect, as has the Canadian publisher Richard Kasak, but there is still a relative dearth of sophisticated Decadent erotica. There is, therefore, all the more reason to welcome the advent of Robert Irwin's *Prayer-Cushions of the Flesh* (Dedalus 1997). The title is derived from a novel by the Chinese writer Li Yu, but Irwin's novel is far more reminiscent of the Middle than the Far East, as one would expect of a renowned scholar in the field of Arabian and Middle Eastern History. I say "reminiscent" because the tale has no particular setting; nor has it any assignable antiquity, belonging instead to a kind of mythical "dream-time"—as also might be expected from a man who published a definitive Companion to the *Arabian Nights* in 1994.

The protagonist of *Prayer-Cushions of the Flesh* is Orkhan, the son of a Sultan who has been raised alongside all his brothers in a cage from which the only prospect of release is—or seems to be—succession to the sultanate or murderous disposal. When Orkhan *is* released, however, he is brought into the labyrinthine halls of his father's harem, where he soon discovers that authentic temporal power does not reside where he had always supposed—in the throne and the phallus—but in the ingenious machinations of the women of the harem. The winsomely mercurial Anadil, the philosophically captivating Mihrimah and the energetically masochistic Roxelana, under the instruction of his mother, the Valide Sultan, undertake a strenuous program of re-education in order to prepare Orkhan for his allotted fate: a program that, in spite of its many exotic and exhausting couplings, he relishes only in part. Mercifully, though, whenever Orkhan is forced by circumstance or exhaustion to rest a while, there are dwarfs, eunuchs and washerwomen on hand to tell him wonderful stories, all of which are marvelously implausible, deliciously dirty and very probably false.

Because the British have never been as fascinated as the French by the mysteries of the Orient, the Gothic tradition in Britain has long neglected the support provided by one of the two founding pillars of Gothic fiction: William Beckford's *Vathek*. It is, however, manifestly absurd that we should prefer the leaden and censorious Germanic attitudes of Walpole's rather awkward *Castle of Otranto* to the gloriously perverse magnificence of Beckford's brilliantly-realized Arabian tale. It is entirely right that the Gothically-inclined should prefer dark to day and pallor to suntan, but those who live eternally by night—whether by curse or by choice—do miss out on some few of the glories and comforts of luxury. True Decadents always relish a foretaste of the heat of hell, even if they cannot follow the Caliph Vathek gladly into the heart of its eternal fire, or if they employ it merely to build a thirst. *Prayer-Cushions of the Flesh* is a mere literary confection intended for amusement, but it does nourish the pheromonal appetites. In any case—as Voltaire one remarked—the superfluous is a very necessary thing, and there is a special delight in such fabulous superfluities as this.

In these iconoclastic days it is by no means rare for books to advertise themselves as pornography, and when one comes across an introduction which boasts that "In reading these, the most intimate documents, you are a sadistic voyeur, transforming someone else's passion into your own pleasure." Alas, the book that accompanies the advertisement, *...Or Not to Be: A Collection of Suicide Notes* by

Mark Etkind (Riverside 1997) induces no such delicious sense of guilt. Part of the problem is the ridiculous cod-psychiatric commentary provided by the "author" but the book also testifies to the sad fact that people simply don't pay enough attention to the literary quality of their suicide notes. It seems to matter hardly at all whether they are self-pitying, altruistic, accusative, nihilistic or merely polite, these notes are simply not up to scratch. No respectable Decadent would want to be seen dead with any one of them.

Now that my invaluable guide to *Writing Fantasy and Science Fiction* (Teach Yourself Books 1997) is in print I really must try to persuade the publisher to let me follow it with the definitive guide for would-be writers of suicide notes. If it's the last thing a person is going to do, all the more especially if it's the only work of art that one is ever going to produce, it ought to be done *well*. It is, after all, up to us—the currently-living—to make sure that *Or Not to Be....II* is a real blockbuster.

v.

The market reports in the latest *Science Fiction Chronicle* include notice of the first on-line horror magazine to pay its contributors, sited at www.gothic.net. Its policy statement begins, as many such statements now do, with the proviso "Not interested in vampires". Almost every commercial buyer now agrees that the literary vampire is, at least for the time being, played out. The time has come for this particular reincarnation of Lord Byron to be laid to rest. No doubt he will rise from the grave again, but not until a period of absence has freshened him up a little. But what will take his place as the primary contemporary embodiment of Byronic devilment and Byronic dandyism? Who or what will inherit the vampire's dark reputation and dress sense, and what subtle transformation will be worked in order to make the replacement seem new?

In *Darker Angels* (Gollancz) one of the key remakers of the modern vampire, S. P. Somtow—creator of Timmy Valentine, the 2,000-year-old child rock-star—offers what may seem to some to be one of the least likely candidates: the *zombi* (as he spells it). One must remember, however, that the vampire of folklore was very zombie-like before John Polidori undertook to clean up his image by borrowing Lord Byron's clothes and mannerisms. Could a similar trick possibly be worked again?

Somtow, the great-nephew of a Queen of Siam, is proud to describe himself as the "Terrifying Thai", but he takes his American citizenship very seriously. In *Moon Dance*, aristocratic European werewolves meet their match in Native American shapeshifters, and, in *Darker Angels,* Byron's attempt to resurrect a dead lover only comes to fruition by courtesy of the efforts of a black slave imported to Oxford by an exchange student from Georgia. Byron's inspiration then has to pass, via Edgar Allan Poe, to another American, the Reverend Aloysius Grainger, before the plot gets thick enough to stir. Joseph, in the meantime, follows his own career, which actually began somewhat earlier, when he was transported to America from Haiti alongside Marie Laveau, the so-called Witch-Queen of New Orleans.

All of this is revealed by degrees in a series of tales told to Aloysius Grainger's widow, Paula, who swoons in Walt Whitman's arms while visiting the corpse of Abraham Lincoln. Whitman is keeping very close company with a young war-veteran named Zachary Brown, whose account of his adventures has nested and knotted within it the tales of the boy evangelist Jimmy Lee Cox, the armless Tyler Tyler and the serially-incestuous slave-holder Griffin Bledsoe. As a result of hearing these life-stories, Paula allows her own life to be drastically changed by Joseph's female counterpart Phoebe, a black sorceress and leopard-woman who can trace the record of her incarnations back to the dawn of time.

Because it is a horror novel, *Darker Angels* does not stint on its description of the evils to which America was subjected by the Civil War, but it is also a novel of redemption, and the redemption it celebrates is that of *voudun*, which, as a religion of slaves and ex-slaves, was as desperately hopeful in its nineteenth-century inventions as Christianity was in the days before self-appointed bishops devised the Bible and the Church. Alas, it is not the *zombi* that ultimately emerges as the chief symbol of fruitful rebellion within the novel but the panther-woman, gifted by nature with far greater beauty, power and passion (not to mention a stylish black coat). Byron's involvement with the plot is both peripheral and fleeting, and he is not sorry to see his *zombi* lover returned to the grave. We shall probably have to wait for a British writer to take up the severed thread and draw it out, imagining the secret passed from one poet to another until a whole company of resurrected aristocrats is accumulated in Victorian England, with an army of *zombi* laborers at their beck and call to help them through the later phases of the Industrial Revolution.

Keats would probably be in this company, and Shelley too, but the one man who *must* be included is the man who inspired Byron to adopt the lifestyle fantasy which Polidori then appropriated for the literary vampire: George "Beau" Brummell. It was a fictionalized study of Brummell by the French dandy Barbey d'Aurevilly that inspired Baudelaire to create the blueprint for the Decadent lifestyle whose literary embodiment was Jean Des Esseintes, designer of the original black feast. It was because of Brummell's stylistic rebellion against the absurd colors and frills worn by the courtiers of late eighteenth-century England that Baudelaire decided that the only "color" he would ever wear would be black—and it was partly because Edgar Allan Poe wore black in his extant portraits that Baudelaire was prepared to consider him an honorary un-American.

Anyone seriously interested in the history of Decadent and Gothic style will find a treasure-trove of information and inspiration in *Rising Star: Dandyism, Gender and Performance in the Fin de Siècle* by Rhonda K. Garelick (Princeton University Press), which throws new light on such intriguing questions as why the great symbolist poet Stéphane Mallarmé briefly edited (and wrote the entire contents of) a women's fashion magazine. The book explains how the modern cult of celebrity grew out of an unholy alliance between Brummell-inspired dandies and female stage performers, and offers in the process a far more coherent account of the personality and endeavors of Oscar Wilde than the execrable recent film starring Stephen Fry.

The main problem with *zombies*, of course, is that even the good sartorial advice of Beau Brummell could only go some way to redeeming their reputation. Even S. P. Somtow acknowledges the evil influence of *The Night of the Living Dead* in feeling obliged to represent his *zombies* as cannibals whose table-manners are on the crude side. I cannot believe, however, that this is an insuperable problem. If blood-drinking can be tidied up and redefined as a superorgasmic sex-act, cannibalism can surely go one better. Vampires are, after all, more-or-less compelled to take their nourishment raw; cannibals can and ought to take advantage of the accumulated culinary wisdom of the great gourmets. (Perhaps, if the great Anthelme Brillat-Savarin had already rotted beyond redemption, we could recruit Mrs. Beaton—who died bearing her twelfth child at the ripe old age of twenty-nine—as chief cook to our company of Victorian *zombies*.)

There is, I am sure, much more that might be done with this brilliant idea, but discretion requires me not to reveal too much at this stage.

PART TWO

REVIEWS FROM *HOLLYWOOD: THE 100 BEST NOVELS*

A Voyage to Purilia by Elmer Rice (New York: Cosmopolitan, 1930)

Elmer Rice was primarily a playwright, and he had deep convictions regarding the theatre's responsibility to react to—and, if possible, to change—prevailing social conditions. His greatest success was the surreal satire *The Adding Machine* (1923), but he also produced realistic plays railing against the economic sickness of the Depression and warning against the rise of Fascism. He was a socialist, and he clung fast to those ideals when McCarthyism made them dangerous, defending his left-wing friends against the tide of hysteria. It is not entirely surprising that such a man, contemplating the use to which Hollywood had put its powerful and popular medium, should have been utterly appalled.

A Voyage to Purilia is cast as a Utopian satire in the vein of Samuel Butler's *Erewhon*; the unnamed narrator and his friend Johnson take off in an aeroplane called a Cellula and head for the vast bank of pink cloud that hides the mysterious world of Purilia. They find its air cloying but breathable, and are only mildly disconcerted by the fact that their ears are constantly afflicted by music. They soon become used to strange optical effects that focus on particular aspects of the environment and blow them up to colossal size, and are quite grateful for the mysterious Presence that is continually on hand to introduce people and places, albeit in somewhat sententious terms.

The narrator and his friend find Purilia a strangely hyperactive world, in which there are always hectic chases of some kind going on, and where certain citizens are perpetually inflicted by all kinds of bizarre—but happily non-injurious—misfortune. In spite of its constant frank defiance of the principles of probability, however, they find the world congenial enough, and soon become involved in the mainstream of its social intercourse by becoming fond of two young women, Pansy and Mollie. In Purilia, alas, becoming enamored of a young woman is the inevitable prelude to inordinately complicated adventures, and the two protagonists are whirled away into a complicated and unfathomable web of intrigue.

The narrator eventually concludes that Purilian society involves five principal castes. The Umbilicans are aging females much given to grieving over the fates their children (although there is no evidence in Purilia of pregnancy or childbirth). The Pudencians are chaste young women forever in the grip of emotional crises, often as a result of being relentlessly pursued (with what purpose is unclear) by the lecherous old men of the Vaurien caste, from whose evil clutches they are always saved by the handsome young Paragonians. The Paragonians are the natural counterparts of the Pudencians, and every Paragonian is destined eventually to marry his Pudencian soul mate, but marriage in Purilia is invariably followed by a fatal fade into obliteration, so it is not entirely clear why it is so devoutly desired. The Vauriens, however, rarely thrive in its avoidance, for they invariably meet an unpleasant death, as do their female counterparts the Bordellians.

In spite of their superficial resemblance to human beings, the reproductive system of the Purilians remains utterly mysterious to the visitors—as does their economic system, for the greater part of the apparatus of Earthly industrial life is nowhere to be found in Purilia. There is little in the way of factory production, or indeed of routine labor. The legal system is astonishingly inefficient, the prisons being full of men convicted of capital crimes on the flimsiest of evidence, who are consistently saved from execution in the nick of time. On the other hand, Purilian medical science is mysteriously efficacious, most wounds healing without any evident treatment and many men being wooed back from death's door by nursing practices that seem to consist entirely of fond glances. It is, alas, a world marred by crude and cruel racism, although the harsh and contemptuous treatment meted out by whites to other races seems to cause remarkably few political problems, at least in a domestic context (fortunately, wars fought in the remoter part of the world are very easily won, with negligible losses on the part of the white forces).

The adventures that the narrator and Johnson undergo while attempting to rescue Pansy and Mollie from the consequences a remarkable series of misunderstandings, abductions, encounters with white slave traders, bouts of amnesia, etc, etc, take them to every part of Purilia before poor Johnson neglects to observe one of the more peculiar customs of the land and is shot. The narrator succeeds in bringing his romance to the very brink of the only conclusion sanctioned by Purilian custom, but decides at the last possible moment that a fade-out is not climactic enough for him, and makes a dash for the Cellula so that he can fly home to a quieter, saner and less disorganized world.

A Voyage to Purilia is perhaps the most sustained and most vitriolic attack on the politics and ethics of the Hollywood "dream factory" ever penned. Its scathing sarcasm is primarily directed against the sheer silliness of the conventions of melodrama and censorship that controlled the silent movies, but the underlying argument of the book is that this surface absurdity overlies an authentic moral disease. To some extent, the escapist quality of the movies in question was a mere reflection of the generalized popular culture of the pulp magazines, but Rice lost no opportunity to stress the many ways in which the movies isolated and magnified the superficialities of pulp melodrama, by transposing them into a visual code unsupported by any text other than mere captions.

Rice's target is not the cinema medium *per se*, and he might well have been prepared to make exception for the work of some of Hollywood's best directors; what appalled him was the way in which Hollywood had so quickly applied the methods and philosophy of mass production to the making of movies. Perhaps he considered the developments that he was able to witness in the following forty years (he died in 1967) a dramatic improvement, but he might well have retained his sense of horror. One thing that would not have pleased him at all, were he still alive, is the fact that modern readers picking up *A Voyage to Purilia* are highly likely to find it an amusing account of a supposedly-long-gone era, to be read with a light heart and nostalgic affection.

Laughing Gas by P. G. Wodehouse (London: Herbert Jenkins, 1936)

Laughing Gas is the only wholehearted fantasy penned by P. G. Wodehouse, Britain's most prolific and most esteemed comic writer of the period between the two world wars. It is a late addition to the rich tradition of identity-exchange stories initiated by Robert Mac-

Nish's "The Metempsychosis" (1826) and boosted to best-seller status by F. Anstey's *Vice Versa* (1882).

The story is narrated by Reggie, third Earl of Haverstock, who is unfortunate enough to have to visit the dentist while visiting Hollywood. He is rendered unconscious by gas at exactly the same moment as child star Joey Cooley, who is receiving treatment in the adjacent surgery. When he wakes up again, Reggie discovers—much to his consternation—that some jiggery-pokery in the fourth dimension has resulted in his consciousness being decanted into the wrong body.

The exchange of corporeal habitats is, of course, something of a disaster so far as Reggie is concerned. He has come to Hollywood in search of his alcoholic cousin Eggy, having been commissioned to do so by one of those awful Aunts who serve throughout Wodehouse's canon as levers with which to set plots in motion. While *en route*, however, he has fallen under the spell of the actress April June, whose tenderness and nobility of soul have captivated his soul.

The displacement of the aforesaid soul not only makes it impossible for Reggie to carry forward his romance, but threatens to capsize the whole project, because Joey Cooley (who is currently wearing his appearance) loathes April June almost as much as April June loathes him. The situation is further complicated by the fact that Reggie's one and only old flame, Ann Bannister—an American girl he met in Cannes but contrived to put off by attempting to kiss her on the back of the neck, while quite forgetting that he had a lighted cigarette in his mouth—is Eggy's fiancée, Joey Cooley's minder and April June's putative press agent.

The situation would be much worse if Reggie had not read any identity-exchange stories, but he is fortunate enough to have done so. Forewarned is forearmed, and he adapts fairly readily to the reality of his situation, reconciling himself to the utter impossibility of persuading anyone else that he is not really Joey Cooley. He does his best to cope with all the problems he inherits from Joey. These include the monstrous Miss Brinkmeyer, sister of his producer, who rules his life with a rod of iron, as well as various rivals he has displaced in the public affection—who now wish to rearrange his features—and the consequences of a number of practical jokes that have not quite come to fruition. The worst inheritance of this sort by far is, however, a veritable legion of doting female film buffs whose dearest ambition is to kiss him. His morale is somewhat undermined by the knowledge that Joey has adapted equally well, and is taking advantage of Reggie's well-developed physique to punch out everyone who has ever offended him, following a list that will lead inexorably to April June.

As with all protagonists of identity-exchange stories, Reggie is in dire need of learning some important lesson, which his experience serves to make abundantly clear to him. The particular lesson he has to learn is that *everyone in Hollywood is an actor*. Everyone he encounters, from Mr. Brinkmeyer's household staff to the kidnappers who abduct him, is just playing a part in the hope of getting into the movies. Their relatively humble deceptions are, however, as nothing to the deceptions of the people who are *already* in the movies. From the standpoint of Joey Cooley, it is easy to discover that April June is a cynical social climber, who is playing him for a sucker for the sake of his title, and even easier to understand that Joey himself has been forced by the expectations of others to become something too horrible to contemplate.

By the time another bout of simultaneous unconsciousness allows the fourth-dimensional glitch to be ironed out, both parties have been liberated. Reggie's delusions about the reliability of appearances have been shattered, and so—through Reggie's carelessness rather than any malevolent or altruistic design—has Joey Cooley's public image. Reggie is free to repair his relationship with Ann, having arrived at a vestigial comprehension of the ways in which his previous ineptitude had upset her, while Joey is free to return to Chillicothe, Ohio and some semblance of a normal boyhood.

It is, of course, no news nowadays that Hollywood is a place where artifice is taken not merely to its logical limit but absurdly far beyond, or that the feverish idolatry of the "star system" is a corrosive force making monsters of those it plucks out of the avidly ambitious herd. In 1936, though, the few scandals that had made headlines could still be regarded as unfortunate exceptions rather than evidence of endemic sickness. *Laughing Gas* is a thoroughly amiable work, as cheerfully frothy as all Wodehouse books, which does not aspire to satirical criticism, but it is by no means as ingenuous as its narrator.

A key aspect of the book's humor is that the adult Reggie is rather more childish, and far more innocent, than the juvenile Joey—and, in spite of his eventual enlightenment, he remains so. Reggie belongs to a world that had already become obsolete, while Joey belongs to an enterprise that is riding the crest of the wave. Although Wodehouse would never have said so straightforwardly, if only because he was far too polite, *Laughing Gas* does contrive to make it clear that, while Reggie's standards of behavior are altogether admirable and utterly doomed, Hollywood's—as briefly reflected and refracted by Joey—are not in the least admirable, and absolutely certain to conquer the world.

The Little Sister by Raymond Chandler (Boston: Houghton Mifflin, 1949)

The Little Sister was the first of Chandler's post-war novels, separated by a six-year gap from *The Lady in the Lake* (1943), the last of the four novels in which Chandler had "cannibalized" the work he had done in the 1930s for the pulp magazine *Black Mask*. The earlier novels, as befitted their pulp heritage, had been taut thrillers animated by Philip Marlowe's attempts to solve mysteries that he had been hired to investigate. The later novels are significantly different, by virtue of the fact that Marlowe's motivation comes from within rather than without, and by virtue of the fact that the "solutions" to the mysteries that confront him no longer seem to function as goals worth seeking.

The Little Sister starts conventionally enough, with a client turning up in Marlowe's office asking him to find her missing brother, but the momentum thus provided is immediately compromised by her reluctance to pay him and his reluctance to accept the inadequate sum she offers—a sum they eventually pass back and forth so often that whatever meaning it might have had is lost in a haze of surreality. When Marlowe actually sets out to investigate the missing man's last address, he claims to be moved by nothing but boredom, but it is clear that he is fascinated by the client, and that his fascination is a peculiar admixture of sexual attraction and mocking derision.

Chandler was never charitable in his treatment of female characters (he was ultimately to lose his impetus completely when he finally allowed Marlowe to pair off at the end of *Playback*, 1958) but it is *The Little Sister* that displays his peculiar attitude to womankind to the fullest extent. This is where Hollywood comes in, for the one "good" woman in *The Little Sister* is a budding film star, and the one thing genuinely at stake in the plot is her career. This may seem bizarre, in that the plot features several murders, but at no point does it ever really matter who committed any of the murders, or why. Marlowe does not succeed in preventing any of the murders (including the murder of the man he was initially hired to find), nor does he succeed in bringing any of the murderers to book; his one and only success is to keep the starlet's name out of the affair, saving her from embarrassment. His motives for doing so are entirely his own; he has to go to extraordinary lengths to co-opt her as a client, thus to provide some "official" sanction for a whole battery of crimes (hiding evidence, giving false testimony, etc, etc). He neither seeks nor obtains any real reward for this service—not even the thanks of the lady in question.

It goes without saying that this is a very peculiar kind of mystery story. The mystery itself is, in spite of its tortuous convolutions, merely a peg on which to hang a series of confrontations between Marlowe and three women: Mavis Weld, the actress who retains her virtue in spite of having a gangster for a boy-friend; Dolores Gonzalez, the nymphomaniac actress; and Orfamay Quest, the "little sister". The real subject of the book is the role played by sexual attraction in the corrupt world through which Marlowe moves—a world whose corruption cuts far deeper than the activities of drug-peddlers, bent policemen and sleazy hotel detectives. Although it is the sexually aggressive Dolores who seems to represent the ultimate evil (and takes the ultimate fall as the plot unwinds) her part is actually rather cursory; the far more fascinating figure of repulsion is Orfamay, whose superficial gaucherie seems to conceal a hidden beauty but turns out in the end to be a mask for rapacious greed.

The contrast between Mavis, who is faithful after her fashion to her not-altogether unworthy boyfriend, and Dolores, who is utterly devoid of fidelity, is not the most interesting in the story. The most interesting comparison is that to be drawn between Mavis and Orfamay, the two half-sisters. Orfamay is, and remains, Chandler's and Marlowe's idea of a quintessential small town girl: undeveloped, unfulfilled and ultimately unredeemable. Mavis, on the other hand, has transcended her similar background, and *has* been redeemed, and what is interesting about the book is that the means of her redemption has been the movies.

This is certainly not because the movie business is any less corrupt than the rest of California, in Chandler's eyes; that would be an absurd proposition, although Marlowe's encounters with certain Hollywood grotesques—an agent and a studio head—while he is trying hard to be recruited to Mavis Weld's team do imply, rather unfashionably, that Hollywood is no worse than the culture of which it is a part. Nor is it because Chandler or Marlowe is a movie fan. It seems, in fact, to be an oddly plaintive recognition that the only way anyone can hope to shake off the filth of the mean streets is by discovering some kind of vocation, and that whatever faults Hollywood might have, it does offer scope for a sense of vocation.

In Chandler's earlier books, being a private eye was itself a kind of vocation—perhaps the highest vocation of all—but *The Little Sister* makes it perfectly clear, without ever actually saying so, that Marlowe has lost the sense of vocation that his profession once provided, and is floundering in consequence. He was to flounder a lot more in *The Long Goodbye* (1954), before finally getting hung out to dry in *Playback*, but in *The Little Sister* he is vouchsafed a glimpse of a different and better destiny—just as Raymond Chandler had been granted a glimpse of further horizons when he wrote such film scripts as *The Blue Dahlia* (1946). Just for a moment, before the awfulness of modern American existence overwhelmed him again, Marlowe was allowed to think that there might be something (embodied in Mavis Weld) truly worth fighting for and something (embodied in Orfamay Quest) that was truly worth fighting against. One is tempted to wonder how differently things might have worked out for Philip Marlowe had Raymond Chandler's career in Hollywood not fizzled out and died after its promising beginning

Screen by Barry N. Malzberg (New York: Olympia Press, 1968)

Martin Miller, the narrator of Barry Malzberg's *Screen* works— as Barry Malzberg once had—as an assessor for the Welfare Department, but his position there is under threat by virtue of his persistent dereliction of duty. For Martin, life does not begin until he can get away from work—and, for that matter, from every other aspect of the mundane world. For him, life is something that can be achieved only by means of the movies, which provide his only release from the appalling stresses and strains of an actuality that is not life at all, but merely a form of lingering death. His immersion in the fantasy world that the movies provide is absolute, all the more so because he has won free of the limitations imposed by the scenes and plots inscribed in the celluloid. For him, a movie is a magical doorway that allows him privileged access to its female star, with whom he can engage in vivid and passionate sexual intercourse.

While his boss bombards him with pleas to pull himself together, or at least to resign his post with some decorum, and a female co-worker tries in vain to make meaningful contact with him, Martin has sex with Sophia Loren and Elizabeth Taylor, with Sabrina (one of several models he can enjoy in the comfort of his own home, thanks to his projector and the local porn shop) and Brigitte

Bardot, and ultimately with Doris Day. These couplings grow increasingly desperate as pressure builds from without, but the desperation only increases their necessity. Martin's one attempt to find temporary refuge in another kind of fantasy-world—at the race-track—is cruelly subverted by the implacable hostility of the odds, which no punter can ever beat in the long run and which he cannot even beat for the space of a single race.

In one sense, Martin's cinematic adventures are mere masturbation fantasies, but in another sense there is nothing "mere" about them; their intensity is a measure of the extent to which he has to go in order to blot out the horrific pressures of mundane existence. They are not a second-rate substitute for real sex, as is made clear by his development of an authentic sexual relationship with Barbara, which is useless to him precisely because it cannot take him out of the claustrophobic grip of actuality.

The problem is not that Barbara also works for the Welfare Department, doing the kind of work that has helped in no small measure to drive Martin to the edge, although that is certainly not a helpful circumstance. The real problem is that she belongs, heart and soul, *to the world*, insistent upon the necessity of compromising with its pressures, of soldiering on under its burdens. Sex, in such a context, promises no real release, but merely an extension of captivity and crushing affliction. Only the kind of sex that the movies offer, or seem to offer, has the power to act as an antidote to the grinding corrosion that threatens his obliteration. By the time the story begins, alas, even that medicine has begun to lose its potency, and by the time it ends—with Martin knowing, as he fucks Doris Day, that he is in some sense fucking America itself—it is perfectly plain that there is no hope for him at all.

Like all Barry Malzberg novels, *Screen* is a tale of unfolding personal catastrophe, whose protagonist loses, by slow and agonizing degrees, the last vestiges of control over his destiny and the last ghostly semblance of existential coherency. The reader enters a Malzberg novel in order to share in and empathize with the tragic disintegration of a man who cannot any longer maintain the pretence of coping, and Malzberg is careful to leave no room within his narratives for readers to distance themselves from this process. A reader cannot pick up a Malzberg novel with the intention of playing the casual *voyeur*; there is no third-person discretion to be found there, and no reflective narrative pauses for re-appraisal and re-evaluation. The reader enters a Malzberg novel as absolutely and as irredeemably as Martin Miller enters a movie, and that is as it should be, for, without such total commitment, the reader could not even begin to grasp the essence of the message that Malzberg is desperate to get across to us all—which is that the world that surrounds us is hell bent on distressing and disappointing us, and that, if we seek to avoid such a fate, we are going to have to try an awful lot harder than we ever imagined.

In one particularly memorable passage, *Screen* puts forward an extraordinarily spirited defense of the movie medium. When Barbara tells Martin that Hollywood is just a factory making lies, whose dreams are poisonous because they tell us that nothing is important except what happens on the screen, Martin is outraged. The truth, he says, is that the movies are as close to reality as most people can get, because most people are neither good enough nor brave enough to exist at all, except through the medium of fantasy. If he is right— and he certainly has a case—then the movies are not the luxury we sometimes think they are, and Hollywood is not the junk factory it sometimes admits to being. If Martin is right, the movies—or something like them—are a vital necessity, without which many of us would have no inner lives at all: no real hopes, no real sensations, and no real identities.

With defenders like that, of course, Hollywood needs no detractors, for no condemnation could possibly compare, in terms of horror or alarm, with that kind of justification, but that is not the point at issue. The real point at issue is the question of whether it is true. Is fucking Doris Day in the private recesses of the vaulting imagination really the closest most of us can ever get to fucking America, or the closest most of us can ever get to incandescent bliss and some marvelous coin of vantage from which life almost seems to be worth living?

One of the reasons why Martin is unintimidated by the threats and pleas showered upon him by his anxious boss is that he is hoping—and, indeed, expecting—to hear, any day now, from one of the many movie studios to which he has applied for jobs in casting or publicity. He is not exactly confident that his attempts will bear fruit, but he persists in the hope. He will go on persisting to the bitter end, and probably beyond; we know this, and we pity him, because we understand.

Marion's Wall by Jack Finney (New York: Simon & Schuster, 1973)

Walter Braden ("Jack") Finney attained considerable success as a writer of daydream fantasies. Most of his stories, long and short alike, are about characters much like himself—but drawn sketchily enough to be almost anyone—who get to do the kinds of things that they would absolutely love to do, were they not illegal, immoral, or frankly impossible. Where frank impossibilities are concerned he is usually content to be entirely frivolous, as in *The Woodrow Wilson Dime* (1968), but there is one kind of impossibility that he was *almost* capable of taking seriously, to the extent that he could inject a measure of real conviction into his self-indulgent fantasies. That was the notion of a "timeslip", which might allow past and future to make brief contact with one another. In his one and only masterpiece, *Time and Again* (1970), Finney contrived to take the notion to a sentimental extreme that became desperately earnest, and there was sufficient fervor left over to fuel the more consciously self-indulgent but nevertheless heartfelt *Marion's Wall*.

Nick and Jan, a young couple decorating their new apartment in San Francisco—an apartment where Nick's similarly-named father once lived—strip off the penultimate layer of wallpaper to find a message scrawled in lipstick on the remaining one: MARION MARSH LIVED HERE JUNE 14 1926. READ IT AND WEEP. Nick senior reveals that Marion Marsh was a girl he loved before meeting Nick junior's mother, but that they split up when he refused to go with her to Hollywood. There, her burgeoning career was cut short while her first really significant film was in production, necessitating her replacement by the then-unknown Joan Crawford.

Soon after this discovery is made, Jan points out to Nick—an ardent silent movie buff whose own collection is severely handicapped by lack of means—that the one film in which Marion Marsh briefly appears is to be shown on TV. Nick watches it avidly—and so, it transpires, does Marion Marsh's ghost, which speaks to him afterwards, under the impression that he is his father.

Having made that first step back to reality Marion quickly finds a way to make a second, and she "possesses" Jan, whirling Nick away to a hectic night of uninhibited pleasure. This brief taste of life only whets Marion's appetite for more, and she pleads to be allowed to borrow Jan's body for a more extensive period, to see if it might be possible to take up her career again. Nick is dubious, until she tells him that one of her old admirers—who is still in the Los Angeles phone book—made illicit copies of many of the legendary films of the era, including many that have since been lost. Jan, who is none too pleased about her husband's adultery, even though hers was the body in question, takes rather more persuading, but Nick ultimately wins her consent.

Masquerading as her own granddaughter, the reincarnate Marion goes to Hollywood to call in a favor from yet another old admirer. Such is her star quality that she captivates everyone even in a second-hand body, and is immediately cast in a part—but she is devastated when she finds out that the scene in which she has been tested has been spliced into an absurd piece of animation to make a TV commercial. Thoroughly disillusioned, she decides that the future is no place for one such as her, but fulfils her part of the bargain by taking Nick to an old mansion, where a crazed collector really does have a refrigerator filled to overflowing with all the lost masterpieces of the silent cinema.

Spoilt for choice, Nick agrees to watch a version of the film (based on a novel by "Walter Braden") that Marion was making when she died, in which her devoted admirer has carefully replaced all the scenes that she made. Such is their hurry and confusion, alas, that they start a fire, which serves as a cruel but necessary *deus ex machina*, obliterating all trace of the lovely dream.

On the surface, *Marion's Wall* is about a brief and deliciously sinful love affair between a young man and the ghost of an aspiring silent movie star, whose career was nipped in the bud by a fatal accident. Beneath the superficial veneer, however, it is very obviously about a fervently nostalgic love of the silent movies themselves. The painful sense of loss incarnate in Nick's fascination with Marion Marsh's aborted career and interrupted life is not merely recapitulated but redoubled in his tragically brief encounter with all the lost movies. The point is made several times over that what killed Marion was the innocent and utterly uninhibited love of life that was the *zeitgeist* of 1920s America and 1920s Hollywood.

Jan is a duller character by far than Marion—although the ease with which she is persuaded to acknowledge the fact and step aside in Marion's favor does not ring entirely true—but the real contrast drawn by the narrative is not that between the two women, but that between the two eras. The real gulf that separates Marion from the present is that between the technologically-primitive but hopeful and artful Hollywood products of the 1920s and the technologically-sophisticated but cynical and crass Hollywood products of the 1970s.

It is easy to forget, especially in the grip of a daydream, that the word "nostalgia" was coined to describe a form of mental illness, and that the habit of looking at the past through rose-tinted lenses is a kind of self-deception. There is, however, something to be said for the argument that a little forgetfulness is a good thing, not merely in the sense that it facilitates pleasure but also in the sense that it facilitates well-being. If accurate knowledge of the real past cannot adequately show up the follies and failings of the present, then there is a useful role to be played by rose-tinted images of an imaginary past, and by literary vehicles that bring such images into fruitful collision with present experience. The Hollywood of Marion Marsh is not a Hollywood that we have lost but a Hollywood that never was—but this should not prevent us asking whether it is the Hollywood that ought to have been, and a better Hollywood by far than the one we have.

The Passion of New Eve by Angela Carter (London: Gollancz, 1977)

The Passion of New Eve is a surreal apocalyptic satire, in which an English Candide is forced by unkind fate to travel into the dark heart of the American Dream—which lies, of course, in Hollywood. American writers do not necessarily see the American Dream in that way, but English writers inevitably do, for it is the invasion of the British Isles by the products and images of Hollywood that is and always has been the sharp spearhead of cultural coca-colonization.

The hero and heroine of Carter's novel is Evelyn, who is male when he first travels to New York to take up a teaching post in a university. He finds the city trembling on the brink of anarchy, and his attempts to keep chaos at bay by immersing himself in a love affair with the beautiful Leilah come to nothing, so he sets off westwards. He is captured by militant feminists and forcibly subjected to a sex change, but the resultant new Eve escapes before she can be impregnated with the stored sperm of the old Evelyn. She is soon captured again, though, and is raped by the one-eyed and one-legged "poet" Zero, who believes himself to be a god and keeps a harem of adolescent wives to worship him.

The inarticulate Zero, who howls his wordless poems to the desert sky, is obsessed with one-time screen goddess Tristessa St Ange, who retired to lonely seclusion a generation before. The sterile Zero holds Tristessa responsible for his psychological castration, and hopes to recover his potency by her ritual murder. When he locates her hideaway, he flies there with his wives in a helicopter and runs riot through the glass palace in which she has entombed herself. When the times comes for the execution to take place, however, Zero discovers that Tristessa is actually a transvestite, who was able to become the perfect embodiment of feminine attraction because he was incarnating his own romantic ideal.

Instead of killing him, Zero decides to marry Tristessa to Eve, and forces him to consummate the marriage. The glass palace collapses around them; Tristessa and Eve are the only survivors. They are captured yet again, this time by an army of pre-puberal children who are preparing to take their stand in the Final War that is raging across America. The colonel of this strange army, who has a copy of Leonardo da Vinci's *Last Supper* tattooed on his chest, shoots Tristessa dead for trying to kiss him, leaving Eve to be reunited with Leilah—now calling herself Lilith—on the Pacific shore. After descending into a "womb" of rock, in which time has gone into reverse, Eve is reborn, and sets forth across the sea in search of her new Eden.

The Passion of New Eve is primarily a commentary on modern sexual mythology: a phantasmagorical exploration of the female condition, and the myths of femininity and maternity. It has perforce to deal with the parallel myths of masculinity, but the goal towards which the narrative is orientated is the liberation of women from the prison of male-imposed imagery; no redemption is offered to the incarnations of masculinity featured in the plot (the principal one is not called Zero without reason). Chief among the chimeras that must be slain in pursuit of this quest—though not without pity—is Tristessa, whose amalgamation of all the great Hollywood beauties makes her the very essence of idealized femininity.

Tristessa has played all the "great" feminine roles. She has been Catherine Earnshaw in *Wuthering Heights*, Marguerite in *Faust* and Emma Bovary, but Eve—who "worshipped at Tristessa's shrine" when she was Evelyn—remembers her most fondly as poor pale Madeleine, risen from her premature grave in *The Fall of the House of Usher*. Although her career was not restricted to the silent movies it is to that era of mute emotional extravagance that she truly belongs, her long retirement emphasizing the extent to which the advent of sound and color made the movies much more like real life. She is a creature of dreams, unreal at every level, making no concessions to human nature until the very end of her symbolic reign, at which point she becomes a "fallen angel" whose role in Eve's story combines that of Adam with that of the serpent. (The fruits that carry the knowledge of good and evil do not need to be picked in this re-creation myth; the tale is saturated with the stench of their rotting.)

Angela Carter's fascination with the iconography of popular culture extended from fairy tales and pornography to the stage and the circus, but almost all the works in which she transmuted other patterns of imagery are set in Europe. *The Passion of New Eve* is different, not merely because the image of America is most perfectly incarnate in its films, but also because the imagery of the cinema leads inexorably to America, and thus to Hollywood. In Carter's fairy tale fantasies and her accounts of the magic of drama there is a certain stability—an awareness of a long and continuing tradition that might be inverted but cannot actually be shattered by a surfacing consciousness of the arbitrariness of the myths enshrined therein, but her examination of the myths of Hollywood is very different. Here, transience and decadence are taken for granted; the iconography of the silent movies is perceived as something essentially meteoric and self-defeating. However harsh the judgment may seem, it certainly works to the advantage of the melodrama of the narrative, which is as sumptuous, as spectacular and as superabundant as the most lavishly overblown of Griffith's or de Mille's epics.

The Passion of Eve does not regret the passing of the myths of femininity that the early Hollywood enshrined—and, indeed, actively seeks to hasten their demise—but it does acknowledge their splendor and their seductiveness. It pays a kind of homage to its idols even as it exposes their feet of clay and casts them down, admitting the glory of the glass palace even as it smashes the edifice into a million glittering shards. It is, after all, Tristessa St Ange's fertile seed that Eve will carry into the new Eden, not that of the ghastly Zero or her own ineffectual former self.

Ancient Images by Ramsey Campbell (London: Legend, 1989)

Sandy Allan, the heroine of *Ancient Images* is a film-editor whose colleague Graham Nolan is an indefatigable researcher with a keen interest in locating and restoring "lost" films. Graham has discovered a print of *Tower of Fear*, a 1930s film starring Boris Karloff and Bela Lugosi, which had been suppressed after completion following the sudden violent death of its director. Tracking down a copy has been difficult, because everyone involved in the making of the film felt very uneasy about it at the time, and the survivors still feel uneasy—with good reason, given that some of them seem to have been permanently marred by the experience.

Sandy arrives at a private screening arranged by Graham just in time to see him leap off a roof, apparently fleeing a pursuer she cannot see; the film, of course, is gone. The story follows her quest to retrace the course of her dead colleague's enquiries, searching for another copy of the elusive film and for some explanation of his curious death. While she pursues her enquiries, it seems that she is, in turn, pursued by shadowy figures she can never quite make out—until, of course the climax of the hunt arrives, when they and everything else become horribly clear.

Ramsey Campbell is a past master of the suspenseful horror story, and he brings all his careful craftsmanship to the unraveling of this fairly predictable plot. His great strength as a writer is his ability to build sinister elements by slowly-amplified degrees into a narrative that is full of realistic detail, extrapolating the artistic method of M. R. James to novel length. He is able to do this without relying on the *grand guignol* violence typical of modern horror fiction, although he can and does insert gruesome passages into his plots when they require it.

The greatest difficulty faced by writers of suspenseful horror stories of this relatively subtle kind is to maintain their readers' patience and sympathy with characters who cannot know (as the reader inevitably does) that the pattern of events enveloping them really are significant of something unutterably nasty. In such a context, the use of a film as a McGuffin is artful and productive, because it allows the plot to echo its own problems and to reflect upon their paradoxicality. *Tower of Fear* is an artifact, whose authentically horrific quality is concealed by a surface of exploitative pretend-horror, and the quest to expose and understand it resonates with the author's mission to achieve a workable communion of naïve character and knowing reader.

In an early scene which seems, on the face of it, merely to be a satirical red herring, Sandy—having only just begun her search— visits a group of horror buffs associated with a fanzine called *Gorehound*. They had been in communication with Graham, but it turns out that they cannot help her. The incident does not move the plot along at all, but it does allow Campbell to provide an elaborate description of their salivating fascination with the bloodiest scenes of the crude video nasty that they happen to be watching. The heroine finds the encounter curiously disturbing, and, in the fullness of time—although Campbell does not labor the point—it transpires that this scene does have a contribution to make to the story, albeit a metaphorical one. The "ancient images" that give the story its title are of a very similar nature to those that flit across the video screen in this brief interlude, and the peculiar avidity of the three weird horrorschlock-addicts is exactly what is made incarnate in the supernatural pursuers whose image has been unwisely incorporated in the lost film.

When they are not busy harrying those who have come into contact with their cinematic representation, the monsters in *Ancient Images* have a ritual function to perform. This cruelly predatory activity is aided and abetted by the passive acceptance of the morally-anesthetized inhabitants of the fertile land they nourish with violently-spilled blood—an acceptance that is mirrored by the passivity and seeming moral anesthesia of consumers of horror movies.

It might seem odd that Campbell, who makes a living writing horror stories, should cast a jaundiced eye upon the motives and appetites of fans of gruesome excess, but one of the key roles of the horror story is to confront its users with awkward questions about their own impulses, appetites and secret fantasies. If Hollywood's reduction of "horror" to a marketable product, served up with derisory and contemptuous cynicism, has any virtue at all, it lies in the concealment of real discomfort and disturbances beneath a superficial and titillatory gloss.

When the heroine of *Ancient Images* ultimately contrives to see the long-lost movie, she finds that its cinematic imagery brings into sharp and provocative focus issues that are blandly unengaging in the written story that is its basis. This does not occur because the film is more carefully constructed, or more artful, than the story, but simply because of the power of the visual image. Horror is more an aesthetic response than an emotion; it is an essentially *voyeuristic* sensation, and, by virtue of that fact, it is very easily adaptable to the movies. The facility with which the movies can handle horror is, however, a double-edged sword, for the appearances that so readily generate horror are mere masks, and, no matter how sophisticated the make-up and special effects may become, the masks remain masks, stubbornly obscuring that which lies behind them.

A book about a movie can never be as brutally horrific as the movie itself, but it can explore more carefully and more comprehensively what might lie behind the movie's force, not merely in a fanciful sense but in a true sense. That is what *Ancient Images* tries to do, and succeeds in accomplishing.

The Night Mayor by Kim Newman (London: Simon & Schuster, 1989)

Kim Newman made his first reputation as a film critic, a profession he followed exclusively for a decade before becoming a prolific novelist. Much of his fiction is heavily influenced by the cinema, examining and reflecting the manner in which the contemporary mythologies of popular culture have been formed and focused by cinematic imagery.

The Night Mayor is a thriller set in a hypothetical future, when the media can be directly hooked into the nervous systems of their consumers. The equivalents of today's Hollywood hacks are "Dreamers" who assist experience-synthesizing computers with their plotting and characterization, adding a gloss of human interest and emotion to what is basically a mechanical process. When ingenious super-criminal Truro Daine "escapes" from maximum security imprisonment by establishing his own private dream-world within the information network, it quickly becomes clear that the despised Dreamers are the only people who might have the necessary expertise to hunt him down and destroy his infectious dream, before it can grow to corrupt and conquer the entire information-world.

Tom Tunney—alias Richie Quick, private detective—is promptly conscripted by the powers-that-be (here known as the Gunmint) to go after Daine. He is quickly absorbed into the dream world established by the "Night Mayor", which is compounded out of images borrowed wholesale from a particular sub-genre of the old-fashioned and obsolete "flattie" films, whose influence on the Dreamers' own dubious art-form inevitably remains considerable. The sub-genre in question is American *film noir*, and the private universe over which the Night Mayor reigns supreme is a compound of such films, populated by countless avatars of Humphrey Bogart, Edward G. Robinson and their numerous contemporaries.

Unable to compete with Daine in a world where the rules are set to his advantage, Richie is reduced to the status of a mere minor character whose role exposes him to constant peril. A second Dreamer, Susan Bishopric, has to be sent in to rescue and support him. In order to carry through their mission, the two Dreamers must adapt their tactics as well as their expectations to the codes and narrative conventions of the *film noir*. They get to meet a host of old-time actors playing their typical roles, including such figures as Dan Duryea and Thelma Ritter, and gradually learn to exploit their knowledge of typecasting and the plot-strategies of hackwork. They also encounter the enigmatic "Bard of the Boulevard", who eventually turns out to be far more than the stock John Carradine character he seems at first to be.

The mock-casual style and breezily pyrotechnic action of *The Night Mayor* combine to make it as witty as it is vivid, allowing it slyly to poke fun at the conventions of the *film noir* genre, while celebrating the charm and seductive power of its exemplars. In deploying the special artifice of the genre to construct its own scenarios, the story conducts a quirky but sophisticated interrogation of the essential appeal of such films, but the process eventually moves beyond this kind of affectionate satirical homage into new imaginative territory.

When the time finally comes to bring its own plot to a suitable climax, the novel has to break out of the constraints of the genre, transcending their limitations in order to bring down a villain whose expertise allows him to have every conventional plot-twist covered. The resolution of the plot thus provides an ingenious transfiguration of typical *film noir* assumptions about the possibility of heroism in an institutionally-corrupt world.

Despite the nostalgic element in its celebration of *film noir* atmospherics, *The Night Mayor* is essentially a book of the video age. As a film critic, Kim Newman had been obliged to spend a significant fraction of his early adult life watching films, day in and day out, thus achieving a state of mind where they could easily be run together as a seamless stream of experience. Twenty years ago, it would have been very difficult indeed for anyone except a film critic to duplicate that experience, but the advent of video has made it possible for anyone to be a collector and connoisseur of any genre they may choose, and to dedicate themselves to cultivating exactly the kind of expertise embodied in Truro Daine's private universe. The elaborate stocks of visual images built up by Newman in the course of his first career are undoubtedly fuller and more coherently-organized than those that most of his readers have, but they are not different in kind from those that any interested cinema buff can nowadays accumulate.

The Night Mayor is in some ways a nostalgic novel, which relies for its appeal on the knowledge that the imaginary world of the *film noir* is long gone, many of its visual conventions having been swallowed up by superior technical expertise. It is, however, a novel that reminds us that the present is always finding better ways to preserve and recover the past, permitting its periodic re-emergence.

Such re-emergences are not so much new leases of life as new kinds of "undeath", and it is entirely reasonable that to the novel should take up a position in the borderlands where two other popular genres—science fiction and horror—uneasily overlap. The novel's commentary on the role that the media play in society, and in the process by which individuals construct and design the narratives of their own lives, is as intense and as sophisticated as one might expect from a critic of the first rank.

PART THREE

REVIEWS FROM *NECROFILE*

The Angel of the West Window by Gustav Meyrink (Sawtry, Cambs.: Dedalus, 1991, 421 p.).

Gustav Meyrink (1868-1932) is best-known as the author of *Der Golem* (1913; in book form 1915), which was first translated into English in 1927. He went on to write four more novels, none of which has ever been translated into English until now. Dedalus reprinted the 1927 translation of *The Golem* three years ago, and have now followed it up with this translation of Meyrink's last novel, *Der Engel vom Westlichen Fenster* (1927).

Meyrink was born in Vienna, the illegitimate son of an aristocrat and an actress. Between 1883 and 1906 he lived in Prague, a city that plays a vital role in several of his books; there he lived an active and somewhat controversial life, and the enemies he made while attempting to fight duels with army officers probably helped bring about the downfall of the bank whose co-owner he was. He began writing for the satirical journal *Simplicissimus* soon after the turn of the century, while convalescing from a bout of tuberculosis; by the time he moved on to novels he was becoming increasingly involved in studies in the occult, editing and translating documents written by the esoteric philosophers and magicians of previous centuries. *The Angel of the West Window* is directly derived from these studies, dealing in detailed fashion with the life and thought of the most famous of all English occultists, John Dee.

It is rare for credulous men to be successful writers of occult fiction, partly because their credulity undermines their aesthetic judgment, and partly because the insistently *recherché* quality of their work often makes it tedious. It is not clear precisely how credulous Meyrink was in regard to the occult writings that so intrigued—and perhaps came to obsess—him, but if he was a true believer he certainly did not let that inhibit his flair for melodrama. *Recherché* though it is, *The Angel of the West Window* is filled with extraordinarily rich and striking imagery, and its plot is intricate and suspenseful. It is undoubtedly a masterpiece, and many readers will prefer it to *The Golem*, on account of the greater scope of its fantastic imagery and its rampant eroticism. Because the details of John Dee's career have recently been popularized—and his reputation partly rehabilitated—by the historian Frances Yates, there is probably now a larger audience capable of appreciating Meyrink's novel than ever existed before, and this will hopefully allow *The Angel of the West Window* to be as widely read and as widely appreciated as it deserves to be. Given the influence that Yates has exerted on the recent novels of John Crowley, there must be a good many fantasy readers well equipped to get a grip on *The Angel of the West Window*, which attempts in its own fashion to do for John Dee what the novel that Crowley began in *Aegypt* set out to do for Yates' other Renaissance hero Giordano Bruno.

As well as being a significant dramatization—perhaps *the* most significant dramatization—of the authentic occult tradition, *The Angel of the West Window* is also an archetypal product of German neo-Romanticism. It makes reverently efficient use of the literary method of E. T. A. Hoffmann, and in some respects is strongly reminiscent of Hoffmann's "Der goldene Topf" (1813)—as are *The Golem* and a notable novel by Meyrink's contemporary Paul Busson, *Die Wiedergeburt des Melchior Dronte* (1921; tr. 1927 as *The Man Who Was Born Again*), which was reprinted with *The Golem* in the Dover edition edited by E. F. Bleiler. Like these predecessors, *The Angel of the West Window* features a contemporary protagonist who finds himself at a crucial interface between his everyday reality and another, and merges his existence with the other reality to the extent that he acquires a greater self. The narrator of *The Angel of the West Window* is a descendant of John Dee, who comes into possession of various documents relating to his ancestor, including fragments of his diary. By virtue of his perusal of these documents—and his evolving relationships with three other characters, who have mysterious affinities with key figures in Dee's life—gradually discovers that he is, in some sense, the same individual as John Dee, charged with the duty of taking up the thread of Dee's appointed mission and attempting to bring that mission to its conclusion. In order to do this he must do battle—as Dee did—with the agents of the sinister goddess Black Isaïs, the ultimate *femme fatale*. As the novel progresses, the past and the present become increasingly and dangerously entangled, until the climax of John Dee's career, as represented in the documents the narrator studies, becomes the narrator's own personal crisis.

John Dee's story as recounted here is fairly faithful to the belatedly-reported events of the actual Dee's life, save for the outcome of the demand made by the crystal-gazer Edward Kelley that he and Dee must share their wives. It is, however, speculatively embellished in various ambitious and highly dramatic ways. Meyrink's Dee is the sponsor of the revolutionary Ravenheads and their amazing leader Bartlett Greene, to whose imprisonment and torture by the sadistic Bishop Bonner he is a reluctant witness. It is Greene who introduces Meyrink's Dee to Black Isaïs, planting a seed that comes to fruition when Dee—who is ambitious to become the husband of the future Elizabeth I and to rule a British empire in the west—responds to a hitch in his relationship with the capricious princess by raising a succubus in her image. After this, Dee can never quite escape the grip of the goddess, who has seized (but not fully established her claim upon) a talisman that is the key to Dee's destiny.

Dee's subsequent career in England and in Prague—where he and Kelley come under the uncertain protection of the Emperor Rudolf and Dee meets Rabbi Löw, the golem-maker—is constantly blighted, but his damnation is never quite completed. His descendant must decide whether to take up the cause, and face in his turn the threats and temptations of Black Isaïs, in order to settle once and for all the matter of her entitlement to possession of the talisman, and thus to John Dee's soul. The eponymous angel is the supernatural being summoned by Kelley with the aid of the black skrying-glass that Dee obtained from Greene, whose ambivalent role in Dee's later affairs leads him to confusion and almost to despair.

Anyone with a serious interest in the history of occult fiction has cause to be delighted that *The Angel of the West Window* is at last available in English. The translation is by Mike Mitchell is excellent, and it is welcome news that he is already at work on a translation of Meyrink's second novel, *Das grüne Gesicht* (1916), to be published by Dedalus next year as *The Green Face*. General readers of weird fiction will also find the book rewarding; the passages dealing with Bartlett Greene's imprisonment and execution, and those dealing with the various temptations of Black Isaïs, are as gripping as any one is likely to encounter anywhere. Although it deals with ostensibly esoteric matters, and certainly has its own mystical axe to grind, *The Angel of the West Window* is by no means an esoteric book; although a little prior knowledge of John Dee's career and the traditions of Renaissance magic will certainly enhance the reading experience they are by no means essential to an enjoyment of the book, which is more easily approachable than either *The Golem* or *The Man Who Was Born Again*. It bears repeating that this is an authentic masterpiece, one of the greatest supernatural novels ever written. All specialist dealers should take steps to stock it.

Candlenight by Phil Rickman (Duckworth, 1991, 363 p.)

Candlenight is a first novel by a Lancashire-born journalist who has lived for twelve years in Wales. In 1987 he made a radio documentary called *Aliens*, which explored the attitude of the Welsh to the leisurely "invasion" of their land by the English—whose penchant for buying picturesque cottages in rural areas for use as weekend "holiday homes" is much resented by local people who cannot afford homes for themselves because of the consequent price-inflation. The research that Rickman did for *Aliens* is redeployed in *Candlenight*, which is probably not the first ever Welsh Nationalist horror story, but is surely the first written in English by an Englishman. With the characteristic zeal of the convert, Rickman goes to great lengths to establish that he is not at all like other Englishmen who have taken up residence in Wales, and he takes great care to show off the fact that he has taken the trouble to make Wales his true home, even to the extent of learning to speak Welsh. Curiously, however, if one looks beyond the book's painstaking didactic passages—which explain how callously insensitive most English incomers seem to the Welsh, and offer propaganda for the more moderate wing of the Welsh Nationalist Party, Plaid Cymru—to study the actual plot, one can easily find evidence of a more profound ambivalence. This is, of course, entirely appropriate; what are horror novels for, if not to give voice to deep-seated feelings of uncertainty and unease?

Because of the author's long journalistic experience *Candlenight* reads more smoothly than most first novels. The prose is lean and clear, possessed by a seriousness of purpose that helps to maintain its urgency even in those fairly long sections of the plot where nothing much actually happens. If the whole seems slightly less than the sum of its parts, this is presumably because the author is used to working in short lengths, and is not entirely at home constructing an edifice of this size and complexity. The reader is introduced to one character after another, more than once falling into the trap of accepting as a central viewpoint a character who subsequently falls over and dies, to be replaced as a narrative anchor by someone who had previously seemed to be a mere spear-carrier. This does not prevent the novel from being a moderately gripping and rewarding read, and the story's casual way with human characters might easily be deemed acceptable, given that the true central character of the narrative is not a person at all; it is the village of Y Groes (The Cross), which used to be called Y Groesfan (The Crossing-Place).

To sum up very simply what the book takes enormous pains to establish, Y Groes is the only place in Wales that remains steadfastly and unconquerably Welsh, and it achieves this partly by committing supernatural murder every time an Englishman has the temerity to try to move into it. Nor is it keen on visiting antiquarians who attempt to uncover the secrets of its secretly un-Christian church—one of which might or might not be that Y Groesfan was the place to which Owain Glyndwr (known as Owen Glendower to Shakespeareans and other Englishmen) was brought to be buried. Not that many Englishmen have the chance to move into Y Groes, given that its houses never come up for sale—even the undertaker from a neighboring village, who thinks of Y Groes as a kind of paradise, can never find an opportunity to buy one—and its victims are mostly the spouses of those natives who marry out. (One presumes that Y Groes has no objection to an occasional influx of English genes, because it has some occult intelligence of the notion of hybrid vigor, but it is reluctant to put up with the carriers of said genes any longer than is strictly necessary.)

Y Groes has an equally profound, but very different, effect on those of its own people who are lineal descendants of a group of four families whose allotted task it is to carry forward the almost-eclipsed tradition of the Black Bards. Some such individuals occasionally move out, but when their turn comes to take up the thread of their duty they are brought back to Y Groes and completely absorbed into its mysterious soul, ruthlessly stripped of the detritus of any ordinary lifestyle they might have acquired (including, of course, English spouses). It is events of this kind that move the somewhat convoluted plot of the story, generating a supply of interested outsiders who try hard to penetrate the secret of Y Groes.

The task of characterizing Y Groes is handled with considerable skill, although Rickman seems to be a little embarrassed by the supernatural apparatus that he deploys. This discomfort eventually

61

leads him to understate the climax, which would surely have been more effective had he been more vividly and whole-heartedly nasty-minded. In the end, the restoration of normality brings the book closer to the *modus operandi* of the contemporary thriller, and horror story fans may be disappointed to see the Black Bards so easily thwarted. In the implausibly upbeat conclusion, the virtuously moderate Welsh Nationalist wins the local by-election; he, it seems, and not Y Groes, is a symbol of the honest and worthy ambitions that the Welsh people ought (in the humble opinion of the English author) to embrace.

Rickman's journalistic conscience occasionally gets in the way of *Candlenight*'s pretensions. He is, for instance, fully aware of the fact that what nowadays passes for "traditional" Welsh culture—the world of Eisteddfods and white-clad "Bards"—is a nineteenth-century fake, without any authentic roots, which was arbitrarily cobbled together by a handful of scholarly fantasists. His awareness that his own invention of a more ancient "authentic" order of Black Bards is no more than an inversion of a folly is seemingly inhibiting; he is unable to muster much conviction in detailing the powers and responsibilities of the hypothetical magicians. One is inclined to wonder, though, whether this invention—half-hearted though it is—reveals more than the author intended about his *true* feelings about Wales and the Welsh.

On the surface, Rickman's rhetoric is insistent that the Welsh (apart from a few lager louts such as one might find anywhere in the British Isles) are polite, pleasant and entirely pragmatic in their quest to preserve their land from the unthinking depredations of rich foreigners. Beneath the surface, though, the novel takes it for granted that the "real" Wales is a dark and murderously malevolent place inhabited by cackling hags and fanatical grotesques, whose heritage is essentially narrow, mean and steadfastly opposed to progress. Is this what Phil Rickman, in his heart of hearts, really feels when he pops into his local for a pint and displays his virtue by conversing with the locals in their own (fiendishly difficult) language? If not, why isn't he writing nostalgically twee Celtic fantasy, like everyone else?

Satanskin by James Havoc (Creation Press, 1992, unpaginated); *Red Stains* edited by Jack Hunter (Creation Press, 1992, 137 p.)

New technologies of book production have facilitated the recent proliferation of small presses, many of which specialize in the off-beat and the outré. A number of small British publishers of this kind have been successful enough in the 1980s gradually to expand their production, including Atlas Press, whose list is dominated by surrealist works, and Dedalus, which specializes in "literary fantasy". Now the Creation Press (which publishes its non-fiction as the Annihilation Press and runs a mail-order business under the name Cease to Exist) is attempting to put through ambitious plans to expand its list and establish its own niche in the English publishing scene. The aims and interests of the press are more idiosyncratic— and likely to be rather more controversial—than those of its predecessors, and it will be interesting to follow the progress of the expansion project.

Creation Press was launched in 1989, its first publication being James Havoc's *Raism*, an "anti-novel" embodying the supposed credo and flights of imaginative fancy of Gilles de Rais, who was executed in 1440 for the torture and murder of more than a hundred children, allegedly carried out in the process of Satanist rites. Of all the people ever convicted of Satanist sorcery, Gilles de Rais is the one most universally believed to have been guilty, partly by virtue of the fact that physical evidence of his crimes was presented at his trial and partly because he confessed without having been tortured. It is, however, worth noting that his enemies did not have the authority to have him tortured before conviction, the Inquisition not having yet been established in his native Brittany, and were thus forced to bring forward physical evidence to secure his condemnation. He confessed *after* having been sentenced to death, that being the one means by which he could avoid torture, having earlier denied everything. It is probable that he was fitted up for political and financial reasons, just like his friend and one time *protégée* Joan of Arc—and if he was, there is a certain delicious irony in the fact that Joan was eventually made a saint, while he became an icon of evil of sufficient authority to warrant his use in a Satanist extravaganza like *Raism*.

Gilles de Rais had, of course, earlier been given a key role in Joris-Karl Huysman's lurid symbolist novel about Satanism in con-

63

temporary Paris, *Là-Bas* (1891), whose hero's biography of him is interwoven with the main text. Huysmans had earlier (in his comic study of the personal politics of decadent lifestyle fantasy *À rebours*, 1884) identified a French tradition of literary Satanism extending from the Marquis de Sade, which he undertook to carry forward until he got religion and became a lifestyle fantasist of a more orthodox species. It is this tradition of literary Satanism that the Creation Press is ardent to revive, revitalize and carry forward; Havoc's new book *Satanskin* and the anthology *Red Stains* offer paradigm examples of the method that the publishers intend to follow. *Satanskin* contains a condensed version of *Raism,* which is to be used as the text for a "graphic novel" illustrated by Mike Philbin (who is a contributor to *Red Stains* and whose *avant-garde* novel *Red Hedz* was published by Creation Press under the pseudonym Michael Paul Peter in 1990). *Red Stains* follows up an earlier Creation Press anthology called *The Black Book* (1989) edited by Tony Reed; it contains an ad expressing the intention to issue a regular magazine of "pieces of a serious nature which touch on interesting and dark extremes".

As the Creation Press's friendly competitor the Temple Press has recently received some unwelcome tabloid attention, because of its links with Britain's most notorious Satanist lifestyle fantasist, Genesis P. Orridge, it may be as well to spell out here that "literary Satanism"—like Satanist lifestyle fantasy, but more reasonably and more respectably—is essentially a species of iconoclastic response to moral taboos, which applauds a (purely symbolic) Satan as a heroic rebel against Godly despotism. It turns icons of evil like Gilles de Rais and modern serial killers into similarly symbolic rebels against the most taken-for-granted moral taboos, not because it wishes to advocate torture and mass-murder as real-life activities, but rather because it wants to offer the sharpest possible challenge to the moral ideas and ideals whose adherents try to shield them from criticism by representing them as the commandments of an (imaginary) God. It also revels unrepentantly in the delicious power to shock that comes from the wholesale violation of taboos; for this reason it typically combines the most horrific imagery it can discover with a calculatedly perverse eroticism, thus producing a kind of fantasy that is always striving (perhaps hopelessly, and perhaps pointlessly) to go beyond the limits of the Sadean imagination.

Satanskin features, in addition to the condensed *Raism,* twenty more-or-less extended poems in prose, which reach out for the limits of erotic/horrific expression. In so doing, they also test the limits of the English language, sometimes to destruction. Havoc has a vocabulary that outdoes Clark Ashton Smith's its calculated exoticism, but which fails to retain Smith's studious respect for the actual meanings of words. It is not quite as extreme in this respect as *Raism*, which refused to have any truck at all with such mundane trifles as storylines, and strung together phrases like "scion of the quinquephallic pig dwarfs" and "ingots of flayed lotus incarnate" as though they were false pearls on an interminable rope, but it still runs into frequent trouble because its grating gear-changes continually evade the clutch of meaning. Generous readers may well feel that a certain amount of linguistic chaos is a small price to pay for the privilege of witnessing a series of attempts to explore vividly exotic literary *terra incognita*, but those not inclined to such generosity may find the texts difficult to assimilate. The pieces do, however, have storylines of a sort—all involving messily revolting processes of destruction—and these impart a certain welcome discipline to the displays of pyrotechnic imagery.

The stories in *Red Stains*, by various hands, including James Havoc's, stick much more closely to orthodox narrative formats. One or two of them are let down by simple literary incompetence—as one might expect of stories that are mostly by inexperienced writers—but only Aaron Williamson's relentlessly *avant-garde* "Catalepsy #1" is likely to seem literally unreadable to the majority of readers. Some of the pieces are excerpted from as-yet-unpublished books, a couple of which are on the Creation Press agenda, and two are reprinted: Ramsey Campbell's "Again" from *Twilight Zone* and *Dark Feasts* and Terence Sellers' "Tourniquet" from *The Correct Sadist* (previously published in the UK in a Temple Press edition handsomely illustrated by Genesis P. Orridge). Apart from a typically-enigmatic piece from the darling of the British semi-professional dark fantasy scene, D. F. Lewis, the other items are by writers with names that are unfamiliar to me outside the context of the Creation Press. The most polished of these are "The Nostalgia for Desire" by Clint Hutzulak (which is seemingly excerpted from a novel in progress) and Tony Reed's "Monsters", but these still suffer by comparison with the slickness of Ramsey Campbell's prose. In any case, literary polish is not really a point at issue here—the aim is to be as disgusting as possible, and rough-hewn prose is sometimes a means to that end. The most stomach-churning items—or so it seemed to me at the time of reading—are Havoc's atypically off-hand "Love Comes in Fragments" and Paul Marks' "...And the Sun Shone by Night", but I must admit that my preference for a delicate touch made the rather less gross and gruesome Campbell story seem all the more effective for its unusual (in this context) refusal to go the whole hog.

Taken one by one the stories in *Red Stains* are less effective than the editor probably hoped, but, if one looks at the book as a whole, it is an interesting literary artifact. I was intrigued by its prepublicity, which advertised it specifically as a collection of dark *biological* fantasy, concentrating on processes of mutation and metamorphosis; this is an area of considerable interest to me (cf my "Dark Chamber" essay in *Necrofile* 4). Actually, the one story in the book that does involve processes that are allegedly gene-directed rather than arbitrarily reflective of psychological degradation, David Conway's "Eloise", is sadly let down by its author's apparent total ignorance of biological science, but I had already realized by the time I got to it that I had misunderstood what the originators of the anthology actually meant by "biological fantasy". In fact, the underlying philosophy of the collection takes its warrant from the idea—recently popularized in no uncertain fashion by the runaway success of *The Silence of the Lambs*—that the underlying psychology of repetitive rape-and-murder has something to do with the serial killer's desire for self-transformation. Fully half the stories herein accept as paradigms of the almost-unthinkable the hypothetical thought-processes of habitual murderous rapists, and attempt to dramatize them in these terms. Whether Thomas Harris is actually right to imagine the phenomenon of serial murder in this fashion remains, of course, a matter for speculation, but if *Red Stains* accomplishes nothing else, it certainly demonstrates that this is a notion whose time seems to have come.

In the remaining months of 1992, Creation Press plans to publish numerous other books. It intends to extend its series of "Creation Classics" (which already includes items by Edgar Allan Poe and the Marquis de Sade) with *Blood and Roses*, a volume of nineteenth century vampire stories that will include some new translations. Other projected titles include mixed collections of fiction and non-fiction by *Red Stains* contributors Jeremy Reed (who may or may not be related to Tony) and Adele Olivia Gladwell. It remains to be seen whether the press can reach an audience large enough to sustain this level of activity, but I shall follow its progress with considerable interest.

"Seeds of Inspiration": *Tales of the Dead: The Ghost Stories of the Villa Deodati.* **Translated by Sarah Utterson; Edited and Introduced by Terry Hale. Chislehurst, Kent: The Gothic Society, 1992. 143 p.)**

Everyone knows the story. In June 1816, Byron, Shelley, Mary Shelley, Claire Clairmont and John Polidori spent a stormy night at the Villa Deodati frightening one another by reading aloud from a book of ghost stories. In consequence of the perverse pleasure they obtained by this experience, they undertook to produce horrific tales of their own. Most of the stories conceived that night withered in the womb and were miscarried, but the chain of causality that was set in progress ultimately resulted in the production of two of the foundation-stones of modern horror fiction: Polidori's *The Vampyre* and Mary Shelley's *Frankenstein*. The book that started it all off was *Fantasmagoriana* (1912), a French translation of tales taken from the early volumes of the German *Gespensterbuch* (1811-15), edited by Friedrich Schulze and Johann Apel. An English translation of tales from the same source, considerably overlapping the French volume, had been issued as *Tales of the Dead* (1813); this has now been rescued from long and regrettable oblivion by the Gothic Society.

Tales of the Dead contains six stories; it omits three of the eight stories that were in *Fantasmagoriana* but adds one extra item not in the original: "The Storm", an original composition of the translator, Mrs. Utterson, based on an anecdote she had heard. Three of the stories—"The Fated Hour", "The Death's Head" and "The Death-Bride"—are known to be by Schulze. One, "The Spirit-Barber", is by Musäus, and is much better known, in Thomas Carlyle's later and fuller translation, as "Dumb Love". The author of the sixth story, "The Family Portraits", remains unknown. With the natural exception of "The Storm", whose heroine coyly and infuriatingly refuses to reveal exactly what it was she saw in the haunted chamber, the stories are typical examples of the German tales of fantasy and terror that were very fashionable at the time. The Musäus story belongs to the subgenre of *Kunstmärchen* ("art fairy-tales"), in which the horrific element is typically subservient to a more elaborate moral allegory, and "The Death's Head" also has more muted *Kunstmärchen* elements. The remaining three items are closely modeled on traditional ghost stories, featuring restless ancestral spirits that harass the living in stereotypical fashion, visiting the sins of the past

67

upon the present generation. "The Fated Hour" and "The Death-Bride", both of which employ the familiar German device of the *doppelgänger* and favor vengeful endings, are rather more effective than "The Family Portraits", in which an over-convoluted family curse is ultimately lifted.

Tales of the Dead is now of historical interest only, but its historical interest is considerable. Any reader inquisitive about the ways in which folkloristic material was first transmuted into the apparatus of Gothic fantasy will find it a useful handbook. The fact that there is nothing whatsoever in it that reappears in either *The Vampyre* or *Frankenstein* is highly significant, in that it demonstrates very clearly the radical break with folkloristic motifs that initiated the modern tradition of horror fiction. The inspiration it provided was in no way an imitative impulse; what Polidori and Mary Shelley eventually did—after having discarded their first thoughts—was to search out new materials that could duplicate the *effect* of the stories in *Fantasmagoriana* without employing an apparatus that had grown tired.

They achieved this goal by throwing out the traditional subtext of the stories in *Tales of the Dead*, which refers to matters of lineage, inheritance and filial obligation—and which had, of course, become far less appropriate to a world in which individualistic values and *laissez faire* economics had replaced feudal values and economics—and substituted a much more highly-charged sexual subtext that had far more power to generate unease for their contemporaries. One can see the primitive seed of such a sexual subtext in "The Death-Bride", in which a bridegroom is spirited away by an evil spirit that mimics the form of his wife-to-be, but the emphasis of Schulze's story is on the matter of contractual obligation—the groom is recapitulating the fate of predecessors who have, like him, abandoned former fiancées in order to seek more advantageous marriages; in Mary Shelley and Polidori such *formal* apparatus has become irrelevant, and the murky depths that lurk beneath centre stage are inhabited by the liberated forces of individual pride and lust.

In the 174 years that have passed since that fateful night, we have gradually relaxed our anxieties regarding pride and lust, allowing vampires and other monsters to overcome some of their initial stigmatization, but the stress-points and crucial ambiguities that haunt our secret hopes and desires are exactly the same nowadays as they were then (at least among such *avant-garde* figures as the exiles of the Villa Deodati). By setting *Tales of the Dead* alongside the works that casually broke its mould, the present-day reader is better enabled to appreciate the width and depth of the abyss of feeling that had to be crossed in the making of the modern world. All serious students of the history of the horror genre ought to take this rare and fortunate opportunity to acquire a copy of *Tales of the Dead*.

"Italian Gothic": *Fantastic Tales* by I. U. Tarchetti (San Francisco: Mercury House, 1992, 191 p.)

This is the first translation into English of nine weird tales by a writer who died at the age of thirty, when seemingly poised for a successful literary career (his second novel had been well-received and his death interrupted the serialization of the third). Although the quotation reproduced on the back cover of this handsome little volume refers to Tarchetti as "a kind of Italian Poe" it must remain a matter for speculation as to whether he might, had he lived longer, eventually have earned such a reputation. The tales that he actually produced remain insufficient in bulk to fill a book without considerable assistance, requiring the present offering to be padded out with an introduction (20 p.), a memoir by one of the author's contemporaries (17 p.) and the texts of two short stories by Gautier and Erckmann-Chatrian, from which Tarchetti lifted ideas (28 p.). In addition, the translator scrupulously points out that one of the nine tales signed by Tarchetti is in fact an unacknowledged translation of Mary Shelley's "The Mortal Immortal". What remains, considered as an entire career in fantastic fiction, understandably seems a little thin. On the other hand, the stories are certainly not without interest, and, in spite of the their derivative nature, they exhibit sufficient flair to make one regret that Tarchetti did not survive to build upon the foundations he had laid.

Tarchetti was born in 1839, a year before Giovanni Verga, who went on to become the most notable Italian novelist of that generation, and three years before Antonio Fogazzaro. He began his career at a time when the once-strong tradition of Italian short story writing initiated by Boccaccio and carried forward by Straparola had languished for two centuries, since the death in 1632 of Basile. The Romantic Movement—which had a profound effect on German, French and English fiction, regenerating and abundant interest in fantastic fiction—had not greatly affected Italian literature, and relatively little of its relevant produce had been translated into Italian. Laurence Venuti's introduction cites the principal (and perhaps only) exemplars available to Tarchetti in his own language as a translation of Hoffmann's tales and a volume that set Adalbert von

Chamisso's "Peter Schlemihl" along two stories by Edgar Allan Poe, the latter translated from Baudelaire's French versions rather than the originals.

Given these circumstances, it is not surprising that Tarchetti's ventures in Romantic horror-fantasy are thematically primitive, or that they show the strong influence of works that he read in English and French (he was fluent in both languages and earned his living—such as it was—as a translator). Even so, the fact that he made his debut as a writer of weird tales in 1865, with a translation whose original author he chose not to acknowledge, is hardly conducive to favorable prejudice.

Of the other eight tales collected here, one—"Captain Gubart's Fortune" (1865)—is a trivial non-fantasy, and one—"The Lake of the Three Lampreys" (1868)—advertises itself, presumably honestly, as a retelling of a local legend. "A Dead Man's Bone" (1869), which borrows the central idea of Gautier's "The Mummy's Foot" (1840), but leaves out the Orientalia and the eroticism, also reads weakly, although Tarchetti could not have known how commonplace stories of dreamers who wake up only to find some physical evidence of the "truth" of their dream would ultimately become. "A Spirit in a Raspberry" (1869), which lifts the central idea of Erckmann-Chatrian's "The Burgomaster in the Bottle" (1862), is, however, a more interesting adaptation.

The Erckmann-Chatrian tale, which is reproduced here in a much better translation than the one previously published in the Ward Lock collection *The Polish Jew* (c. 1875), is essentially a joke; a man who drinks a bottle of wine is possessed by the spirit of a burgomaster who was buried beneath the vine from which the grapes were plucked, but ultimately manages to excrete the spirit in the usual manner. Tarchetti treats the notion earnestly, and effectively describes the disorientation that overtakes a nobleman when his body becomes host to the spirit of a murdered servant-girl; she is eventually able to discharge her duty as a revenant by identifying her murderer, but the heart of the story is the strange manner in which she alters people's perceptions of her host, including his own—and the deftly casual way in which it is revealed that he was once numbered among her lovers.

The least of the original tales are "Legends of the Black Castle" (1867), a timeslip story that revolves around dark secrets written in a book, but coyly refuses to reveal what they are, and "The Letter U" (1869), which is a madman's account of his phobia regarding that letter (Tarchetti was also not to know how tediously commonplace first-person accounts of idiosyncratic monomania were to become). It is the two longest stories that are the real basis of Tarchetti's claim to be taken seriously as a contributor to the rich tradition of nineteenth century fantasy, and they do indeed sustain such a claim, despite the fact that they are so few in number.

"Bouvard" (1867) is a deeply felt tale of alienation, in which a deformed young man can find no intimate human companionship, in spite of his genius as a musician. He falls in love with a girl, but as she responds so coldly while she is alive, he cannot begin seriously to woo her until she is dead. Although the ensuing necrophiliac orgy comes to an altogether expectable end, it is described in a remarkably intense and languorous fashion. Tarchetti liked to fancy himself an irredeemable social outsider—he identified strongly with the Milan-based Bohemians who styled themselves the *scapigliati*, who fervently embraced deviant behavior and literary unorthodoxy, in imitation of the French writers who inspired the Decadent Movements—and his depiction of this particular anti-hero constituted his principal adventure in extremism along these lines.

"The Fated" (1869) may be another story that borrows its central idea from Gautier—this time from the novella *Jettatura* (1856)—but, unlike Gautier, who gives the power of the evil eye to his hero, so that he must kill himself lest he destroy his beloved, Tarchetti takes the more orthodox line of offering an onlooker hero, who first becomes aware of the activities of the agent of doom and then feels compelled act to save the girl to which the other attaches himself. What makes the story interesting is the method by which he undertakes to accomplish this end, which introduces a curious *doppelgänger* element into the story.

Few readers will come away from this collection convinced that Tarchetti is a neglected genius, but, as a literary curiosity, he is certainly worthy of some attention. Lawrence Venuti has done an excellent job of translation (it is interesting to compare his retranslation into English of Tarchetti's version of Mary Shelley's story with the original) and has done everything possible to make this a nice volume to have on the shelves. The illustrations by Jim Pearson are apt and well-executed and the publishers have done an excellent job of designing the text and the book itself. It is a book that will look well on the shelf, and it is not so very esoteric that it has nothing to offer the casual reader. The connoisseur will undoubtedly be grateful for "Bouvard" and "The Fated", and will not resent the rest of the contents—only the reproduction of the over-familiar Gautier tale really constitutes a waste of space.

"Somme Enchanted Evenings": *Lovedeath* by Dan Simmons (New York: Warner, November 1993. 310 p.)

A collection of five novellas is an oddity in a day and age when Conventional Publishing Wisdom holds that collections of any sort are only to be published with the greatest reluctance, as a kind of sop to the vanity of money-earning novelists—a sweetener to persuade them to sign up for multi-book contracts, or to keep them happy while they work on their next blockbusting cash cow. A writer has to have real clout these days to get a book like this through that muddy minefield, strewn with the mangled corpses of a million frustrated endeavors, which used to be the English language publishing business. The front flap blurb and the publicity handout both assure their readers that *Lovedeath* is "in the tradition of Stephen King's *Different Seasons*"—which, roughly translated, means "now *another* of the bastards has got us so far over the barrel that we're having to pander to his whims". All discriminating readers ought to rejoice in this victory of Art over Circumstance, and show their gratitude in the usual way.

Dan Simmons has become a highly successful writer without ever playing by the publishing industry's "rules". He has hopped from one genre to another with a blithe disregard for maintaining consistency of product in any respect save for the quality of his prose, which has always remained lucid, vivid and gripping. He is, in fact, one of those rare writers who can command attention for whatever he happens to want to say, even if his readers had no idea until they started reading that they were interested in the particular topic under consideration. He is not only a writer of considerable elegance and great panache, but one who is never content to devote his theatricality to the service of well-worn tricks; he is always enthusiastic to do something new, something different. This is worthy of admiration, because rather than in spite of the fact that it is a policy that carries certain risks. The well-tried routines can always be relied upon to strike a chord with readers who have had their heartstrings thus twanged in the past, but every expedition into literary *terra incognita* is at hazard of ending—in the mind's eyes of at least some of its camp-followers—up shit creek.

Speaking as a reviewer attempting to pass objective judgment, my verdict is that *Lovedeath* is an altogether admirable book, of uniformly high quality. I would dearly like it to be a great success, critically and commercially, on the grounds that every such success is a hammer-blow upon the blunt end of a stake that might one day be driven through the diseased heart of that loathsomely undead monster which is Conventional Publishing Wisdom. This judgment is, as it ought to be, quite unclouded by the fact that there are things in the book that I do not like; indeed, one of the great merits of books like this is that there are things in them that engage the intellect and the imagination sufficiently to sow seeds of doubt, confusion and distress. Paradoxical as it may seem, I found the book all the more fascinating and engaging because certain aspects of it rubbed me up the wrong way. The following comments are not intended to suggest that *Lovedeath* is a bad book or that Dan Simmons has made any kind of error of judgment in doing what he wanted to do the way he wanted to do it; at worst they reflect a disagreement on a few essentially contentious points of principle or a difference in psychological complexion.

The author's foreword informs us that he wanted to call the collection *Liebestod*, but settled for a translation, because not everyone in America knows German and because he wanted to avoid the risk of being thought of as a Wagner fan. He then publicly declines the opportunity to write "something superficially profound here about the themes of Eros and Thanatos that circle through these five tales like hungry sharks in a crowded pool", pointing out that almost all successful fictions embody these elements. He offers brief descriptions of the first four novellas—the off-handedness of which descriptions seems tacitly to assume that there is little in them to stir up controversy—but devotes the greater part of the foreword to a much longer (and much more defensive) explanation of the nature and origins of the final story in the book, "The Great Lover".

"The Great Lover" is a story about the Great War (aka World War I) and about the uniquely rich crop of poetry that it produced. Some of that poetry is reproduced in the story, credited to its true authors by a series of footnotes but represented within the text as the work of its central character, an entirely fictitious individual. Simmons anticipates that the legitimacy of this move will attract some debate and offers, by way of excuse, the explanation that the story was written "as a personal form of illuminating and explaining the power of this particular poetry", which became important to him as he "came to grips with my own possible involvement in the nightmare that was Vietnam". "In a real sense," he adds, "I had little or no choice in the matter". This statement echoes an earlier "explanation" of the fact that he took time out to write the five novellas in the collection, even though he had not planned to and the moment was not convenient, and the fact that love and death are "almost obsessive topics in my fiction"; of these matters too he is prepared to say, flatly, that "I have no choice in the matter."

I must admit that I am always profoundly suspicious of defenses claiming that the perpetrator of an action had no choice, whether the perpetrator in question is a war criminal who was only following orders, a murderer bidding to be classified as a victim of mental illness, or a not-so-great lover recruiting the notion of helpless infatuation to the justification of infidelity. I am, of course, aware of the fact that there is a quasi-metaphorical way of talking that some writers routinely adopt, which implies that they are mere instruments of characters who "demand to be written about" and who then proceed to "live their own lives", but I have never been entirely sure whether to attribute this to grotesquely false modesty, compulsive tweeness, calculated silliness or barking madness. It is so difficult to suspect Dan Simmons of any of these follies that I am tempted to conclude that he is being subtly ironic, in a way I cannot quite fathom, but, if he is not, then this is surely a classic example of Sartrean bad faith. The simple fact of the matter is that every act, and creative acts most of all, are exercises of choice; Dan Simmons really is the *author* of *Lovedeath* and of "The Great Lover", and if "The Great Lover" is to any extent an act of plagiarism and willful distortion then Dan Simmons is the guilty party. I shall return to this point, but, in the meantime, let us examine what the rest of *Lovedeath* has to reveal about the manner and configuration of its author's "almost obsessive" involvement with love and death.

The first (and shortest) story in the book, "Entropy's Bed at Midnight", is about the anxieties of an insurance claims adjuster regarding the safety of his daughter, following the death of his son in an accident as freakish as any of those with which his work brings him into contact. The story interleaves an account of a precipitous ride, which puts the protagonist's hypostatized fear to a severe test, with a set of sample cases drawn from the "Orange File" in which he dutifully tabulates the most blackly comic of the everyday tragedies with which he has been peripherally involved. The text reveals in meticulous and relentless detail the manner in which the death of his son has so contorted his world-view as to destroy his marriage and threaten the last atom of community remaining from it, and celebrates the small triumph of the eventual loosening of the rigidity that grips him. It is a fine story, and a beautiful beginning to the collection—but it is worth noting that (on the surface, at least) it is devoid of any erotic component. It is about love, but it is not about Eros; in this, it contrasts with the next two stories in the collection, which are about Eros, but not—not, at least, to any conspicuous degree—about love.

"Dying in Bangkok" also interleaves two narrative threads, one set in 1992 and one in 1970. In the flashback sequence the protagonist, on leave from service in Vietnam, comes to Bangkok in search of cheap sex and ends up funding his companion's adventure into the furthest hinterlands of sexual adventure: an encounter with a vampiric snake-tongued fellatrix that proves indirectly but horribly fatal. The scenes related in the present tense describe the protagonist's hard-won vengeance, ostensibly wrought in the name of love (following the belated discovery of a homosexual attraction to his dead friend) but carried out in a strictly clinical fashion. It is, of course, absolutely *de rigueur,* in the hyperinflationary economy of contemporary horror, to go for gross, so it is a compliment of sorts to observe that this is a profoundly nasty-minded story. I have no way of knowing whether it can be said to capture some metaphorical essence of the city of Bangkok or of the Vietnam War, although I assume—perhaps wrongly, I admit—that this particularly horrid version of the *vagina dentata* is not to be interpreted as a straightforward expression of male sexual anxieties.

A more familiar image of the *vagina dentata* plays the central role in "Sleeping with Teeth Women", but this too is transfigured into a political symbol of (to me, at least) dubious import. Here, a Sioux medicine man, who cannot pass on the wisdom contained in the oral tradition whose heir he is to children and grandchildren who have been hopelessly corrupted by modern America, confides his most precious fabulation to a tape recorder. Both the narrator and the author state that they are reacting against the appalling condescension of the film *Dances with Wolves,* trying to preserve— against the irresistible weight of circumstance—an image of the Sioux as a proud and masculine tribe whose descendants might one day recover the ground lost to the much prouder and even more masculine race that over-ran and overwhelmed their ancestors. It is a remarkably lively and witty story, related in a brilliantly precise narrative voice, which abundantly makes up in charm what it lacks in plausibility. Like its predecessor, though, it has far more death in it than love, although it is not short of sharkish lust.

"Flashback" has no *vagina dentata* in it, but, in spite of its context, it is remarkably short of lust, let alone love. It features a future USA that is in rapid and terminal economic decline, largely due to the fact that its citizens spend too much of their time obsessively reliving their memories, with the aid of a drug that may or may not be a sabotage device launched by the wily Japanese. The story focuses on three of the drug's victims: an adolescent, egged on by his friends to commit the murder that will provide him with the ultimate experience on which to flash back in future years; his mother, clinging desperately to the jejune measure of contentment and joy that life has afforded her; and her father, cursed by some unexplained and inexplicable whim of fate to flash back obsessively on somebody else's memory of failing to prevent the assassination of John F. Kennedy. Their separate tragedies, which have comprehensively isolated them from one another in the unfolding, converge with black irony into a single bitter climax. In spite of Simmons' cautious introductory disclaimers, I do not mean it as an insult when I say that this is the most Wagnerian story in the book, noisily celebrating the irresistible movement of a kind of Fate that is far more assertive than meek, mild entropy.

It may be worth pausing at this point to reflect that the Wagnerian *Liebestod* derives from a version of the story of Tristan and Isolde. Although we tend to view that legend through the lens of modern romantic fantasy, which assumes axiomatically that sexual love is a thoroughly good thing, whose consummation is devoutly to be desired, we ought perhaps to remember that it was originally composed to demonstrate that powerful erotic attraction was a terribly bad thing, which threatened the whole social order by putting such a dire strain on objective obligations of duty and allegiance. The first four stories in Simmons' *Lovedeath* do not come remotely close to an examination of any similar dilemma; none of the characters so far encountered has really had to weigh contrasting objectives in the balance. They make decisions to do things, it is true, and the decisions they make are important because they are matters of life and death, but they are never torn as Tristan was torn, between desire on the one hand and duty on the other, so that whatever they do must involve paying a price, calculated in the currency of pain and death. The connections that Simmons makes between love and death are, in fact, much simpler and much more direct than the ones implicit in the classic scene in Wagner's opera that Simmons (uncharacteristically) chooses to describe as "a huge lady in a brass brassiere belting out an indecipherable dirge for her dead boyfriend". All four of the stories so far discussed—even the first—are horror stories because their fundamental worldview is one in which love of any kind is so heavily overshadowed by the darkness of death as to become at best a perilously fragile barrier against it, and at worst its helpless instrument. "The Great Lover" provides a peculiar but by no means inapposite climax to the collection, at first appearing to take this line of thought inexorably to its conclusion but swerving violently on to a new track at the last possible moment.

Simmons says that one of the things that contributed to the evolution of "The Great Lover" was spending Remembrance Day in England in 1991 and realizing how much the Great War still meant to the descendants of its survivors. As chance would have it, I read "The Great Lover" in the week following the 75th Remembrance Day, having seen the usual array of cursory but deeply touching TV interviews with the last remaining survivors of the Somme and the three battles of Ypres, and having heard the usual crop of heartfelt verses used as voiceovers to archive film; this undoubtedly heightened my reaction to the story. In other circumstances, I must admit, the story might have seemed less of a travesty than it did then.

The main part of the text of "The Great Lover" takes the form of a diary in which an officer wounded at the Somme, having become convinced that he will die there, interrupts descriptions of the sequence of battles with accounts of a series of hallucinatory encounters with a "lady", whom he identifies with the figure of Thanatos in G. F. Watts' symbolic painting of "Eros and Thanatos" (reproduced in *Lovedeath* as a frontispiece). He records in great detail the scenes of death and destruction that surround him, occasionally pausing to dramatize them in verse (the earnest verses are actually by Siegfried Sassoon, A. G. West, Wilfred Owen and Charles Sorley, but there is also a savagely scathing exercise in satirical doggerel by A. P. Herbert). In the meantime, his episodic dream moves towards the symbolic act of sexual intercourse which, he assumes, will mark his death. The last and fullest poetic work that he "produces", however—closing the diary—is the poem by Rupert Brooke that gives the story its title, which embodies an attitude very different to that embodied in the previously-cited verses. A coda then explains what happened to the protagonist after this last entry was penned.

I am extremely uneasy about the propriety of this story, not so much because it borrows verses that are not the author's own, as because it deploys those verses in such a way as to pervert and falsify them. In those instances where he is simply placing his protagonist in situations where the true authors might indeed have found themselves, honestly trying to recover some sense of the experiences that might have inspired them, his sin might be considered venial, but that is not what he does with "The Great Lover", which is here used to "mean" something radically different from what Rupert Brooke meant by it—a transformation much more distortive than the shift of meaning imposed on Watt's painting. I do not wish to spoil the story for readers who might take some delight in its unexpected narrative *bouleversement* (although I fear that the mere revelation that it turns such a somersault might undermine the surprise) so I will not describe the move that Simmons makes in detail, but I will say that it seems to me to be a blatant cheat, unworthy of a man of his artistry. Given that he is a writer of no mean ability, why should he not have written his own poetry to enshrine his own philosophy?

The notion of honesty in fiction is a tricky one, and there is a sense in which it is absurd to charge a writer of fiction with not telling the truth, but when a writer aspires to the kind of realism that is inherent in the greater part of the narrative of "The Great Lover" it seems to me that one is entitled to question the moral legitimacy of his literary devices, and I feel as uncomfortable with the supernatural embroideries of "The Great Lover" as with its use of borrowed verses. I understand why Arthur Machen wrote "The Bowmen", in which St George brings a company of ghostly bowmen to the battlefield in order to help cover the retreat from Mons, but I also understand why Machen became upset when some people started believing that Heaven really had taken a hand in that battle. It is precisely because it is so very easy for writers to take up their pens and write "and then there was a miracle" that those who aspire to seriousness and profundity must be very careful of their reasons for doing that sort of thing. The world of a story has an inherent moral order, because the author has the omnipotence required to see that the good end happily and the bad unhappily *if he so chooses*, but if a writer wishes to persuade his readers that the world in a story is the real world, or some careful transfiguration of the real world that stands in a meaningful allegorical relation to it, he must use this power sparingly and responsibly. Even—perhaps especially—writers who speak of their work in terms of "I had no choice but to write this story and to write it this way" may be called to account if they are guilty of sharp practice.

The problem I have with "The Great Lover" is that it seems to me to turn its hijacked poetry and its sexy dream sequence into an escatological device of such blatant arbitrariness as to make a mockery of the moral that the story hopes and intends to enshrine—a moral which, incidentally, has been not merely denied but stridently derided by three of the four stories that precede it. The only way in which "The Great Lover" might be said to complete this particular set of meditations on the way in which Eros and Thanatos "circle....like hungry sharks in a crowded pool" is that the kind of love-life it endeavors to glorify turns out in the final analysis, as in the introductory tale, to be contentedly non-sexual. Dan Simmons, it seems on this evidence, is no greater fan of Eros than he is of Wagner; even when Eros is artificially transexualized into a beautiful, genteel and generous individual, she is only a way station to something even more refined.

Personally, I would like to think that it is possible for human beings to contemplate the everpresence of death without either the morbidly pseudo-pornographic fascination with mutilation that drips from the greater number of these pages or the eccentrically sentimental affirmation that serves as its upbeat ending. But then, if I were asked to dream up my own symbolic representation of Eros and Thanatos I would be even less inclined to think of hungry sharks in a crowded pool than Watt's bouncing baby bowman and bashful buxom belle. *Chacun à son goût*. For all its undoubted elegance, panache and gripping intensity, I fear that *Lovedeath* left me, in the end, with a sadly sour taste in my mouth.

"Double, Double, Toil and Trouble": *The Dark Domain* **by Stefan Grabinski, translated by Miroslaw Lipinski (Sawtry: Dedalus & New York: Hippocrene, 1993. 153 p.)**

The career of Stefan Grabinski (1877-1936) appears to have run along much the same lines as many other notable contemporary writers of supernatural fiction. He worked in lonely isolation, commercially unsuccessful and largely ignored by critics, gradually weakened and eventually destroyed by poor health (lifelong tuberculosis), sustained meanwhile in his idiosyncratic labours by stubborn determination, and perhaps by the sheer intensity of his unusual preoccupations. He died poor, his passing virtually unnoticed in a country that was about to be plunged into a catastrophe on a far grander scale than anything a compiler of tales of individual psychological disaster could ever have imagined, only to undergo a gradual process of rediscovery and achieve belated recognition of his achievements in more peaceful times. This slim collection of eleven stories, introducing Grabinski to the English-language market, represents the latest phase of that rehabilitation.

The most striking features of the work assembled here are the author's obsessively repetitive use of *doppelgänger* figures and his fascination with trains. His characters are prone to haunting themselves, unwittingly dislodging fragments of their own personality that become independently incarnate. These distorted doubles are usually hated adversaries, as in the grotesque "Strabismus" and "Saturnin Sektor", but "Szamota's Mistress"—whose incarnation is more problematic than most—is an elusive *femme fatale*. Sometimes the lost part of the self manifests itself in unhuman form, as in "The Area", where artistic creativity runs riot. Even when there is no solid secondary manifestation, the leaching away of some aspect of the self can bring about a fatal confrontation, as in "The Glance", or open the way for a deadly demonic possession, as in "The Vengeance of the Elementals". In all of these cases, there is an implication that the process of fragmentation and ultimate self-destruction amounts to a kind of poetic justice, although it is hard to say what crime the protagonists are supposed to have committed. The fire-chief in "The Vengeance of the Elementals" seems to be a heroic benefactor of mankind, and yet the impression remains that the elementals are somehow entitled to their revenge. One suspects that Grabinski, like many writers of a parallel stripe, was no great admirer of his fellow men, nor even of himself.

As a writer of psychological horror stories, Grabinski is inevitably at his most powerful when his narratives are at their most intimate. He is by no means a clinical writer, and becomes less interesting when his viewpoint is more objective. "Fumes" is another tale of personality fragmentation, but the protagonist is merely an observer, albeit an erotically-entangled one. "A Tale of the Gravedigger" is another story of exotic possession, but the enigmatic gravedigger is too oblique a case-study to command the wholehearted involvement of the reader. "The Wandering Train" is far the least of the three railway stories, because it too must be watched from the sidelines. The other train stories, by contrast, make much of the supposedly-delicious sensation of being on a fast-moving train, exaggerating it to extraordinary effect. "The Motion Demon" is yet another tale of metamorphic *doppelgängers*, more effective than "Fumes" even though it lacks the fierce eroticism of the latter story, "In the Compartment"—which *is* fervently erotic—is more effective still in its account of a meek man driven to sexual and murderous excess, while temporarily in the possessive grip of a train's thrust and momentum.

According to the translator's biographical introduction, Grabinski's supernaturalization of the experience of riding on a train is linked to his fascination with the philosophical works of Henri Bergson and the particular notion of *élan vital*. One suspects that Sigmund Freud would offer a rather different interpretation, although Freud might well have preferred it if Grabinski's sexual displays had not been so forthrightly literal. Where Bergson's influence does show up very clearly, however, is in the brilliantly phantasmagoric "Saturnin Sektor", in which the dissociated personality-fragments of the narrator embody contrary theories of time, so that the inevitable climactic murder becomes overtly symbolic of a supposedly-imminent shift in the popular conceptualization of time.

"Saturnin Sektor" is a very fine story—as are "Strabismus" and "The Vengeance of the Elementals"—but it suffers more than most of the stories in the collection from the failure of the translator to handle its central imagery in a sensible fashion. The sensitive translation of mythical figures from one linguistic context to another is, of course, a very difficult thing to contrive, and perhaps too much to expect of a man who is presumably translating out of his first language into a second, but it is disappointing to experience this kind of let-down effect while reading a story of such evident power. In simpler stories, like "Fumes", and even in vivid but straightforward visionary fantasies like "The Area", one can simply overlook Lipinski's idiosyncratic way with English grammar and his woefully inelegant handling of idiomatic phraseology, but his ham-fistedness becomes more annoyingly conspicuous when he is dealing with symbolic and allegorical materials. I dare say that native English speakers who are capable of literary elegance in their own right and also fluent in Polish are rather thin on the ground, and might well prefer to work on projects more likely to win the approval of the literary establishment, but it is a pity that this book could not at least have been put into the hands of a competent copy-editor.

The ads at the back of *The Dark Domain* announce the forthcoming publication of a *Dedalus Book of Polish Fantasy*, which might contain more Grabinski stories, and certainly ought to allow English and American readers and critics to get a clearer idea of the historical context in which his work ought to be viewed. Madeleine Johnson's brief critical afterword to the present volume is singularly unhelpful in this regard; she contents herself with drawing a parallel between "The Area" and a modern children's book in order to justify the title of the collection. (The book in question is left perversely unnamed but I presume the reference is to Catherine Storr's excellent *Marianne Dreams*—although, if so, the plot summary is incorrect in one detail).

There is ample evidence in this volume, despite the slight botching of the translations, to demonstrate that Grabinski was a highly accomplished writer, whose work certainly deserves to be firmly established within the canon of supernatural fiction greats. I cannot help wondering how many more embittered ghosts of similar stature might be wandering amid the shelves of moldering libraries, hidden behind barriers of language and the legacies of past neglect.

"Life's a Bitch, and Then...": *Strange Angels* by Kathe Koja. (New York: Delacorte Press, May 1994. 277 p.)

According to Martin Heidegger, the underlying *angst* ensuring that the life of the mind is set on a permanently uneasy foundation is the consciousness that the aforesaid life will at some future moment (perhaps the very next) cease, and vanish into oblivion. In pursuit of some sense of existential security, we may try all manner of ingenious ploys, some of which may half-succeed in the short term, but all of them fail in the end; there is no way in which we can finally avoid knowledge of the doom that overhangs us like the sword of Damocles.

Writers of horror fiction have long understood that the situation is not quite as straightforward as this, and is, in fact, significantly worse. There are, alas, even darker anxieties, which—were they to take full possession of a person—would remake even death in a merciful image. According to the logic and historical tradition of horror fiction, another and potentially more menacing kind of *angst* is the consciousness that the apparent order of the external world might break down, either by virtue of its own supernatural subversion or because the apparatus of consciousness itself develops a fault. In this view, the difficult—and ultimately futile—pursuit of existential security requires far more than a tactical means of dodging the knowledge that we must one day face extinction; it requires a strategy by which we may continually reassure ourselves that the order of the world is safe, or recoverable, or less precious than we assume. Conscientious Sadducism can take care of the supernatural version of the anxiety, and has the not-inconsiderable philosophical advantage of being true, but fear of mental breakdown is not so easily displaced or assuaged.

Horror fiction's own role in the tricky business of dealing with the *angst* that is its essence is neither clear nor simple. If its sole purpose and effect were to taunt us with corrosive assurances of the hopelessness of our plight, it surely could not be so popular; we are obliged to look for a subtler explanation. Perhaps the virtue of horror fiction is that it allows us to confront our anxieties in a safe arena, so that we might pretend to be brave without undue risk. Perhaps such books and films act as a kind of repository, into which we are continually trying to decant our anxieties by means of a (purely symbolic) rite of exorcism. Perhaps such acts of reading constitute a kind of mockery, by which we subject our anxiety to a process of caricaturization, hoping thereby to make it seem absurd and ridiculous, and hence less dangerous. Perhaps, on the other hand, the writing and reading of horrific fantasies really is a kind of bravery: a process by which we attempt to get to know the substance of our anxieties more intimately, in the desperate hope—as futile as all the rest, of course—that we might in fact be able to live with them and come to terms with them.

Strange Angels, like most horror novels that are short on grue and long on literary pretentiousness, invites consideration on the last of these grounds. It is a story that attempts, not to understand madness, but rather to snuggle up to it, to indulge in elaborate foreplay with it, and in the end to retreat with it into the sour disappointment of post-climactic *triste*. It poses as a brave book, and perhaps it really is, although unsympathetic readers might cynically suspect it of being merely perverse.

Strange Angels confronts the reader with the story of a man who attempts to confront, domesticate and make peace with the madness of another; in studying his methods, motives, hopes and ambitions so intently, the narrative might be thought to be holding up a mirror to readers indulging a similar—if far less risky—flight of fancy. The man in question is Grant Cotto, a failed photographer shacked up with an art therapist, who becomes fascinated with drawings made by a schizophrenic patient named Robin Tobias. He befriends Robin and ultimately sets up home with him, tacitly replacing his troubled relationship with a girlfriend who is in every way his social superior with one that is superficially more difficult, but is safely asexual, and provides no scope for any challenge to the comforting assumption that he is the one in charge, the one with responsibility.

This move is passed off by Grant as an act of defiant compassion, which places him on a higher moral plane than all the other would-be careers who continually let Robin down. Because the flow of the narrative is so closely tied to Grant's stream of consciousness, unwary readers might be tempted for a while to go along with this interpretation, but it eventually becomes obvious that there is not an atom of reason in Grant's obsessive fascination, or his relentless pursuit of it. The tentative delusions by which Grant tries to persuade himself that Robin might simply be possessed of a different way of seeing, or might even be undergoing some strange process of metamorphosis—ideas supplemented and amplified by the problematic intervention of another schizophrenic, whose feminine charms profoundly disturb Grant's delusions of being in control—are, in the end, shown up for shallow folly. When Robin dies, Grant has no alternative but to recognize his own insanity.

Koja's story, like its central character, feigns compassion for the mad, but the primary form in which this compassion is expressed is a calculated demonization of the sane. The un-mad characters are uniformly (if peripherally) portrayed as unreasonable, unfeeling, over-demanding individuals, whose relentless struggle for control of their fellow human beings is ever wont to decay into frustrated and jealous rage. Grant is, of course, more than a bit like that to start with, but he gradually mellows as his last few marbles slip away. A weaker writer might have fallen prey to the temptation to contrive sunnier outcomes for the mad characters by way of moral reparation (authors, of course, have the power to do that, being in sole control of Miracle Central for the duration of their plots) but Kathe Koja—even if her work is, of necessity, merely posing as brave—is certainly not weak. Her ultimate distribution of rewards and punishments demonstrates that she is fully aware of the fact that metaphorical demons, whatever their failings, are infinitely to be preferred to metaphorical angels, and that anyone who thinks otherwise is off his (or her) head.

As Heidegger observed (in a slightly more long-winded fashion), life's a bitch and then you die. Writers of psychological horror fiction, of whom Kathe Koja is far from being the least, add the corollary that there's no earthly point in trying to go by the scenic route.

"In the Prison of the Past: *Nevermore* by William Hjortsberg (New York: Atlantic Monthly Press, October 1994. 299 p.)

William Hjortsberg enjoyed a considerable success with his offbeat mystery *Falling Angel*, which was filmed as *Angel Heart*. *Falling Angel* is, of course, a difficult act to follow, not merely because of its success but because of the way that success was obtained, which involved an explosive breakage of the conventions of the genre to which the story at first appeared to belong. The melodramatic flourish that converted the seeming part-boiled detective story into a supernatural thriller was the kind of trick that cannot work twice, because it relied on the reader innocently walking into the narrative ambush. Moreover, it is at least arguable that, were it not for the panache with which the surprise was delivered, the plot of *Falling Angel* would have had considerable difficulty standing up to the skepticism of reasoned argument.

Nevermore belongs to the same chimerical subgenre as *Falling Angel*, but it wisely makes no attempt to repeat the trick that made the fortune of the earlier novel. It is entirely upfront about the fact that it has one foot in either camp, to the extent that its two main characters embody diametrically opposed attitudes to the supernatural. This time, Hjortsberg has tried to enliven his story by choosing characters from life; his heroes are Sir Arthur Conan Doyle (usually referred to, rather quaintly, as "the knight") and Harry Houdini (alias "the magician"). The story is set in the 1920s, during one of the American tours Doyle undertook to popularize the spiritualist beliefs to which he became an enthusiastic convert after the death of his son in World War I. In the course of the tour, Doyle's friendly relations with Houdini are disturbed by Houdini's fervent determination to prove that all mediums are charlatans, who employ exactly the same tricks as stage magicians to dishonest effect. As in all products of the American "buddy mythos", however, true loyalty cannot be subverted by mere intellectual differences, especially when the buddies in question find themselves under threat by a homicidal maniac.

Hjortsberg's strategies of characterization tend to be rather awkward, even when he deals with invented characters. If he ever thought that it might be easier to deal with actual ones—who arrive, in a sense, ready-characterized by their careers and biographers—he must have found out very quickly that he was wrong. He does not attempt to tell his readers very much about the thought-processes going on inside the heads of Doyle and Houdini, but what he does tell us is conveyed in an oddly impersonal fashion. He continually seems to be laboring under the burden of a coy embarrassment, perhaps arising from a sense that he is invading the privacy of real people. This is most obvious in the horribly stilted sex scenes, but it extends to all the beliefs, attitudes and opinions of the main characters. Hjortsberg's account of the thoughts and feelings of Doyle and Houdini hovers uncertainly between the concerns and mannerisms of today and yesterday, never sure whether it should aspire to punctilious pedantry or modern raciness, and never attaining either. The difficulty that the reader might find in believing that the real Doyle and the real Houdini could ever have manifested the kind of emotional actions and reactions foisted on them by Hjortsberg is, however, only one among many factors generating the overall impression that *Nevermore* is about as authentic as a nine dollar bill.

The plot involves a series of bizarre murders committed in imitation of various short stories by Edgar Allan Poe, which involve victims whose connections with Houdini grow more intimate at each step. It soon becomes evident—to Houdini and the reader, at least—that the series might well be intended to reach its climax with the murder of the great magician himself. Doyle becomes involved partly by virtue of his acquaintance with Houdini, partly because the gentlemen of the press—making much of his Sherlock Holmes connection—keep asking him whether he intends to "solve the Poe murders", and partly because he continually meets up with the ghost of Edgar Allan Poe.

The newspaperman who first observes the connection between the murders, and thus gains an inside track on their reportage, is Damon Runyon, but this turns out to be of no real consequence, save to maintain Doyle's supply of tickets to big sporting events and to multiply opportunities for celebrity name-dropping. Constant exposure to Hjortsberg's writing style (e.g. "All along Fifth Avenue, facing the park north of the plaza, a mile-long row of châteaux and palazzi, each deserving a country estate, crowded together cheek by jowl like an overdressed chorus line rudely competing for the limelight") might, however, serve to conjure up wistful fantasies in the mind of the reader, in which Damon Runyon would be entrusted with writing the story instead of merely strutting and fretting his hour upon its rickety stage.

In trying to fit his materials together into a coherent whole, Hjortsberg takes a few liberties with history, dutifully listing the anachronisms in his prefatory note. By and large, though, he remains faithful to the known facts about the period in question and the people in question. In pursuit of verisimilitude he is prepared to go to some length in making certain selected aspects of the story plausible—for instance, in explaining why Runyon, who was a sports reporter, might in this particular case have turned his attention to crime—but his sense of priorities is, to say the least, questionable. His research into matters of detail is fairly conscientious, but he is to be one of those writers who is absolutely determined that no allegedly-fascinating tidbit of discovered information should go to waste, and his tour-guide trivia frequently become irritating.

As good historical novels readily demonstrate, the past is a fairly flexible prison; all kinds of events can be slipped into it without disturbing the pattern of the known, provided that they remain carefully self-enclosed. Nevertheless, the accomplished past *is* a prison; there are solid walls and locked doors within it that even Houdini could not get past. The more famous the characters are with whom a historical novelist chooses to work, the more their actual careers limit what can be done with them. The real history in which Hjortsberg's plot is incarcerated is, alas, consistently detrimental to the cause of narrative suspense.

When Doyle and Houdini are entrapped by their mysterious adversary we know perfectly well that they are in no danger, but that problem can be set aside with a little goodwill on the part of the reader. More serious difficulties arise by virtue of the fact that Doyle has a lecture tour to do and Houdini a career to extend; while they are out on the road, nothing much can happen. Hjortsberg attempts to fill in these lacunae by bombarding us with the flotsam of his research, and arranging cameo appearances by Buster Keaton, W. C. Fields and so on, but the fact remains that the plot keeps grinding to a halt. In addition, neither main character can undergo any serious development; neither Doyle's commitment to spiritualism nor Houdini's skepticism can be seriously threatened. This means that their attempts to unravel the mystery confronting them can never properly harmonized—cannot, in fact, ever really *come together,* except when the action is fast enough to prevent significant questions from being raised and discussed.

Mystery stories are at their most compelling and their most suspenseful when the whole substance of a text can be placed at the disposal of the mystery. Actual history and actual biography inevitably resist that kind of enslavement, and it requires great cleverness on the part of a writer to weave actual history and actual biography into the texture of a mystery plot. The particular materials with which Hjortsberg has chosen to work simply will not permit that kind of cunning weaving. To make matters worse, many of the ingredients stirred into the pot turn out to have no real relevance to the mystery. Runyon and the bit part players make no contribution at all to the working out of the mystery, and the only purpose Poe's gloomy phantom presence serves, in the end, is to leave the reader with the uncomfortable choice as to whether Doyle (the only person who sees the ghost) is barking mad or Houdini utterly mistaken in his convictions about the dishonesty of all would-be ghost-seers. Perhaps Hjortsberg felt equally uncomfortable with his own dithering inability to make that choice or to examine its consequences.

This unsettled issue might no be so awkward in the context of the novel, were it not that the question of whether some mediums really do have supernatural powers is vital to the reader's assessment of the chief suspect, the enigmatic *femme fatale* Opal Crosby Fletcher. Some readers, at least, might consider that the question of what Opal Crosby Fletcher is doing, and how (not to mention why) is far wider and considerably more interesting than whether or not she occasionally dresses up in a monkey suit in order to ape the murders in the Rue Morgue. Hjortsberg's eventual "solution" does inform us as to the identity and ironic fate of the homicidal maniac, but it does so in a remarkably brusque and oblique fashion that deliberately leaves all the more interesting questions unasked and unanswered.

Unfortunately, and in spite of all its calculated bizarrerie, the mystery at the heart of *Nevermore* never acquires the least hint of intricacy or aesthetic convolution. Nor is there ever any sense of anything much being at stake, because nothing really *can* be at stake; history cannot be disrupted, and unreconciled matters must be left unreconciled. The attempt to make some kind of virtue out of this irreconcilability—which is what the author seems to be doing in the peculiar and strangely pointless final chapter—is bound to fail in the context of a mystery story, where unraveling is supposed to be the order of the day. *Nevermore* is, alas, an ill-omened and sadly disappointing book.

"Lust in Vain": *Love in Vein: Twenty Original Tales of Vampiric Erotica* **ed. Poppy Z. Brite (New York: HarperPrism, November 1994. 405 p.);** *Love Bites* **ed. Amarantha Knight (New York: Richard Kasak, February 1995. 202 p.) and** *Blood Kiss: Vampire Erotica* **ed. Cecelia Tan (Boston: Circlet Press, 1994. 66 p.)**

Given that all vampire stories are erotic, covertly if not overtly, the notion of anthologies filled to bursting point with "vampiric erotica" carries a slight hint of pleonasm—but this is by no means inappropriate, for, if the brief offered to writers by these three anthologies differs from that of other anthologies of vampire stories, that difference lies in the hope, if not the insistence, that they must go right over the top and keep on going.

This is not an easy challenge to meet. It is, one imagines, bad enough to be invited to contribute to an anthology of vampire stories, whose packaging will ensure that no story can possibly exploit the shock value of its characters discovering, as if by ambush, that what they are dealing with is—oh horror! horror! horror!—a VAMPIRE! How much worse must it be to be required to kit out one's latest head-birth for sliding into a slot where it will rub shoulders (not to mention everything else) with somewhere between seven and nineteen other super-slick gushing-wet dream-fantasies? The contributors to these three volumes must have set out knowing that they had little or no chance of shocking anyone, no matter how relentlessly they might go for gross, and no chance whatsoever of hiding their stories' crucial moments of enlightenment behind some obligingly-camouflaged façade of mundanity.

The blurb carried by Poppy Brite's anthology (for which she is unlikely to be responsible) boasts that horror itself has become passé. "Now," it assures us, "there is a controversial new literature of the macabre that goes deeper than horror, beyond fear, to explore our darkest, most intimate hungers. The ones even lovers are forbidden to share." As come-ons go, this has a certain charm, although antiquarian grammar-fetishists who lament the extinction of the colon might be too busy wincing and sighing to drink its fascination to the full. What, exactly, *does* lie "deeper than horror" and "beyond fear", on the far side of aesthetic and emotional experience?

Fortunately, it is not necessary to take any elaborate census of the thirty-nine stories included in these anthologies in order to answer this question, because Poppy Brite has cunningly arranged *Love in Vein* —which contains twenty stories—so that its climactic item, Robert Devereaux's "A Slow Red Whisper of Sand", is a kind of summary of all that has gone before. This extraordinary *tour de force* condenses into its thirty-seven pages not merely the whole riot of improbably various, impractically cruel and impossibly orgasmic sexual intercourse that greases the other pages of both books but also—and more importantly—the entire tangle of miserably narrow-minded, morosely intense and plaintively inchoate aspirations that guide the entire enterprise. The unstated but very pointed moral of "A Slow Red Whisper of Blood" is *plus ça change, plus c'est la même chose*—or, to put it less obliquely, *vampires might get their kicks differently, but at the end of the day, they're no better off than the sad individuals who place and follow up contact ads*. The message—and it really *is* a message—which finally emerges from these anthologies, when they are considered as a set, is that there really is no perfect relationship to meet your imagined needs; substituting a vampire for the boy/girl next door might seem to promise something more, but it can't and won't deliver.

On average, the contributors to Cecilia Tan's *Blood Kiss* and Amarantha Knight's *Love Bites*, both of which are produced by publishers specializing in erotica, are more optimistic about the redemptive possibilities of vampiric attachment than the contributors to *Love in Vein*. When they place themselves, imaginatively, in the vampire's shoes (and they are *much* more keen to do that, even if the shoes prove to be ill-fitting, than they are to imagine themselves as mundane victims) they get a bigger and more immediate kick out of it than the more contemplative contributors to Poppy Brite's anthology. The star of Tan's collection, Renée Charles' "Cinnamon Roses" is a blithely blissful fantasy of pubic shaving. The most interesting item in Knight's retinue, David Dvorkin's "Reign of Blood", is a cruelly witty account of a vampire member of the French *ancien régime*—who is, of course, as serenely indifferent and ill-informed regarding the condition of the proletariat as Marie Antoinette—recklessly saved from Revolutionary justice by the pseudonymous Englishman Sir Percy Blakeney.

The stories in these anthologies are more often inclined to view conversion to vampirism as a kind of liberation than as a form of subjugation, although the liberation in question is sometimes hardwon. In *Blood Kiss,* Raven Kaldera's "Predator" is a bracingly brisk dystopian romance, while Pat Salah's "The Perfect Form" is a mincingly masochistic tale of transsexual transubstantiation, but both tales move sure-footedly towards a crucial moment of "true" identity revealed and realized. In *Love Bites*, "Pleasure Domes" by Kathryn Ptacek, "The Color of Her Eyes" by James A. Moore, "Smiling Eyes and Haunted Face" by David Niall Wilson and "Dark Seduction" by Nancy Kilpatrick (aka Amarantha Knight) are all fairly straightforward—albeit rather highly colored and slightly traumatic—celebrations of immortality found.

The neatly-twisted kind of optimism implicit in the stories chosen by Tan is to be expected in the produce of a small-press which seems to have been spawned by a group of Internet users brought together by their interest in sadomasochistic pornography. Upbeatness is even more typical of such endeavors than the kind of cursory narrative structure—here exhibited most brutally in Amelia G's "Wanting" and Dave Smeds' "Loved to Death"—which moves with increasingly hurried thrusts to an unashamedly dismissive climax. The contributors to a collection such as this are at least obliged to pretend that nothing sucks seed like sick cess, and perhaps one or two of them really believe it. Even viewed in isolation, though, the stories in *Blood Kiss* are possessed by an uneasy lack of conviction, and a naïve inability to extrapolate their premises.

Amarantha Knight's collection is slanted towards a more mainstream audience and it is not surprising that vampiric intercourse is usually deployed therein as a ritzy-glitzy alternative to all the more readily available boy-meets-girl games. Those stories that do extrapolate the sadomasochistic element—Ron Dee's "Soulmates", Lois Tilton's "Bite Me" and Nancy Collins' "Dancing Nightly"—tend to take it to extremes that are either hopelessly implausible or (in the last-named example) calculatedly comical. The fiction in *Love Bites* is more polished and more professional than that in *Blood Kiss*—as befits a team of writers that has clocked up an astonishing total of vampire novels—but it lacks a certain self-consciousness and self-analysis. By taking the sexiness of vampires and their predatory activities so completely for granted, they contrive to lose some of the erotic power implicit in stories whose writers were anxiously intent on the demonization of the urges that found symbolic display in their plots.

When they are compared with the stories in Poppy Brite's wider-ranging and more sophisticated anthology, the limitations of the lesser collections become clear. *Love in Vein* is not without its own optimistic fantasies, in which the ritual objects and narrative obstacle-courses of the Harlequin/Barbara Cartland formula luv-story are simply and straightforwardly replaced with their vampy-kinky equivalents, but Ian McDowell's vengeful "Geraldine" is the only really clunky one. Charles de Lint's syrupy "In This Soul of a Woman" barely avoids drowning in its own pretentiousness, but it does achieve a certain dignity, and A. R. Morlan's deftly ingenious "....And the Horses Hiss at Midnight"—which is certainly the *nicest* story of the thirty-nine, if not quite the best—succeeds in tempting the discerning reader with a hint of authentic delight. Inevitably, though, these inclusions are greatly outnumbered and more than abundantly outweighed by celebratory *contes cruels* that move with unerring glee to calculatedly-abortive endings.

Where exotic alternative bliss is fleetingly glimpsed in Brite's pages—as it is in Nancy Holder's "Cafe Endless: Spring Rain" and Brian Hodge's "The Alchemy of the Throat"—it flatters only to deceive. Usually, we know from page one that we are headed for a culminatory deflation that will be savage and thoroughly deserved. The irony of Christa Faust's "Cherry" and Elizabeth Engstrom's "Elixir" is brutally frank in spite of its surface gloss, while that of Kathe Koja and Barry Malzberg's "In the Greenhouse" and Jessica

Amanda Salmonson's "The Final Fête of Abba Ali" is magnificently decorated in the true Decadent style, but the ultimate effect is the same. High hope and vaulting ambition lead not to redemption but to disappointment, and the only winners in the game are those who start without such handicaps, and are thereby enabled to appreciate the true worth of their limited achievements.

In such company as this, where excess is the prescribed destination and exoticism the mapped-out route, it is as difficult for a writer to advance towards an effective nastiness as it is for a writer to retreat towards an effective delicacy, but there are some highly commendable near misses in *Love in Vein*. Wayne Allen Sallee's "From Hunger" only misses being genuinely sick by virtue of being too nakedly silly, and Danielle Willis' "The Gift of Neptune" only misses being genuinely harrowing by being a little too obvious in its build-up and a little too evasive in its ultimate delivery. Gene Wolfe and Thomas F. Monteleone fail to stand out—as writers of their experience ought to, among so many neophytes—only because their contributions are a shade too clever for their own good. In the end, though, the sum total of the various authors' achievements is to demonstrate in a very convincing manner that there really is nowhere to run, and nowhere to touch down, except the line that marks the devastating conclusion of "A Slow Red Whisper of Sand".

For the record, the emotion that lies beyond fear is despair; the aesthetic response that underlies horror is morbid fascination. There are, I know, some critics who disapprove of morbid fascination even more strongly than they disapprove of horror (well, they would, wouldn't they?) but I am not one of them. If I were the kind of person who could adopt poses, I think I would try to pose as a connoisseur of morbid fascination, and it is a matter of deep regret to me that my depressingly mundane mien and relentlessly moderate conduct make it quite impossible for me to carry off any such imposture. I am, however, easily able to perceive that *Blood Kiss, Love Bites* and *Love in Vein* are books that would certainly appeal to connoisseurs of morbid fascination. Such connoisseurs would be condescendingly amused by the buoyantly naïve presumption of Cecilia Tan's amateurs, pleasantly piqued by the accomplished performances of Amarantha Knight's tricksters, and knowingly reassured by the unrepentantly bleak *weltanschauung* of Poppy Brite's dark-flying acro-bats. Readers interested in vulgar titillation would, of course, be wasting their time picking up any of them, but who cares about *them*?

"Mazy Modern Monsters": *The 37th Mandala* by Marc Laidlaw (New York: St Martin's Press, February 1996. 352 p.)

The optimists of the Age of Enlightenment believed that, as science continued its triumphal march, superstition would wither away, so that when all men were literate and learned, intellectual folly would be seen for what it is and discarded.

The optimists of the Enlightenment were dead wrong; instead of withering away, superstition and intellectual folly thrived, steadily increasing their authority until their most enthusiastic prophets felt entitled to proclaim the advent of a New Age.

In his 1902 lecture on "The Discovery of the Future", which summed up the philosophy behind his pioneering work of futurology, *Anticipations*, H. G. Wells contrasted the kind of mind that was intelligently future-orientated with the kind that was bogged down by tradition and precedent, and declared that the day of the latter kind was done—that, in the twentieth century, people would free themselves from the awful burden of the past and commit themselves to the rational and methodical project of designing a better future.

Wells was dead wrong too; as the pace of social change accelerated, and uncertainty as to what the future might hold grew apace, people mostly gave up the unequal task of trying to make rational plans and accepted that life was a lottery beyond their control. The failure of "scientific" futurology was not that it could not anticipate with any degree of exactitude the shape of things to come, but that it could not persuade its users that they had any real power to take an active part in such shaping.

To all rational men, there are horrific thoughts—and their particular horror is what underlies and sustains such distinctively modern novels as *The 37th Mandala*.

The principal anti-hero of Laidlaw's novel (which has no heroes) is Derek Crowe, a hack writer who has come to the conclusion that the easiest path to reputation and riches in today's fading book market leads through the wilderness of New Age philosophies. He has set out to pander to the desperate hunger that so many people have, for the comforting illusion that there is some kind of key that will give them control over the vicissitudes of fate and fortune. His understanding of that hunger is rather vague—like all charlatans he underestimates his own vulnerability to his lines of patter—but he can see clearly enough that magic is a saleable product and that the fact that all magic fails in practice merely increases the demand for new magic (because magic is, after all, a subspecies of hope rather than a kind of substitute science).

The reader meets Crowe while he is in the process of hawking his new book of "mandala rites", anxious because some seedy nightclub owner seems to have ripped off the designs on which he is trying to build his career. Said reader already has the advantage of knowing, however, that the designs in question are charged with a power Crowe does not even suspect, for he too has ripped them off, without knowing how—or how intimately—their history is bound up with the killing fields of Cambodia. In selling them to a gullible public, Crowe is unwittingly selling shares in the appalling cruelty that such dark episodes of human history represent and display.

Given this, the reader is not at all surprised when the wife of one of Crowe's fans—who are both innocents abroad in the occult Underworld of the West Coast—is transformed by the nastiest of all the mandala rites into a monster-in-waiting. The reader knows from the very beginning that everyone who comes into contact with the mandalas will be tortured and destroyed by them, because there is no defense to be found in a time and place so utterly dispirited as to have pinned its hopes to the vacuous philosophies of the New Age.

Laidlaw's plot, such as it is, is merely an obstacle course that brings Crowe and his unwitting disciples to their fateful final meeting in a suitably problematic manner. It dutifully leaks explanations along the way, which record the manner in which Crowe came by the rites. Embedded within that tale-within-a-tale is a further tale-within-a-tale which displays the subconscious wellsprings of his unorthodox career—and it is within *this* tale, rather than the ones that contain it, that the real heart and passion of the text lie.

The main weakness of *The 37th Mandala* is its mazy but not-very-scary monsters. They are vaguely-sketched things with lots of eyes, mouths and tentacles, which hover above people like horrid haloes, feeding their nastiness in order that they may feed on it in their turn. They are similar in many ways to the "vitons" of Eric Frank Russell's Fortean fantasy *Sinister Barrier*, but their forms have become more complicated along with the depravities that they husband and harvest. This weakness is perhaps inevitable; bringing monsters on stage is always the greatest hazard a horror-writer has to face, and there is probably no way to do the job right. As a critic of H. P. Lovecraft once remarked, there is an inevitable sense of letdown in the discovery that the "unthinkable" is only an invisible whistling octopus.

The strength of *The 37th Mandala*, on the other hand, lies in its painstaking attempt to scrutinize and analyze the psychological malaise that lies at the heart of the so-called New Age. The fact that there is not a single sympathetic character in the book does not matter, always provided that the reader can identify with the author's commentary scalpel, which carefully dissects out the rotten moral core that lies within each of them. No matter how far California may be from the darkest corners of Cambodia, there are no innocents here. The mandalas that feed on corruption are just as much at home as they were in their native habitat—and, given their presumed nature, it is hardly surprising that they have taken aboard the delusions of grandeur and dreams of conquest that are so awesomely fecund in the neighborhood.

At the end of the book, of course, there is only the illusion of a conclusion. There are only two ways a horror novel can end, and the kind of horror novel that ended with the banishment of the horror is no longer in keeping with modern sensibility. Honest horror novels don't even bother with an apparent resolution, which is then subverted by a contortive coda; they deal in overt re-emphasis. Laidlaw is writer enough to try to contrive a melodramatic crescendo rather than settling for Lovecraftian underlining, but he is honest enough never to pretend that there is any possible exit from the moral maze that the mandalas symbolize. Some readers will probably find the ending unsatisfying, simply because all the melodrama in the world, no matter how thick and fast it might be heaped up, could not possibly provide an ending more effective than the story's beginning, but that is another burden under which all horror fiction labours. The fact that a clinical eye has been opened is always more significant than the precise form of what it sees.

The 37th Mandala is a thoroughly modern horror novel, competently done. You just have to remember that the horror is not in the mandalas but in ourselves, and in our historical predicament.

"Our Critics, Our Vampires": *Our Vampires, Ourselves* by Nina Auerbach (Chicago: The University of Chicago Press, October 1995. 231 p.)

So, the Lone Ranger's gun is out of bullets and there are none left in his ammunition belt; he's right up against the back wall of the box canyon and the Apaches are hot on his trail, war-whooping away like crazy. "Don't worry, Tonto," he says, bravely, "we've got out of tighter spots than this." "Who's this *we*, paleface?" replies

Tonto, before leaping away and letting rip with the war-whoop to end all war-whoops.

I am not normally one for quoting old and tired jokes, but this one came irresistibly to mind as I read *Our Vampires, Ourselves*, wondering exactly whose vampires and whose selves "we" were supposed to be talking about. Personally, I blame Camille Paglia. Ever since she made it to the Emerald City of TV-land, every slightly-raddled female academic in America seems to have begun to nurse the dream that she too might attain superstardom, if only she could follow the frenzied fishwife formula with sufficient flash and flair:

Contents: one part classic, two parts obscure, two parts pop culture and one part seriously hip. Tone: two parts hifalutin, one part flip, one part scathingly sarky and one part chatty-confessional. Shake or stir vigorously and serve piping hot.

There you have it: scholarship as performance art—well, performance anyway.

There is no such thing, the reader is assured by Ms. Auerbach, as The Vampire; there are only vampires. Well, knock me down with a feather—isn't postmodernism a wonderful thing? In Part 1, "Giving up the Ghost", Ms. Auerbach's vampires (and, one presumes, those of the entire mysterious company encompassed by her "our") masquerade as moon-linked friends in search of a special kind of intimacy—or, rather, as moony *friends* (nudge, nudge, wink, wink) in search of an intimacy that dare not speak its name. Unfriendly vampires, like those featured in William Gilbert's "The Last Lords of Gardonal", are refused entry. So are French and German vampires, probably because of their rampant and unrepentant heterosexual tendencies rather than on racial grounds. It seems that, for the purposes of the argument, Ann Crawford is deemed to have been de-nationalized, if not actually denatured, when she married the Baron von Rabe.

Varney the Vampyre is in Part One (but Smyth Upton's *Last of the Vampires* isn't), although he might have difficulty recognizing himself in such amicable and faintly ethereal company—but then, he always did. Personally, I put his essential incoherency down to the fact that James Malcolm Rymer was making up his adventures as he went along, under the pressure of an editorial instruction to spin it out for a few more months no matter what, but Nina Auerbach and her like-minded host are not madly interested in vampires as products of creative endeavor, preferring vampires as reflections in a darkling glass—and they are, after all, entitled; the past is a free and foreign country, where fanciful historians can do things as differently as they please.

Part 2 introduces the reader to Dracula, here dubbed "A Vampire of Our Own"—which is odd, really, given that the argument places such a heavy emphasis on Dracula's essential alien-ness and his abrupt reduction in the course of Stoker's narrative from hectic volubility to virtual silence (a transition unlikely to be replicated by any literary critic). Ms. Auerbach reads this subtext as a response to the trial of Oscar Wilde, which sure as hell shut *him* up.

(Actually, this is rather an intriguing suggestion, especially when one bears in mind that Bram Stoker had married Oscar Wilde's first sweetheart, Florence Balcombe. Did Bram ever look into the mirror of his wife's eyes and see himself as an Oscar-substitute? Did he ever wonder, as Wilde's star ascended, whether Florence might have regretted the unfortunate bout of syphilis that sundered her first romance? These are, of course, questions that Ms. Auerbach doesn't raise; after all, Dracula is *her* vampire, no matter who his creator and model might have been.)

In Part 3 the scene moves to America, not, as Count Kotor did in *The Vampires of Alfama*, in search of a land fit for vampire alchemists and enlightenment, but because that's where Hollywood is and all films belong to Hollywood, even ones made in Germany (*Nosferatu* and *Vampyr* are allowed to breach the protectionist barrier excluding all literary work in languages other than English). At this point the argument begins to ramble, although its sights make heroic attempts to remain firmly fixed on the many reincarnations of Dracula, here uplifted as "Our Vampire, Our Leader".

Feminism enjoys a formal emergence, as a blushing debutante, in the last subsection of Part 3 (although keen-eyed observers might have noticed her, skulking in the bushes like a Welsh Methodist at an orgy, in earlier subsections). Once out, she deftly paves the way for Part 4, whose title moves with breathtaking rapidity from alliterative punning to calculated bathos: "Grave to Gay: Reagan's Years". It is in the familiar territories of the recent past that the Paglia formula can really come into its own (so to speak), with Queer Theory and political pseudocommentary rubbing up against one another in a louchely lubricious fashion.

Perhaps I'm just being nostalgic, but it seems to me that there was once a time when literary critics were content to be the reader's friend, gently leading her (or even him) through a neatly mapped-out text, feeding her information judiciously, in such a manner as to improve her appreciation of its loveliness. What innocent and joyous days those must have been (assuming, of course, that they actually existed.) Then, if I remember rightly, F. R. Leavis and his unholy kin arrived like some supernatural emperor rising from the tomb, and the Great Critic mesmerized that same hapless reader with the awesome force of his authority, instructing her as to the enormously long list of books that were simply not worth reading. And the Great Critic cast his terrible blight over the greater part of the century, while the Groves of Academe quivered and quaked.

(Personally, I could never understand why there are English Literature Departments in universities at all. I can understand why historians might be interested in the history of literature, why sociologists might be interested in the sociology of literature, and why philosophers might be interested in the aesthetics of literature, but I have never been able to figure out exactly what intellectual credentials literary critics are supposed to have—but then, I'm the kind of person F. R. Leavis utterly abhorred, even though I didn't laugh on the one occasion when I saw him fall downstairs.)

It's all different now, of course. Postmodernism has determined that texts don't have objective meanings, so literary criticism has been freed from the necessity of pretending to maintain any intellectual standards at all. All texts now belong to the critics, who can own them as utterly as they parasitize them. All texts have become *our* texts, reflections of *our* selves; like Dracula's plaintive brides they have nothing left to call their own. Jonathan Harker—and everyone else who ever inhabited a printed page—belongs to the lordly vampires now, and it's absolutely no wonder that your average slightly-raddled apprentice harridan can look into a literary genre full of bloodsuckers and see nothing but herself multiplied a thousand times.

I make a guest appearance in *Our Vampires, Ourselves* as a token un-American, along with Kim Newman and Tim Powers (who seems to have been de-nationalized, if not actually denatured). I am introduced with the accusation of "characteristic murkiness", to which I freely and gladly admit. Well, it's better than being bloody *obvious*, isn't it, darling? So, here's three quirks for Misther Murk, a gripfruit juice for Jimmy Joist and a Hi-hoh Silver for good old Tonto. As an honorary American might say, with a certain ironic insouciance, I'm out of here.

"As in Ancient Days": *Tales of Zothique & The Book of Hyperborea* by Clark Ashton Smith (West Warwick, RI: Necronomicon Press, June 1995 & July 1996. 224 p. & 173 p.)

These two collections assemble the elements of Smith's most important series, presenting them in the order of composition and employing the author's original texts wherever possible. Each collection has an introduction and postscript by Will Murray, who edited the first collection in collaboration with Steve Behrends and the second solo. These provide information as to the origins of the stories and their initial fate in the marketplace, making it clear that, at the time of their composition, Smith hoped to collect each of his story-cycles into a book. That object had been so long frustrated by the time Arkham House finally began to put his work between hard covers that he seems to have suffered considerable demotivation, settling instead for the reprinting of the published versions of his stories in a series of representative collections begun with *Out of Space and Time* (1942). These two volumes are as close as we can now come to seeing Smith's prose fiction in the form for which its items were designed, but they are of course "incomplete", by virtue of the fact that each series lost its impetus in the absence of adequate encouragement, and was eventually dragged down into the Slough of Despond.

The roots of Smith's work are embedded in the literary loam of nineteenth-century France. His poetry traces it ancestry back to such late Romantics as Charles Leconte de Lisle and to the man who perfected what Gautier was to call "the Decadent style": Charles Baudelaire. Baudelaire's translations of the works of Edgar Allan Poe had made Poe's fantasies far more influential in France than they ever became in America, and the American writers who attempted to resuscitate a Poesque tradition in the early twentieth century—including Ambrose Bierce and Robert W. Chambers—had to recognize that the trajectory of that tradition had been diverted via Paris.

When Smith developed his own version of the Decadent style, his first recourse was to write tales set in the imaginary French province of Averoigne, which was separated by a metaphorical *massif* from James Branch Cabell's Poictesme but was nevertheless part of the same figurative landscape. Like Rémy de Gourmont, in the tales collected in *D'un pays lointain*, however, Smith found that he was drawn to even remoter regions of the past, first to Atlantis and then to Hyperborea, whose dubious civilization had flourished before the last Ice Age and had been extinguished thereby.

Two of the Hyperborean tales look even further back, to the limits that the imagination may reach in that direction. In "Ubbo-Sathla" a modern occultist briefly shares a magical vision of primordial chaos conjured up by the sorcerer Eibon, while the luckless hero of "The Seven Geases" descends through a series of Underworlds to the ultimate fount of Creation: Abhoth "the father and mother of all cosmic uncleanness". These termini having been reached, Smith naturally turned the lens if his imagination in the other direction, where he found the ultimate Decadence in the imagery Zothique, the last continent of the dying earth, where "sorcery and demonism prevail again, as in ancient days". Hyperborea is a world in eclipse, facing obliteration by ice, but Zothique faces a much more profound and final annihilation. After Zothique, there was no further limit to beckon the imagination on, and this may have something to do with the fact that, when Smith's tales of Zothique began to lose impetus (after "Necromancy in Naat", although he went on to write half a dozen more), his career stalled.

Tales of Zothique consists of sixteen stories and a verse play, plus a few fragments. As the supplementary material of both collections points out, one of the stories—"The Voyage of King Euvoran"—has a tone far more reminiscent of the Hyperborean tales, but, in the absence of any version with that setting, it had to be omitted from *The Book of Hyperborea*, which is left with ten stories and three fragments, although it is bulked out by the inclusion of the more familiar abridged version of "The Coming of the White Worm". The links between the gods of Smith's Hyperborea and those of H. P. Lovecraft's Cthulhu Mythos are carefully explicated, with appropriate quotes from the two men's correspondence, although due note is given to the very different manner of their address. Both books are, of course, labours of love, executed with care and passion; every library in the English-speaking world should make copies available and every parent should make sure that his or her children are equipped with their own personal copies. This recommendation may seem excessive to some, but it does not to me, for reasons which I shall try, briefly, to explain.

I first encountered Clark Ashton Smith's work in the early 1960s, when I was in my teens. It attracted me then with a power that still seems as uncanny as it was unique. Since then, I have read most of these stories half a dozen times, most recently in the "unexpurgated" editions issued by the Necronomicon Press, which I was avid to read as soon as I had heard of them. It was through Smith that I first encountered Baudelaire, and because of Smith that I eventually became intensely interested in the history and ideology of the Decadent style and its spin-off. No author I have encountered since has awakened such a forceful resonance within me and I have often sought an explanation of that fact. One of the first fanzine articles I ever wrote was about Smith, and I have written a dozen more since, culminating in the title-piece of my recent collection *Outside the Human Aquarium* (Borgo Press, 1996).

There are, I know, many people who believe that literary work can only be worthwhile if it deals with the human and the possible, and that it declines in value the more remote it becomes from the realm of actual experience, but I have never felt that way. If my conviction to the contrary is perverse, it is a deep-seated perversity. I have never had the slightest doubt that people who think otherwise are victims of a strange delusion, which is so deleterious to their mental lives as to be classifiable as a disease.

For me, Clark Ashton Smith has always been the ultimate writer: the man who piloted the literary imagination to its proper destination; the one man who really understood the politics of escapism. For him, as it is for me, the point of literary escape is not to assuage (in an essentially pusillanimous fashion) the oppressions and frustrations of confrontation with the real by fleeing to an imaginary realm that is cozy and hospitable. For him, as it is for me, the point of literary escape is—and ought to be—boldly to *defy* those oppressions and frustrations, by embracing an imaginary world in which all moral and material boundaries have been shattered.

What is set free in this kind of escape is the power of artifice, and, in my view, there is nowhere that power can find better opportunities. Zothique is, as the first story set there boldly states, "The Empire of the Necromancers"; it is not their only empire but it is their most glorious—and what, after all, is literary creativity but necromancy in the broadest sense: an essentially *black* magic, whose core is divination by consultation with the spirits of the dead.

Smith's Hyperborean tales—especially "The Testament of Athammaus" and "The Seven Geases"—are more blatant in their disposition of the ironic wit that cannot help but saturate the most honest expressions of the Decadent style, but the subtler humor of his best tales of Zothique—"The Empire of the Necromancers", "The Dark Eidolon", "Xeethra" and the unfortunately unrestored "Necromancy in Naat"—is so beautifully black as to seal the

Ouroboros circle that units comedy and tragedy in self-devouring mutual annihilation.

I am very glad indeed to have these books, because their editors have done everything practically possible to assemble the true texts of the stories and to arrange them as they ought to be arranged. There is no contradiction in also saying, however, that there is a sense in which they make very sad reading, by virtue of cataloguing so minutely the awful difficulty that Smith had in getting the texts into print and reaching an appreciative audience. Like Sisyphus and Tantalus, and all others condemned to special Hells of frustration, he found that, no matter how hard he tried, he simply could not break through to a viable audience. There is a certain treasurable irony in the fact that such rewards as he did garner came from the editors of pulp magazines notorious for their crudity, but the real tragedy that devoured that particular comedy was the fact that his creative impetus suffered such a terrible diminution within a couple of years of having found its *métier*.

On the other hand, things could have been worse. If Smith had started writing tales of Hyperborea and Zothique five or ten years later, he might never have got into print at all.

"The Body (and Mind) Fantastic": *Writing Horror and the Body* **by Linda Badley (Westport, CT: Greenwood Press, 1996. 183 p.),** *Sacrament* **by Clive Barker (New York: HarperCollins, 1996. 447 p.), and** *Servant of the Bones* **by Anne Rice (New York: Knopf, 1996. 387 p.)**

Linda Badley's *Writing Horror and the Body* is introduced as a "continuation of the business" of her earlier book on *Film, Horror and the Body Fantastic*; she had initially conceived the two books as a single volume. She admits that the university course that gave rise to the project was "a flagrant appeal to what had all the symptoms of a fad" and that the horror movies with which she had previously been familiar were "a long-time guilty pleasure" reflective of "a taste for camp". She observes that she "had heard of Stephen King's popularity with students, although [she] had not read any of his books".

In other words, this is an exercise in academic slumming, conducted by a bog-standard literary snob, who has condescended to descend temporarily from her ivory tower to see what the common people are doing, in the hope of currying favor with an audience slightly larger than that at which most academic books have perforce to be aimed. Ms. Badley has consented to read a few best-sellers strictly in order to pontificate about them, but she doesn't know anything—and cares even less—about their situation within the wider context of popular literature. (Did you know that people can actually get paid for doing things like that? Do you realize that they actually *cut down trees* in order to produce books like this?)

I am not familiar with the first part of this study but I can see how it might have made sense as a project. "The Body Fantastic" might be a useful hook on which to hang an examination of horror movies because the characters in movies are all body and no mind. A movie audience consists of voyeurs, who watch the characters doing things—and, more relevantly, *undergoing* all manner of hideously-contrived processes—without any significant advice as to what might be happening inside: the feelings; the thoughts; the suffering. Books, of course, relate to their audience in a completely different way; texts consist of coded information that turns the reader's eyes into a processing-device. Events are described, but nothing is seen; if there are bodies at all, they are virtual bodies, existing solely in the reader's imagination, and the characters who possess them are all mind and no flesh: their feelings, thoughts and sufferings are what the text is all about, because that is what texts do. So, when your average academic slummer has covered the movie ground, BodyFantasticwise, how much can she carry possibly over into a study of texts? The answer, of course, is Sweet Fanny Adams (as people sometimes say in England when they are in company too polite to allow uneuphemistic speech).

Actually, the two chapters (68 p.) in which Ms. Badley deals with Stephen King's work aren't all that bad. At least they cover the ground at a reasonable pace, in reasonably good order. They do not have a lot to say, but they say it with a certain relaxed grace. The two chapters (66 p.) dealing with Clive Barker and Anne Rice are, however, a different kettle of fish; they are crowded and chaotic and utterly without use or ornament. The one thing you can say for them is that they are not nearly as crowded or blatantly incoherent as the Afterword (6 p.), which pretends, hollowly, to set what has gone before in some sort of context. The book's only coherently-stated thesis is that Freudian psychoanalysis is not an adequate theoretical framework for the analysis of modern horror fiction. This did not come as a surprise to me, and I doubt that it will come as a surprise to anyone else; we common people have known that for a long time.

Linda Badley might well have been delighted to find that the title of Anne Rice's new book is *Servant of the Bones*. Bones are bits of body, after all and the gold-impregnated bones in question definitely qualify as a Body Fantastic. She might have been less pleased to discover, however, that Azriel, the so-called servant of the bones, isn't *really* a servant, and that his bones turn out, at the end of the day, to be utterly irrelevant to his fortunes. Azriel is, in every meaningful respect, a free spirit whose presence is essentially virtual. He can put on textual flesh if and when he needs it (in order to commit murder or—in one instance—enjoy sexual intercourse) but he can discard it just as casually. He is a thoroughly textual kind of guy, as different as can be from the sorts of chap one sees in the movies.

Azriel is, of course, a replacement for the Vampire Lestat, who Got Religion in *Memnoch the Devil* and decided that he'd had enough of being an Icon of Evil. Azriel is a much nicer chap, who obtains problematic immortality by luck and self-sacrifice and then undergoes a prolonged existential crisis before deciding that what he really wants to make of himself is an Avenging Angel. Having made that decision, he is fortunate enough to select, out of all the readily-available avengeable acts, one that also allows him to save the world from a fiendish plot hatched by the insane leader of a modish cult. In the meantime, he talks about himself, obsessively and repetitively—which, given that he has far less to explain, excuse or justify than your average vampire, eventually gets a little tedious.

Like Stephen King, Anne Rice has now become a "brand name author", having long since transcended the limits of genre packaging. Her fans will presumably not mind at all that *Servant of the Bones* is in no sense a horror novel. Its plot adopts a conventional thriller-movie formula in which the hero is working against a deadline to save the world from devastation by an evil genius, but it lacks the suspense such plots sometimes generate, because an Avenging Angel is absurdly over-equipped to deal with such problems. Azriel is as invulnerable as Superman, and he has no fear of Kryptonite—in fact, the only thing standing between him and the inevitable *deus ex machina*, once he has proved himself immune to magical compulsion, is his own verbal diarrhea.

Unlike the Vampire Lestat, I doubt if the cult-killing Azriel will generate a cult of his own. There is, alas, little that can be done with him in serial terms. Once upon a time, there used to be abundant literary work for Avenging Angels to do, but modern popular fiction has more-or-less exhausted the available supply of Interesting Villains. The cult leader with vast stockpiles of ingenious weaponry has, I fear, been done to death even in the real world, and there is no one with an ounce of charisma waiting in the wings to take his place.

The *real* weakness of *Servant of the Bones* is, however, its lack of eroticism. Nobody ever read Anne Rice for the plots, after all; they read her because her work was so thoroughly besodden with kinky lust. It is, alas, painfully obvious that the one and only sex scene in *Servant of the Bones* was slotted in just for form's sake; it is not only gratuitous but tediously conventional. The irrelevance of Azriel's body is no mere matter of winning independence from the prison of his bones; it cuts much deeper than that. This is a book so repressed that even Freud might have approved of it—and might well have been able to explain it, hypothetically if not provably. We common people might buy the book, for old time's sake, but we will like it even less than we liked *Memnoch the Devil*, which at least had the virtue of parading its sickly piety so frankly as to make us want to vomit.

Clive Barker's *Sacrament* is not a horror novel either—or so the blurb assures us. There is still a lot more body here, in terms both of injury inflicted and lust unleashed, than there is in *Servant of the Bones*, but, if one compares it with Clive Barker's earlier works, it is a model of restraint—and its real concern, inevitably, is with mind rather than matter, sensibility rather than stigmata.

The hero of *Sacrament* is a world-renowned wildlife photographer who specializes in chronicling the injury done to the natural world by the relentless march of civilization. He focuses his lens on the degraded and the dying, conveying the message that those species Man is disposed to destroy he first makes wretched. An encounter with a particularly wretched polar bear lands him in hospital, and, while he remains comatose, he relives the childhood meetings with the murderous Jacob Steep and the lustful Rosa McGee that initiated his vocation. When he wakes from his coma into the AIDS-ravaged world he briefly forsook, he realizes that a further "awakening" is necessary before he can really claim to have recovered his life.

I cannot help but wonder whether there might have been a point in the planning of this book when Jacob Steep and Rosa McGee might have been pure figments of the hero's dream, symbolic rather than actual—and when the hero's apparent awakening from his dream might (as is formally suggested in the plot) have been merely a gear-shift within it. Had that been the case, *Sacrament* would have been a visionary allegory—a Pilgrim's Progress—rather than a generic dark fantasy in which there really is an alien entity discovered, exploited and made wretched by an actual mage. Perhaps a Pilgrim's Progress was what Clive Barker wanted to write, but thought it best to desist, on the grounds that his audience would expect *hard* fantasy with *real* magic, and fleshy symbols capable of spilling good red blood, at least of a textual/virtual kind.

Sacrament will not disappoint Clive Barker's fans nearly as much as *Servant of the Bones* will disappoint Anne Rice's, partly because he is a much more skilful writer, and partly because he has actually done more to keep them happy. Call me fickle if you will, but, whereas I wish that *Servant of the Bones* were more like *The Vampire Lestat* than it is, I wish that *Sacrament* were just a little less like *The Damnation Game* than it is. The difference is that, whereas Anne Rice seems to me to be quite incapable of writing a sensible allegory, and thus—in my opinion—should not try, Clive Barker is good enough—and then some—to leave out the knee-jerk horror motifs entirely and concentrate on the real heart and soul of his work. When it deals with matters of real concern—the dereliction of the planet and the soul, the awkward division of the self, the grief of living in a plague-stricken community—*Sacrament* is a much better and more gripping book than it is when it labours so hard to import a schlocky melodramatic fever into its manufactured climax.

Sacrament is a good book, which some might justly consider to be the best thing Clive Barker has so far done—and Freud certainly could not come close to figuring it out. Its true gold is, however, alloyed with a lavish helping of sterling silver, and I think it probable that its author can and will do even better in time to come, if he ever cares to take the risk of testing the patience of his loyal fans. (If *Servant of the Bones* serves no other function, it might at least inspire other best-selling writers to test the patience of their loyal fans to the very edge of destruction.) If not, we can at least be glad that there is true gold to be found in his work, and that even his manufactured climaxes are nowhere near as tawdry as the made-in-Taiwan climaxes favored by his less able peers.

It is interesting, by way of conclusion, to note that, of the three books considered here, the only one that ranks as an exercise in unalloyed cynicism is the only one that cannot hope to become a best-seller. That is, I suppose, a measure of the desperation that has infected the groves of Academe in recent years. In fairness to Linda Badley, however, I ought to note that, however cynical and badly-constructed her book might be, it is not without intelligence. Although it does not fit in with her ostensible theme at all, she does know, and is prepared to say, that the imaginative politics of Clive

Barker's work are only superficially concerned with bodies and their stigmatization. Having read his books, she is able to reinterpret his films, realizing that "the imagery of violence and the experience of pain are aspects of his metaphorics of transformation". If there is one idea in her book worth carrying away it is that one—and it is worth noting, too (although Ms. Badley does not), that what Anne Rice is dealing with, in her own more forthrightly artless fashion, is her own "metaphorics of transformation".

We common people cannot, in the end, take up careers as Avenging Angels or world-renowned wildlife photographers, and even university teaching may be beyond our mediocre reach—but as long as we continue to deal with texts, as well as going to the movies, we can nourish our minds as well as our bodies, and make what progress we can in the difficult art of self-transformation. What possible excuse could anyone have for doing otherwise?

"Brutal Judgment": *The Panic Hand* by Jonathan Carroll (New York: St. Martin's Press, November 1996. 295 p.)

I assume that *The Panic Hand* contains all, or almost all, the short fiction that Jonathan Carroll wrote alongside his eight novels during the last decade and a half. The earliest item in the book, "The Jane Fonda Room", was published in 1982, in between *The Land of Laughs* (1980) and *Voice of our Shadow* (1983); the most recent of the previously-published pieces is "A Wheel in the Desert, the Moon on Some Swings", which appeared in the same year as *From the Teeth of Angels* (1994). The twenty items herein represent, therefore, a less intense but slightly more detailed spectrum of this highly idiosyncratic writer's preoccupations than the novels that have gained him his deserved reputation as one of the most accomplished and distinctive contemporary fantasists.

By virtue of their relative brevity, only a few of the items included in *The Panic Hand* are able to reproduce the characteristic pattern of Carroll's longer works, in which an engaging and usually sentimental account of the central character's domestic situation is distorted—gradually at first—by an oddness that eventually explodes into a casually preposterous metaphysical revelation. Although it is not unknown for Carroll to use such a revelation to provide a climax for his story (he does so in *Voice of our Shadow* and *Sleeping in Flame*) he usually produces these wrenching changes in perspective about two-thirds of the way through the text, so that the naturalistic part of the narrative is coupled with a sustained surrealized extension. The novellas "Uh-Oh City" and "Black Cocktail" have sufficient space to lay out this pattern—and both of them do—but many of the shorter stories are forced to collapse it. It is interesting that only a few do this the easier way, by using the revelation as a "surprise ending"; the greater number move the moment of surrealization to a much earlier point in the narrative, so that the balance between sentimentalized naturalism and metaphysical adventurism is tipped in favor of the latter. One effect of this is that the reader who zips through *The Panic Hand* in a day or two is likely to obtain a clearer view of the perverse anatomy of Carroll's somersaulting imagination than the reader who has read the novels at one- or two-year intervals.

"The Jane Fonda Room" is a simple story in which new entrants to Hell can choose their own "torments". The effect of this is that, instead of being forced to suffer according to their worst fears, they are compelled to have their most cherished affections spoiled by infinite repetition—thus adding an extra ironic turn of the screw to the process of their damnation. "Postgraduate" (1984) is a similar account of strange damnation, based in the kind of dream that often takes adults back to their schooldays. Several of the later stories, notably "The Dead Love You" (1990), "A Quarter Past You" (1990) and "The Life of my Crime" (1992), are equally straightforward accounts of eccentrically horrific damnation, but the World Fantasy Award-winning "Friend's Best Man" (1987) is the earliest story in the book that elects to elaborate this kind of theme in a distinctively Carrollian fashion, imagining a Day of Judgment in which there is no obvious Hell at all, but which is no less brutal in consequence.

Egan, the protagonist of "Friend's Best Man" loses a leg in plucking his dog Friend from under the wheels of a train. While in hospital, Egan befriends Jazz, a dying girl, who combines her own talent for working minor miracles with Friend's in order to steer a few of life's petty rewards his way, before offering him a chance to avoid the apocalyptic revolt of nature that will obliterate the world that humans have made. It is entirely typical of Carroll's method that the protagonist does not tell us whether he will take the proffered chance or not.

Jazz and Friend are quasi-angelic figures of a kind that is fairly common in Carroll's work, operating as intermediaries between the characters and God. Such figures are usually ambiguous, and sometimes sinister, in spite of the fact that they are rarely wrathful avengers. The heroine of "The Sadness of Detail" (1989) is threatened with all kinds of dire eventualities if she cannot produce the drawings which—for unfathomable reasons—keep God sufficiently entertained to prevent Creation evaporating for lack of divine attention. The over-efficient cleaning-lady in "Uh-Oh City" actually turns out to be one thirty-sixth of God, but her role is still intermediary, and, in the course of prosecuting the hapless protagonist, she recruits an accessory far harsher than herself. By contrast, the minor characters in "Black Cocktail" turn out to be four-fifths of the protagonist's own fragmented self rather than agents of some higher power—but, in the end, it makes little difference, as his alliance with them becomes the midwife of an unexpectedly dark deliverance. These stories are the most complex in the book, and, taken individually, might seem the most "difficult", but reading them in series makes their underlying *weltanschauung* stand out in sharp relief. They inform us that, even though we can forget our sins, we cannot disown them, and that, if there is a price to be paid for our hopes, then it must be paid in full.

The first story in the book, "Mr. Fiddlehead" (1989), is one of the simplest but it makes a good starting-point because it displays one of the subtlest—and yet most brutal—damnations of all. The female protagonist falls in love with her best friend Lenna's "imaginary friend", who takes on flesh every time Lenna's misery and desperation become sufficiently strong to solidify him. The lovers' affair is idyllic, but it seems doomed to end when Lenna's increasing contentment begins to banish him from existence. The force of the ending is not so much the decision they make as the ease with which they make it, remaking themselves in the process.

By the gruesome standards of modern horror fiction, Carroll is extraordinarily subtle, but that serves to give his work a special effectiveness. He is prepared to strike a occasional note of optimism, but it is notable that the relatively upbeat conclusions of "Friend's Best Man" and "A Wheel in the Desert, the Moon on Some Swings" are gifted to a man who has lost a leg and a man who is going blind. The sentimentality with which he often dresses his stories is a Trojan Horse, which the wary reader will soon learn to mistrust—but even those who learn to keep it at a distance cannot soften the impact of his stern morality to the extent that it is rendered harmless.

The argument of Carroll's fiction, crudely summarized, is that if that which people imagine were somehow to become real, its actuality would be nightmarish, no matter how innocent the initial process of imagination seemed to be. Most of his central characters are conspicuously nice and fundamentally honest people, who generally try to do their best—sometimes in very difficult circumstances—but cannot ever escape the insidious and cruel assaults of conscience. His curiously seductive and calculatedly-perverse narratives take the view that *no one* is authentically pure in heart, and that love—however ecstatic or faithful it might be—not only cannot save us from the effects of spiritual pollution but is likely to bring such effects more fully into the open.

"Love-Sickness and Its Consequences": *The Dealings of Daniel Kesserich: A Study of the Mass-Insanity at Smithville* by Fritz Leiber (New York: Tor, March 1997. 125 p.) and *Asylum* by Patrick McGrath (New York: Random House, 1997. 254 p.)

The Dealings of Daniel Kesserich was among Fritz Leiber's earliest works; according to the jacket copy it was "drafted" in 1936 but mislaid by the author in the 1950s, eventually surfacing among his posthumous papers. It is advertised in the blurb as a "short novel of cosmic dread and Lovecraftian horror" but there is nothing Lovecraftian about it. The design of the plot is, in fact, very similar to that employed by William Sloane in *To Walk the Night* (1937), one of the few upmarket American novels of the 1930s to borrow a device from pulp science fiction. As in Sloane's novel, the narrator is a passive observer of mysterious events, whose prime movers are an old college friend and their one-time professor. As in Sloane's novel, the key to the mystery is contained in the results of the professor's daring scientific experiments, which are so far beyond the understanding of the small town folk among whom he lives as to be regarded as unholy. As in Sloane's novel, the key characters are motivated by erotic obsession, which leads them inexorably to tragedy.

Sloane's novel was sufficiently successful, both critically and commercially, to prompt its author to produce a similarly-structured sequel in *The Edge of Running Water* (1939), and it is easy to understand how its example might have seemed inspiring to a young writer reluctant to accept that the only remaining milieu for serious and daring imaginative fiction was the pulp ghetto. If Leiber did indeed draft it in 1936 rather than a year or two later the coincidence is remarkable, although it might be explicable in terms of the common influence of H. G. Wells.

It is, however, hardly surprising that Leiber's story proved more difficult to market than *To Walk the Night*. Sloane was careful to leave a substantial measure of ambiguity about the solution to his mystery (and I must confess that I, for one, have never been able to accept the science-fictional explanation as the true one) whereas

Leiber's solution is absolutely explicit and much more challenging. Leiber's story is, in fact, an ingenious and striking adaptation of the notion of time travel, which must be reckoned ahead of its time, even if the true date of the story's composition was a little later than the one suggested. Although it has its moments of crude melodrama, the story is probably too sophisticated in its ideative convolutions to be appealing to pulp magazine editors. I do not want to say too much about the mystery and its solution, lest I spoil the story for readers, but it addresses the phenomenon of time with the same daring and ambition that Wells brought to *The Time Machine* and "The New Accelerator", and there is a hint of *The Invisible Man* about its method and its denouement.

The Dealings of Daniel Kesserich establishes that, even in his twenties (he had been born in 1910), Leiber was a very accomplished writer. It also establishes that his interest in the interaction of science and superstition—which came so strikingly to the fore in *Gather, Darkness*! and *Conjure Wife* (both 1943)—was a long-held preoccupation. The fact that a writer of such obvious literary grace and imaginative power could find no place of publication for such stories as this and "Adept's Gambit"—which must have been composed at about the same time—is striking testimony to the stultifying effect of the awkward division of the 1930s literary marketplace.

Things are, of course, very different nowadays. Writers of up-market fiction are no longer ashamed to borrow motifs from the popular genres, and the whole philosophy of genre marketing—which was brought to perfection and established as a norm by the brand-warfare of the 1920s pulps—is beginning to break down. Patrick McGrath is one of a number of contemporary writers who have begun to rehabilitate psychological horror fiction (or, in a term he helped to popularize, "neo-Gothic fiction") to the upper strata of the marketplace. *Asylum* is by no means as fantastic or horrific as *Spider* or *The Grotesque* but it belongs to the same subgenre of case studies in madness. It has very little in common with *The Dealings of Daniel Kesserich*—whose "mass-insanity" eventually turns out to be a mental phenomenon of an unprecedented kind rather than any common-or-garden craziness—but it does reproduce the earlier novella's assumption that the motive force most likely to engender bizarre and dangerous behavior is erotic obsession.

The case-study presented in *Asylum* is that of Stella Raphael, the wife of a psychiatrist working at a hospital for the criminally insane (obviously Broadmoor, where McGrath's father was medical superintendent for many years). Stella falls in love with a patient named Edgar Stark, an articulate sculptor who murdered his wife after becoming convinced that she was unfaithful with an improbable number of other men. When Stark exploits the affair to prepare for his escape, Stella follows him, thus delivering herself into danger—but it is not until she is safely reunited with her disgraced husband that the worst consequences of her obsession become tragically manifest. The real subject of the novel is not, however, Stella's state of mind but the state of mind of the psychiatrist who is compiling the case-study. This is the more interesting study, by virtue of its paradoxicality—a paradoxicality that lies at the heart of all psychiatric practice, by virtue of the fact that the psychiatrist must somehow combine compassion for his patient with the dispassion of his scientific analysis of the patient's problem.

The path that leads a dull analyst's neglected wife to become erotically obsessed with an interesting patient is, of course, exceptional, despite the commonplace nature of its folly. The path that leads a sharper analyst to become similarly obsessed is not merely unexceptional, but actually constitutes the fast lane of the therapeutic highway; how is artful analysis possible without a degree of obsession, and how is persuasive treatment possible without the partial transmutation of that obsession into emotion and action? In an institution like Broadmoor, *quis custodiet ipsos custodes*? Where would madness end and responsibility begin, if the two were actually separable? Perhaps not within the walls—and perhaps not even without.

Although the link between these two particular works is weak there are several intriguing parallels to be drawn between the works of Fritz Leiber and Patrick McGrath. Leiber was the son of an actor; McGrath is the husband of an actress (Maria Aitken). Both have written numerous tales of mental abnormality in which sexual obsession plays a significant role. It is possible that their work would exhibit much more striking similarities had they not begun work half a century apart, faced with very different spectra of opportunity. In essence, though, McGrath remains—at least to date—a writer of neo-Gothic fiction, for whom the fantastic and the horrific are only interesting insofar as they mirror and amplify the troubles that routinely afflict the human mind. For Leiber, at the very beginning of his career and all the way to its conclusion, there were always more things in heaven and earth. For Leiber it was the human mind that was the mirror and the measuring device of larger forces—and for him, in consequence, love-sickness was an origin and not a terminus.

"When the Chill Sets In": *Night Relics* **(New York: Berkley, April 1996. 385 p.) and** *Winter Tides* **(New York: Ace, August 1997. 346 p.), both by James P. Blaylock.**

After writing a couple of quirky comic fantasies in the early 1980s James P. Blaylock effectively re-launched his career with two surreal melodramas, *The Digging Leviathan* (1984) and *Homunculus* (1986). These novels played a considerable role in establishing the fashionability of "steampunk" fiction—as did roughly contemporary works by Blaylock's fellow Californians Tim Powers and K. W. Jeter—but they had a highly distinctive tone that combined straight-faced humor, stylistic delicacy and a delight in meticulous complication to marvelous effect. Blaylock subsequently directed his attention to the production of fantastic romances with a distinctively local flavor, producing a sequence of texts that extended from *Land of Dreams* (1987) via *The Last Coin* (1988) and *The Paper Grail* (1991) to *All the Bells on Earth* (1995). This sequence was interrupted more than once, firstly to allow the author to revisit his earlier sequences—adding one more novel to the comic fantasy sequence and a collection of three novellas to the steampunk sequence—and, secondly, to embark upon a new venture into the ghost story in *Night Relics*, whose first edition appeared in 1994.

The four novels of Blaylock's third phase offer images of neatly-defined areas of California that are conscientiously re-enchanted by the clever use of such traditional devices as timeslips, alterations of size and the Wandering Jew, and such modern scholarly fantasies as Jessie Weston's *From Ritual to Record*—the last of which was more enthusiastically taken up by Tim Powers, when he too began to produce accounts of a comprehensively re-mythologized California. All the tonal elements that worked so well in Blaylock's calculatedly-nostalgic steampunk novels were transplanted with easy grace into a contemporary setting, investing the new sequence with a charming and unique quasi-anachronistic flavor.

At first glance, both *Night Relics* and *Winter Tides* might seem to be affiliated to the Californian sequence, by virtue of presenting narratives solidly set in very similar carefully-detailed locales, but they are, in fact, the first elements in what must be seen as a fourth phase of Blaylock's career. There are some slight traces in them of straight-faced humor but the traces in question are fugitive and rendered in a *conte cruel* spirit that eventually becomes horridly unfunny. The stylistic delicacy, similarly carried over, also flatters

113

only to deceive, the velvet glove gradually revealing the strength and weight of a rather leaden fist as the unfolding plots of the two novels attempt to grip the reader. Echoes of meticulous complication survive in the careful attention paid to the minutiae of the main characters' eccentricities, and the methodical way they are moved hither and yon across the narrative chessboard, but the story-lines remain essentially linear, building from introduction to climax with a relentlessly purposeful tread.

Now that we have *Winter Tides* to set alongside it, *Night Relics* looks suspiciously like a practice run: an attempt to write a horror story, which proved in the end to be half-hearted, undermined by a squeamish refusal to go the whole hog. On the other hand, it is arguable that the willingness of the second novel to pull no punches in its nasty-mindedness does not work entirely to its advantage.

Night Relics and *Winter Tides* both apply the same narrative formula, subjecting a couple of emotionally-wounded would-be lovers to a strangulatory series of threats, whose left hand is a ghostly echo of family tragedy and whose right hand is an amorous psychopath. In *Night Relics* the two hands never establish a co-operative grip, and eventually fall to wrestling one another, but in *Winter Tides* they co-operate much more closely, and are much more efficient in their murderous malignity. The confusion that handicaps *Night Relics* thus has to be set against the brutality displayed in *Winter Tides*; if the author under consideration were Stephen King or Clive Barker one would unhesitatingly prefer the latter approach, but James Blaylock has never been a writer whose appeal has rested on his ability to be brutal.

The hero of *Night Relics* is Peter Travers, who takes refuge from his broken marriage by setting up a symbolic "new home" in a cabin in a remote canyon. When his ex-wife and son visit him there, the wounds of their relationship are re-opened, and they part on such bad terms that it takes him a week to figure out that they never returned home—and might never actually have left the cabin. Peter's new inamorata, Beth, lives next door to Lance Klein, who is secretly trying to acquire as many of the cabins in the canyon as he can, in the hope of profiting from a government buy-back scheme when it becomes part of a National Park. The legman hired by Klein to approach the cabin-owners is Barney Pomeroy, an expert salesman who also happens to be an extortioner and a stalker.

When the ghosts lurking in Peter's cabin begin a campaign of harassment against him, Pomeroy coincidentally begins twin campaigns of harassment against Klein, whom he intends to blackmail, and Beth, the innocent object of his latest sexual obsession. The three campaigns become accidentally but intricately intertwined, entangling Beth's young son and the owner of another cabin, who happens to be the only survivor of the events that gave birth to the ghosts that Peter and his first family have reanimated. In the end, Peter, Beth and Klein exorcise the ghosts along with their own emotional burdens, while Pomeroy is supernaturally delivered to his just desserts, but the climax is too diffuse to build up the pitch of intensity normally expected of a horror story.

The greatest strength *Night Relics* has is its use of Barney Pomeroy as a leading viewpoint character. This examination of a thoroughly twisted world-view derives considerable power from Blaylock's deftness and meticulousness, and is authentically unsettling—all the more so because it is so calculatedly moderate. The extent of Pomeroy's self-delusion is plainly obvious to the reader, but the reader is also able to see how it might not be obvious to *him*, because he does not disturb the world sufficiently for his confabulations to be utterly incredible. One can accept that everyday stalkers might actually be like this. Pomeroy's story remains a sidebar to the main plot, though, and it is casually brushed aside when the story's climax has to focus tightly on the precise nature of the ghosts and the spiritual mechanics of their manifestation.

The hero of *Winter Tides* is Dave Quinn, who gives up surfing the day he has to go into rough water after two young sisters, but is only able to save one of them. Before being ripped out of his grasp by a wave, the second sister informs him that she had been trying to drown her companion, but this only serves to intensify his subsequent guilt; having considered letting go of the girl, thinking that drowning would have served her right, the fact that her death is actually an accident comes to seem irrelevant. Fifteen years later the underachieving Quinn is working for "the Earl"—the father of a fellow surfer, Casey Dalton, who is forever trying to persuade him back into the water—helping to run a theatre that is the old man's favorite hobbyhorse. Unfortunately, this job brings him into constant contact with the Earl's elder son, Edmund, who cannot wait to come into his inheritance legitimately.

Like Barney Pomeroy, Edmund Dalton is a sexual psychopath, but there is no moderation at all about his appetites or his methods. He is barking mad, and Blaylock's conscientious attempts to conceal the true extent of his pathology, during the early chapters that establish him as a viewpoint character, stand no real chance of success. Unlike Pomeroy, Edmund is central to the plot, in league with the nasty ghost from the moment of its first re-manifestation—which comes about when the surviving sister, Anne, brings her dead twin's nasty effects back to the scene of the tragedy. Whereas Pomeroy's fixation with Beth was understandable, and believable, precisely because of its sheer arbitrariness, Edmund's fixation on Anne has to be based in the mistaken conviction that she is a split personality, who has repressed the "Night Girl" which mirrors his own innate evil. By the same token, the ghost of Anne's evil twin, Elinor, has to be a manifestation of pure, focused and essentially inexplicable malevolence—which the ghosts of *Night Relics* emphatically were not.

The result of these modifications is that *Winter Tides*, as is expected of modern horror stories, soon goes way over the top and keeps right on going. Edmund's career of mass-murder moves up through the gears with unseemly rapidity, his pretences to cleverness dissolving utterly as the corpses pile up in his wake, to the point at which he cannot possibly escape from the prosaic forces of law and order. Elinor remains beyond the reach of such easy disposal, but her one-dimensionality ensures that her eventual exorcism has to be as arbitrary as it is absolute. There can be no subtle negotiation with her, as there was between Peter, Beth and the ghosts that sought to possess *them*; Elinor's fate has to be a more straightforward matter. The payoff bought at this price, however, is that the climax of *Winter Tides* reaches a far higher pitch as the crescendo builds up to its final explosive outburst.

There is much to be said in favor of both these novels. They are the work of a true artist in prose: a writer whose descriptions are beautifully definitive, whose characterization is painstaking, and whose plotting is scrupulously precise. Indeed, the whole *performance* of each text is so minutely-defined that one cannot help but raise an eyebrow at Blaylock's insistence that the one way in which his psychopathic monsters betray their abnormality is their unnatural obsession with *neatness*. James Blaylock must, of course, be as conspicuously pleasant as he is resolutely sane (no one who has read his earlier books can possibly doubt either inference) so one is tempted to wonder whether this strange process of transference represents a certain self-dissatisfaction with these particular texts—a wonderment that lends further emphasis to the question of exactly what Blaylock is trying to do with them. Ordinarily, it is no bad thing for a writer to try to broaden his range, but there will be some diehard Blaylock fans who will be desperately disappointed by the fact that, in *Night Relics*, and even more so in *Winter Tides*, he seems to be consciously trying to set aside everything that makes his work unique, in order to accommodate himself to the conventions of a genre even schlockier than the comic fantasy genre from which he set forth on his creative odyssey some fifteen years ago.

If *Winter Tides'* venture into slasher fiction is simply an attempt to muscle in on a cozy corner of the King/Koontz Klondyke, one can hardly blame Blaylock for trying. That, after all, is where the big money is, and every professional writer in the world who is pushing fifty must be *extremely* anxious about the prospect of having something to live on during the next thirty years, if the chilly tides of circumstance that presently beset the literary marketplace continue to surge and swell. If this *is* the case, the real tragedy is that the ploy probably will not work, unless Blaylock is even more ruthless in sloughing off the remaining vestiges of his exquisite quality and descending even further into relatively style-free depths of viciousness. His all-American psychos might be able to cling to their paranoid concern with appearances, but, if Blaylock is to succeed as a mass-market horror-monger, he will probably have to compromise and go for gross. If he does, we must wish him the very best of luck, and be grateful for the work he has so far produced—it would, after all, be rather cruel to insist that artists ought to apply themselves exclusively to the production of the kind of works that only they can contrive, if the cost of such artistry had to be measured out in bitter penury in the artists' declining years.

The more horrific possibility, of course, is that *Winter Tides* might reflect a real decline in Blaylock's creative energy, or a real darkening of his outlook. It is, alas, the case that the four novels extending from *Land of Dreams* to *All the Bells on Earth* show some evidence of a gradual decline of both inventiveness and liveliness, and that *Lord Kelvin's Machine* is not a patch on *Homunculus*. I simply cannot believe, however, that an author of Blaylock's intelligence, wit and integrity could burn out so tamely—and, for all *Winter Tides'* brutality, it is still a novel whose prose is power-packed. Were it not an obviously minor work by a writer of great and profound ability, it would probably seem much better than it does with James P. Blaylock's signature upon it.

"Ghosts and Scholars": *A Night with Mephistopheles* **by Henry Ferris, ed. S. T. Joshi (East Horam, Sussex: Tartarus Press, 1997. 254 p.);** *The Haunted Chair and Other Stories* **by Richard Marsh, ed. Richard Dalby (Ashcroft, British Columbia: Ash-Tree Press, October 1997. 301 p.)**

The advent of "desk-top publishing" has resulted in a remarkable boom in small press publication, whose products range from slim and scrappy magazines to high-quality hardcovers. A drastic reduction in start-up costs means that it is now possible to produce small editions of a few hundred copies relatively cheaply, so that any book that has a constituency of potential readers on that meager scale can break even at the same sort of prices that mass-market books command. One of the consequences of this situation has been a rapid growth in presses catering to esoteric tastes, such as those that reprint nineteenth century fiction that is nowadays very difficult for collectors to find. One population of collectors very well served in this way is that specializing in ghost stories, which has long been consolidated into a true community by its association with such organizations as the Ghost Story Society and such publications as Rosemary Pardoe's *Ghosts and Scholars*.

Although most publications of this kind are straightforward reprints of elusive antiquarian volumes, the boom has also created opportunities for scholars of the field to compile assemblies of works that were never collected together before, either because the works in question were distributed through non-specialized collections (as in the case of Richard Marsh's stories of the supernatural) or because they never reached book form at all (as in the case of Henry Ferris's work). Lovers of the esoteric have twice as much reason to be grateful for such books as these, and to the assiduous amateurs who labor to put them together. Richard Dalby and S. T. Joshi are among the most knowledgeable of all collectors of supernatural esoterica, and any opportunities they find to make the fruits of their research more widely available are to be greatly welcomed. I am very grateful to have both of these books, and I found them both perfectly fascinating, although they provide a peculiar study in contrasts.

Richard Dalby's introduction to *The Haunted Chair* laments that there are no entries on Richard Marsh in the relevant reference books; he was, alas, no better placed to know that I had written one for *The St James Guide to Horror, Ghost and Gothic Writers* than I was to know that he had found out a good deal of information that I would have been very glad to know before writing it. Unlike me, Dalby had discovered Marsh's real name, and is thus able to give a much fuller account of his career than I was, although I am pleased to note that the hours I spent in the London Library combing through its near-random sample of Marsh texts did produce a couple of data unknown to him. This definitive collection of Marsh's weird tales omits only one item I would have been tempted to include and takes aboard five of whose existence I was ignorant, so I feel confident in my assessment that no one could possibly have made a better job of this compilation than its actual editor.

The problem that remains, when the perfection of *The Haunted Chair and Other Stories* as an editorial achievement has been duly praised, is the fact that Marsh was a high-speed hack who knocked out these stories in a manner that was careless of every priority, save for making money with as little effort as humanly possible. His prose has a certain fluency, but it is obvious that he made up his stories as he went along, and that he had only two strategies with which to deal with a gathering sense of not knowing what to do next: he either pads relentlessly, with acres of repetitive dialogue and authorial commentary, or he simply escalates the scale of his supernatural manifestations until they become preposterously blatant. Marsh appears, in any case, to have been a man in whom the concept of subtlety excited a veritable phobia, and nowhere is that phobia more obvious than in his weird tales. It is transparently obvious that he was a brutal realist, who found all talk of ghosts silly, and, on the relatively rare occasions when he could bring himself to write stories of the supernatural, he was inclined to take the view that, if he must be silly, he might as well be very silly indeed.

This does not make the stories in *The Haunted Chair and Other Stories* uninteresting—indeed, it might be held to add to their bizarre fascination—but it means that they are of interest only to connoisseurs, whose scholarly temperament over-rides mere matters of plot and plausibility. As period-pieces of a particular type, these tales are virtually archetypal; it is probable that no one else wrote so many slapdash shockers with such contemptuous ease in late Victorian times, although "Dick Donovan" and Joyce Muddock—who were, of course, the same person—set the standard that Marsh had to beat. Marsh is far the most obvious literary precursor of the work done by the two stalwarts of John Spencer's *Supernatural Stories*, John Glasby and R. Lionel Fanthorpe, although it is extremely unlikely that either of them had ever read anything of his—except, possibly, the best-selling *The Beetle*, which is a true titan among bad books.

Henry Ferris is a very different kettle of fish. Had it not been for the fact that August Derleth once mistook one of his contributions to the *Dublin University Magazine* for a previously-unidentified tale by J. Sheridan Le Fanu, it is entirely possible that no twentieth century scholar would ever have noticed his existence at all, but when the editors of the *Wellesley Index to Victorian Periodicals* determined by an examination of the DUM's records that "A Night at the Bell Inn" was actually by Ferris, they were able to associate it with more than twenty other items published in that periodical between 1839 and 1851. This led S. T. Joshi to take a look at the rest—and thus to a remarkable treasure-trove of fanciful tales and essays on the occult. *A Night with Mephistopheles* reprints six stories and three essays, with a bibliography of the remainder and some commentary on further items of interest.

Joshi makes only modest claims regarding his discovery, claiming that, although Ferris was a lesser writer than le Fanu, he is an interesting contemporary whose non-fiction might have had some influence on le Fanu's work. He finds Ferris's prose style verbose and slightly awkward, and takes care to point out that some of his fiction is second-hand, consisting of new versions of tales and legends apparently heard during travels in Germany. It is true that Ferris is slightly long-winded, and that his sentences are sometimes too densely crammed with subsidiary clauses, but these were commonplace attributes of contemporary prose. If one compares Ferris's stories with contemporary works of a broadly similar stripe—for instance, the supernatural items in Mrs. Craik's *Avillion* or the works of William Mudford—it becomes clear that it is only by comparison with le Fanu that the six stories included herein seem mediocre.

"A Leaf from the Berlin Chronicles" (1843) offers a version of a German legend about a sojourn in Berlin that the Devil is said to have enjoyed in the guise of a charismatic gentleman. "A Night with Mephistopheles" (1845) is a more original tale of a Faustian bargain, which might well have been inspired by John Sterling's profoundly earnest *Blackwood's* serial "The Onyx Ring"; Joshi comments, dismissively, that it "ends happily" but, in fact, it ends very ironically, and rather neatly. I hope I shall not be giving too much away by observing that "A Night in a Haunted House" (1848) and "A Night in the Bell Inn" (1850) are even more ironic, each of them featuring individuals led by superstitious madness to believe that they are ghosts, whose subsequent behavior creates "manifestations" calculated to convince the keenest skeptic. "The Mysterious Compact" (1850) is a more straightforward story of a conventional haunting, but, like the first item, it is a reproduction of a tale heard in Germany. "Tobias Guarnerius" (1851)—which seems to me to be by far the best of the stories—is carefully enclosed in a frame narrative, suggesting that it too is based on a popular legend. If so, it was presumably the same legend that inspired E. T. A. Hoffmann's much more ambiguous classic "Rath Krespel", which stands at the head of a rich tradition of tales of ensouled violins.

Whether or not these tales are better than Joshi gives them credit for, there is no doubt that they are set in a subtly different light—and, if a near-paradoxical mixture of metaphors is forgivable, thrown somewhat into the shade—by the long essay "German Ghosts and Ghost-seers" (1841). This was the second item that Ferris published in the DUM under the anagrammatic pseudonym Irys Herfner, which he later used on an even longer essay on "Mesmerism" (he also used by-lines G. H. Snogby Esq. and George Hobdenthwaite Snogby, although his later contributions were mostly unsigned). Joshi's comments on Ferris's essays are scrupulously cautious, content to register the evidence they offer of a considerable fascination with the occult and with contemporary attempts either to dismiss all accounts of supernatural experiences as nonsense or to reinterpret them in the light of such notions as "mesmerism" and "animal magnetism". Perhaps wisely, Joshi does not attempt a rigorous analysis of Ferris's own stand on such matters—but it is the cavalier ambiguity of his position that makes "German Ghosts and Ghost-seers" a truly remarkable work.

Readers of *Necrofile* have probably never had occasion to notice the fact, but I regard myself as having a certain amateur skill in the art of sarcasm—not enough, I dare say, to qualify me as a master in my own right, but certainly sufficient to allow me to recognize a true master when I encounter one. You have my solemn word for it that Henry Ferris is such a master, and that "German Ghosts and Ghost-seers" is easily comparable with such masterpieces of nineteenth-century sarcasm as the early phases of Edgar Allan Poe's *Eureka* and Oscar Wilde's "The Decay of Lying", with both of which it has a certain intellectual kinship. The best passages of "German Ghosts and Ghost-seers" are quite hilarious, and the whole is so magnificently eccentric that I am not in the least surprised that no one dared take the risk of reprinting it in book form until now. It clearly demonstrates that Ferris was a man ahead of his time, although his work does have something in common with the parodic fiction of Robert MacNish, Mudford and Walter Herries Pollock, and to the wry moral fables of James Dalton.

The other essays here reprinted are "On the Nightmare" (1845) and "Fireside Horrors for Christmas" (1847). The first draws on many of the same pseudoscholarly sources as "German Ghosts and Ghost-seers" and similarly compares alternative explanations, in such a way as to show that modern "authorities" are no less fanciful than traditional ones, and that neither can exhaust or reduce the fascination of the ghost-seeing experience itself. The second re-emphasizes the fact that Ferris's fascination is with the fascination that other people have with ghosts, rather than with the ghosts themselves. The question of whether there really are ghosts or not is so irrelevant to him that he is content to play exuberantly with a calculated ambivalence of approach (but I am perfectly certain that beneath his ironic rhetoric there lurks a hardened Sadducee); it is the credulity of the ghost-seers and the respectful attitudes of the hearers of their tales that seem to him to be *really* interesting.

Joshi has not found out anything more about Ferris than is recorded in the *Wellesley Index*—which is that he was an "Irish divine" born in 1801 or 1802 and dead by 1853. His name and the mere fact that he was a contributor to the DUM imply, however, that he was actually a protestant of Scottish descent: effectively, a colonist, who was bound to regard the religion—let alone the folklore—of the native Irish as mere superstition. In a way, one of the most interesting aspects of Ferris's work is that it has nothing at all to say about the popular beliefs of the Irish; its stubborn insistence on aiming all of its sarcastic criticisms at German scholars and German believers (whose ostensible Protestantism is often acidically noted) implies that he was a teacher rather than a clergyman, but might also signify that he was diplomat enough not to want to be seen to be crying "foul" on his own doorstep.

It is probably optimistic to hope that there are other writers as wonderfully intriguing as Henry Ferris waiting to be exhumed from the obscurity of nineteenth century periodicals, but, while men like Richard Dalby and S. T. Joshi are prepared to carry forward the great crusade of winkling them out, who knows what yet remains to be revealed? In the meantime, we can be reasonably confident that, thanks to such noble endeavors as Ash-Tree Press and Tartarus Press, modern readers will soon be granted access to such rich but currently-unfamiliar treasures as the works of John Sterling and Walter Herries Pollock. In time, perhaps, even Robert MacNish, William Mudford, James Dalton, "Dick Donovan" and Mrs. Craik will make their reappearance on the modern shelf, so that we can once again view the works of writers like Richard Marsh and Henry Ferris in their proper context.

"Graves and Zombis": *Darker Angels* by S. P. Somtow (New York: Tor, February 1998. 384 p.)

In chapter IX of Robert Graves's *I, Claudius* the young Claudius encounters the man upon whom he bestows the glorious title of "the Last of the Romans". This is not, of course, the emperor Augustus, or the emperor-to-be Tiberius; it is the historian Pollio. Claudius is called upon to arbitrate a dispute between Pollio and Livy, as to which of them writes history in the proper manner. Pollio is a scrupulous marshaler of facts who values minute accuracy above all else, while Livy makes a *story* out of history, recklessly imputing suspiciously modern motives to the men of the distant past in order to draw moral lessons from their fates.

Claudius comes down heavily on the side of Pollio, thus slyly promoting the notion that *I, Claudius* is the kind of history of which Pollio would have approved. But *I, Claudius* is, in fact, a novel whose real author, Graves, is deliberately and purposefully working in the deceptive tradition of Livy. Such is irony: the lie *behind* the lie behind the lie.

The Pollio/Livy debate was still going strong two-thousand-and-one years later. R. C. Collingwood, in his classic analysis of the philosophy of history, *The Idea of History*, argues that the methodology of the historian is crucially unlike the methodology of the natural scientist, because its most fundamental instrument is the act of imaginative identification by which the historian places himself in the shoes of the actor (as carefully fitted by the available facts as is humanly possible) so that he may accurately grasp the actor's motives. Collingwood agrees with Pollio that the point of the exercise is to get at the truth rather than to produce a moral fable, but he agrees with Livy that the only way to do that is to understand the motives of the people whose actions constitute history.

Collingwood does not pay much attention to the likes of Robert Graves, whose intention was to usurp the authority of the historian in order to construct moral fables so powerful and compelling that they might become modern myths—myths so skillfully devised and disguised that they would consume, subsume and displace the myths of old. But then, Collingwood would not have agreed with Shelley that the true legislators of the world are not the ones officially appointed to that task.

Having already seen what serious historians could do—he had obviously read and greatly admired Jules Michelet's *La Sorcière*, the most successful European fountainhead of scholarly fantasies and lifestyle fantasies since the great syncresis of Thomas Aquinas—Graves wrote the scrupulously unserious *The White Goddess*, in order to find out whether he was capable of doctoring the spin of Michelet's Big Lie in such a way as to magnify it into an Even Bigger Lie. (To anyone who thinks it illegitimate for me to credit him with such a mischievous motivation, I can only say: Trust me, I'm a historian.) Graves died, as all historians are fated to do, before he had a chance to see how well his lie would work, but I think he would have been very pleased and proud to see how wide and deep the penetration now is of his carefully-sown infectious ideas. From the fine and private place that was Graves's imagination, a remade myth has flown that millions now embrace.

The moral of *La Sorcière* is that Christianity is essentially evil and oppressive, and that the pagan traditions it stamped out by careful demonization were morally preferable. The moral of *The White Goddess* is that all religions are rooted in the same nexus of myths, but that the People of the Book (the followers of Judaism, Christianity and Islam) have perverted that nexus by de-emphasizing or eliminating the feminine component of the godhead, removing the checks and balances that are supposed to restrain the evil manifestations of masculinity: war, slavery, rape, oppression, and so on. (Actually, these two morals were so wonderfully appealing and so magnificently useful, especially in the breast-beating times in which we now dwell, that they would undoubtedly have been invented, spontaneously, by hundreds of other modern writers had neither Michelet nor Graves ever written a line; but this is history, and history needs heroes—not to mention neat patterns of cause-and-effect—if it is to Livy up to expectations.)

Which brings us to *Darker Angels* by S. P. Somtow, who modestly describes himself in his afterword as the "Terrifying Thai" (quotation-marks in the original). He also puts it on record that his great-aunt was the Queen of Siam and that he only got into horror writing, via sf, as a sideline from his career as a "serious, avant-garde composer". In his foreword (no serious historian ever stints on self-justifying commentary, so there is no cause for surprise in the fact that the book has a foreword *and* an afterword) Somtow explains that the world within his text is "almost identical to, but subtly different from our own" and, in order to give readers a clue to the nature of the subtle differences involved, he explains that it is the same world featured in *Moon Dance* (in which native American shapeshifters and immigrant European werewolves fight an epic battle for hegemony in the American West during the 1880s) and *Vampire Junction* (the story of the 2,000-year-old child rock star Timmy Valentine). *Darker Angels* is perhaps best regarded as a sequel to *Moon Dance*; it begins, as befits the analytical work of a serious historian, a generation before the earlier novel—during the period of national mourning following the assassination of the century's most symbolically-loaded president—and proceeds backwards into deeper layers of buried time..

The format of *Darker Angels* is cleverly derived from one of the key parental works of modern fiction, *The Saragossa Manuscript*, whose own format was derived from the *Thousand-and-One Nights*. Somtow's heroine, Paula Grainger, visits Lincoln's body, out of respect for the high regard in which the president was held by her dead husband, the Reverend Aloysius Grainger. The company of the corpse renders her giddy, and she swoons into the arms of Walt Whitman. Whitman is keeping very close company with a young war-veteran named Zachary Brown, who begins to tell Paula about his adventures in the war. His tale, which extends over several nights, seriously disturbing Paula's sleep-patterns and utterly transforming her view of the world, has a whole series of further tales nested and knotted within it. These include the tale of the boy evangelist Jimmy Lee Cox, the tale of the armless Tyler Tyler, and the tale of the serially-incestuous slave-holder Griffin Bledsoe.

As a result of hearing these intricately-entangled life-stories, Paula learns to see her dead husband in an entirely new light. She discovers that her own doubts as to the truth of the religion he professed were negligible by comparison with his, and she discovers that her respectable widowhood (with becomes considerably less respectable once she has been seduced by Zachary Brown) must be shared with the reverend's second "wife": the liberated slave Phoebe. The mercurial Phoebe, who eventually completes Paula's decline from respectability, by teaching her to turn into a leopard, is a sorceress who can trace the record of her incarnations back to the dawn of time.

The web of tales contained within the novel eventually extends to take in a series experiments in resurrection conducted by Edgar Allan Poe and Lord Byron as well as Aloysius Grainger. These experiments are granted a tiny measure of success, by virtue of having borrowed the merest fraction of the power committed by history to the great tradition of African magic: the quintessentially black art of *zombi [sic]* manufacture. Marie Laveau makes the inevitable cameo appearance, but the principal exponent of the art within the novel, whose strange career is revealed bit by bit in the interwoven tales, is Phoebe's male counterpart, Joseph. Phoebe and Joseph are slaves who are, after their own fashion, masters; they are the ultimate victims who achieve, after their own bizarre fashion, the ultimate triumph.

The moral of the multi-stranded story that Phoebe and Joseph hold together is that Christianity is essentially evil and oppressive, and that the pagan traditions it stamped out by careful demonization were morally preferable, although all religions are rooted in the same nexus of myths. More specifically, the novel proposes that the Christian conquerors of America had long ago perverted that nexus by de-emphasizing or eliminating the feminine component of the godhead, removing the checks and balances that are supposed to restrain the evil manifestations of masculinity: war, slavery, rape, oppression, and so on. It further proposes that one key to the potential recovery of that balance was held by the slaves imported by the conquerors from Africa (*Moon Dance* had already proposed that another was in the keeping of the Native Americans.) Because it is a horror novel, *Darker Angels* does not stint on its description of any of the evils in question; but because it is, at heart, a novel of redemption, it is also generous in its compensatory imagery.

The redemption and compensation in question are, of course, only peripherally applied to those characters in the book who suffer the appalling indignities and predations of slavery and the Civil War. The facts of known history include no provision for *their* redemption or compensation. We must not lose sight, though, of the simple fact that all history is written for the benefit of the present. It is us, the readers, who are really in need of redemption, and it is for *our* compensation that the imagery of shapeshifting and resurrection is so lavishly deployed in *Darker Angels*. We are the *zombies* who are in dire need of the return and repair of our stolen souls; we are the Christians who stand in dire need of a better moral education. (I speak loosely, of course; personally, I am no more a Christian than a slave-holder, and am not even an American, but no one now living, whether he is a Californian or a great-nephew of the Queen of Siam, can escape guilt-by-association for the key events of history. It as, after all, history that shaped the world whose bounty feeds us all.)

As its title implies, *Darker Angels* is not merely a serious work of history, but a Holy Book. It offers not merely a moral, but a kind of confessional, an opportunity to say "Bless me, Mother, for I have sinned...." Any reader who can properly place himself or herself in the shoes of Somtow's characters will not merely learn to understand history, or even simply to repent of it, but also to obtain a tiny hint of forgiveness and the promise of a very slight but nevertheless precious resurrection. We, in our turn, are graciously invited to forgive those sinners of the past who knew not what they did. (We are left to make our own judgments about the extent of the forgiveness we ought to extend to the sinners of the present, who surely ought to know what they do.)

Darker Angels is not, of course, the hind of history of which Pollio would have approved—but it is a bigger and better history than any modern Pollio could have contrived, and it is beautifully told. As a story-teller, Somtow has the kind of grip and flair for intricate complexity that has kept Scheherazade alive, in spirit, not merely for a thousand-and-one nights but at least two-thousand-and-one years. If he is not the kind of writer who could move a *zombie*, no one is—but if we are all *zombies* until the day comes when we may reclaim our souls, we must hope that there are legions of writers capable of moving us with histories and Holy Books and tales-within-tales-within-tales.

The last of the Romans is dead and buried. The Dark Age has arrived, trailing storm-clouds of glory. Let us eat, drink, read and be merry, for, although we died yesterday, the history of tomorrow is yet to be lived, let alone written—and the darker angels may yet see fit to help us redeem ourselves from ignorance. Amen.

"Roma Mater": *Judgment of Tears: Anno Dracula 1959* by Kim Newman (New York: Carroll & Graf, 1998. 291 p.)

It is entirely natural that revisionist horror fiction—which asks whether the classic monsters of the genre, especially the vampire, the werewolf and the reanimated dead, really deserved the knee-jerk stigmatization that appointed them key archetypes of evil—should frequently take the form of alternative history. Given that these monsters emerged to form the core of the horror genre in the nineteenth century, inevitably reflecting the hang-ups and psychological limitations of that era, it is not surprising that many series of re-examinations have begun in that era. Nor is it surprising that others should have delved into more remote eras, when the monsters in question hovered in the margins of actual belief and folkloristic fancy, or moved forward in time to fillet the fancies of the past with the finely-honed cutting edge of more recent history. The reconsidered monster has routinely provided a fresh and distant eye from whose viewpoint the follies and tragedies of all human history can be deftly weighed and re-evaluated. Given that all history is, in essence, fantasy (for reasons I surely need not repeat them here, having summarized them for the umpteenth time as recently as the last issue of *Necrofile*), the use of fantastic viewpoints to enhance it is an entirely legitimate imaginative device.

At first glance, Kim Newman's vampire series begun with *Anno Dracula* and *The Bloody Red Baron* and now concluded (I presume) in *Judgment of Tears* may appear to be merely one more exercise in this sort of reappraisal, whose inventions happen to stand at the end of the spectrum of scrupulousness that is most distant from such minutely-researched historical reconstructions as those of Chelsea Quinn Yarbro and Tom Holland. In fact, however, Newman is doing something markedly different from other writers of vampirized alternative history. Although "real" historical figures from the relevant periods are included in these works in considerable abundance—and sometimes play key roles, as the Queen Victoria who becomes Dracula's bride in the first volume of the series and the Manfred von Richtofen of the second volume do—they are mingled with an equal profusion of imaginary characters borrowed from contemporary popular fictions. It is the latter that are pre-eminent, and the former only figure insofar as they to have been "fictionalized"; the 1897 London of *Anno Dracula* was not the 1897 of memory and history but the 1897 of the popular imagination, which inevitably embraced the folkloristic dimension of certain actual individuals.

As with the straightforward re-evaluators of history, Newman the re-evaluator of modern folklore does not come to praise the imagery of yesteryear but to ram a pointed stake through its very heart. His new take on the 1897 of literary legend made mockery of almost every vainglorious delusion of that popular imagination. His 1959 Rome is a similar figment of the imagination—particularly the cinematic imagination, whose core *zeitgeist* was created, captured and immortalized by Federico Fellini's *La Dolce Vita,* but which also extended into a maze of reflections and refractions compounded of dozens of other movies, especially the stylishly schlocky horror films of Mario Bava and Dario Argento—and he rampages into it with the same satirical zest. It is, of course, a milieu that Newman, as an awesomely knowledgeable and critically adept film historian, knows as well as any man alive, although there remains a sense in which it remains exactly as remote from his own memory as 1897—1959, presumably not by coincidence, was the year in which the author of *Judgment of Tears* was born.

Judgment of Tears begins with a reconfiguration of the opening scenes of *La Dolce Vita*, aptly entitled "Dracula Cha Cha Cha", but complications begin to set in when the neo-vampire starlet who arrives in Rome to a rapturous welcome is slaughtered at the Trevi Fountain by an extraordinarily muscular serial killer known as the Crimson Executioner [appropriated from Massimo Pupillo's *Il boia scarlatto* (1965)]. (As with previous volumes in the series, the existence in the plot of fictional characters still in copyright necessitates a few shallow disguises, while the fact that many of the real people mentioned are still alive necessitates some subtle diplomatic screening; wherever I have supplemented the information given in the text I have placed my amplifications in square brackets.) The second chapter, "On Her Majesty's Secret Service", introduces another neo-vampire, Hamish Bond, who has come to ask the advice of the centenarian champion of the Diogenes Club, Charles Beauregard. The next phase of the plot introduces Bond's Soviet opposite number, a cat-fancier—or, more pedantically, a fancier cat—named Gregor Brastov, whose suitably exotic employees include Olympia [of Hoffmann's "The Sandman" and the ballet *Coppelia*] and the golem. All this, however, flatters merely to deceive, for *Judgment of Tears* is by no means a celebration of Cold War *machismo*.

Charles Beauregard's heroic exploits in the previous two volumes were merely facilitated by his rival vampire protectresses, Geneviève Dieudonné and Kate Reed, but his resistance to being "turned" has now rendered him almost helpless, so these two uneasy allies must look for new helpmeets. It transpires, however, that the idiotically flashy Bond is no further up to the mark than the supercool reporter Marcello [Mastroianni], and everything the vampiresses contrive to do herein is strictly their own achievement. The feminization of the melodrama extends with equal wholeheartedness to the less heroic characters. Beauregard's renegade fiancée, Penelope Churchward, eventually proves far stronger and more capable than her scheming "warm" gigolo Tom [Ripley, as per Patricia Highsmith]. Instead of being the alter ego of an American reporter named [Clark] Kent, as is briefly hinted, the Crimson Executioner eventually turns out to be a lesser figure, and merely the homicidal instrument deployed by the four female incarnations of the thoroughly maternal spirit of Rome. Even Dracula, a paradigmatic symbol of aggressive male potency in *Anno Dracula* and the archetype behind the Bloody Red Baron, is here the merest shadow of his former self, effortlessly outshone in sadistic glamour by his latest intended bride, the Moldavian princess Asa Vajda. The actual 1959 might have preceded the irresistible upsurge of feminism, but Newman's topsy-turvy reconstruction of the mythical 1959 saturates it with male *impuissance*.

As with all Newman's fantasies of alternative history—including, of course, *Back to the USSA* (1997), whose co-authorship with Eugene Byrne allows him to close his extraordinarily scrupulous acknowledgements section with the typically apt claim that he is the author of eight and a half books—much of the delight to be obtained from the text is to be found in the casual brush-strokes of the background. These include, among many others, the observation that the first vampire pop star, Cliff Richard, will probably be able to exploit his eternal youth to go on making hit singles forever, the explanation for the boom in sales of Vimto, and the "autopsy" scene in which Herbert West [the re-animator] and Dr Pretorius [late of *The Bride of Frankenstein*] reprise the comedy turn provided for the first volume by Doctors Jekyll and Moreau. We also learn the suitably ironic fates of such vampires as Casanova, Edgar Poe, Errol Flynn and the Addams family—again, among many others. Even in the background, though, the males of both species are mostly lit in a distinctly unflattering light; the one glaring exception is Orson Welles.

The title of the final chapter—taken, like so many others, from a best-selling book—goes some way to explain why this is case; although it has leapt forward forty years, within the context of the series *Judgment of Tears* follows on from a novel set in the Great War, and Newman knows well enough what effect the Great War had on the more prescient aspects of British popular imagination and ought to have had on the rest. Entitled "On the Beach", the chapter in question ends with a game of tag played out against funerary scenery, echoing (perhaps not calculatedly, given its absence from the acknowledgements) the 1969 film version of Joan Littlewood's *Oh What a Lovely War*—whose original stage version was one of the seed-works of the rich modern tradition of reflective and re-evaluative satire to which Newman's novel is a late and appropriately sophisticated addition. Although it has a bittersweet elegiac quality and a louche fatalism that distinguish it from its excellent predecessors, *Judgment of Tears* is a thoroughly worthy successor to *Anno Dracula* and *The Bloody Red Baron*; it easily qualifies as one of the slickest, wittiest and most original dark fantasies of the contemporary *fin de siècle*.

"Blood Brothers": *The Cleft and Other Odd Tales* **by Gahan Wilson (New York: Tor, November 1998. 333 p.) and** *The Barrens and Others* **by F. Paul Wilson (New York: Forge, December 1998. 379 p.)**

The world has far too many Wilsons in it to make it probable that any two chosen at random will have anything much in common. By the same token, however, it is probable that any reasonably-sized community, profession or vocation will feature at least two of them, whose unrelated approaches to similar issues will facilitate interesting comparisons. The science fiction field had an entire handful at one time, although F. Paul Wilson's migration to the horror/thriller borderline lessened the pressure there in the 1980s, and has now brought him into intriguing—but presumably momentary—juxtaposition with the cartoonist Gahan Wilson, whose thirty-odd-year sideline as an occasional writer of weird fiction has now heaped up enough oddments to fill a book.

In some ways, the two writers are completely different, by virtue of coming to the writing of short fiction from diametrically opposed directions. Paul Wilson is a consummate professional whose craftsmanship—still in development in the stories assembled in his first collection, *Soft and Others* (1989)—has since been honed to a very keen edge. His sense of balance is impeccable; his stories always do enough, and never too much. His method might almost be reckoned a trifle too cultured—the chatty biographical string that links the pearly fictions together is full of lamentations about being frequently nominated for awards but never actually winning, and it is easy to imagine that this might be because they always ran into opposition with a hint of inspired craziness. On the other hand, Gahan Wilson is an obvious *dilettante* as a writer, diversifying from artwork only when the whim takes him, and making not the slightest attempt at consistency of production. He owes his two World Fantasy Awards and his Bram Stoker Life Achievement Award to his deliciously offbeat macabre cartoons, which have carried forward the comic-Gothic tradition initiated by Charles Addams without ever being confined or bogged down by it. Oddly enough, however, Gahan Wilson's prose style seems far more polished than the mildly *faux-naïf* manner of his cartoons; even the earliest stories here show no trace of the awkwardness that might be expected of a man whose imagination works primarily in visual terms. His deftness and versatility are so nearly Thurberish that one is tempted to wonder what he might have accomplished had he ordered his priorities in a different way.

Even if one took the stories in these two books out of their very different career-contexts one could not possibly confuse the two. No Paul Wilson story could be mistaken for Gahan's, even if it came with a heavily-inked caricaturish illo instead of an introductory account of which editor commissioned it and which novel had to be interrupted in its progress to get it done. The opposite is also true. Despite this distinctness, however, there are inevitable echoes and resonances between the two assemblies whose harmonies map certain key concerns of modern weird fiction.

The earliest story in *The Cleft and Other Odd Tales* is "The Book" (1962). The longest story in *The Barrens and Others* is the title novella, first published in 1989. Both derive their inspiration from a notion that H. P. Lovecraft borrowed from Robert W. Chambers, and brought to a new pitch of perversity: the book that so thoroughly corrupts its readers' relationship with reality as to lead them to damnation. Paul Wilson's account of the process is earnest and meticulous, making exceedingly clever use of a unique locale that is perfect for its purpose. Gahan Wilson's is a wry tale in which a collector who thinks he has found a fabulous bargain book is, in fact, being passed a buck that is far too hot to handle, but which also leaves its dread legacy behind. A recognition of the power that texts possess by virtue of mediating our understanding of the phenomenal world, and a corollary anxiety about that power getting out of hand, are likely to be aspects of any thinking horror writer's work, so it is not surprising to find further echoes of the literary and folkloristic heritage cropping up elsewhere in both collections.

Gahan Wilson offers thinly-disguised and ironically-distorted pen-portraits of real writers in "Them Bleaks" (Robert Bloch) and "The Power of the Mandarin" (Sax Rohmer) but pays homage to the power of traditional tales in two decisively modern reworkings written for Ellen Datlow and Terri Windling's anthologies, "The Frog Prince" and "Hansel and Grettel". "The Frog Prince" is a particularly deft psychoanalytic fantasy, which casually disregards the commonplace jokey variations on the theme in favor of one that cruelly turns the superficial humor into a study of morbid frustration. A remarkably similar emotional foundation underlies the twist at the end of Paul Wilson's tale of time-machine-assisted plagiarism "Bob Dylan, Troy Jonson and the Speed Queen". Paul's "The Tenth Toe" provides an ingenious reworking of a well-known item of popular American folklore—the pre-OK Corral career of "Doc" Holliday—which is bitingly witty, while "Definitive Therapy" and "Rockabilly" offer carefully sophisticated takes on characters drawn from the popular culture of the comic books. "Definitive Therapy" is, as its title suggests, a psychoanalytic fantasy, and, if its account of the misadventures of the new psychiatrist at Arkham Asylum who inherits the Joker's case has little in common with "The Frog Prince", that is only because it has so much more in common with "The Book".

As must be expected of a modern collection of horror stories by a canny pro, Paul Wilson's volume is by no means short of sociopaths. The first two stories in the book, "Feelings" and "Tenants", present us with a conscienceless ambulance-chasing lawyer and a murderer on the run, both of whom are textbook cases, and both of whom get their due comeuppance. The last story in the book (whose appendix features two dramatizations, including one of this particular story) is "Pelts", which is also the most gruesome, and the only one where Wilson almost permits himself to go over the top. This too is a morality play, in which human monsters are guilty of the most cardinal of contemporary sins: a lack of empathy for the pain of others. Gahan Wilson usually adopts a more traditional view of the seven deadly sins in such twisted morality plays as "The Casino Mirago" and is quite prepared to punish mere curiosity in such tales as "The Marble Boy". "Mister Ice Cold" is, however, a deftly horrific account of disguised threat, and Gahan comes much closer to the spirit of Paul Wilson's moralistic tales of sociopathy in "A Gift of the Gods" and "Sea Gulls". The two writers are, however, even closer in spirit in their desire sometimes to transcend and interrogate the customary bounds of the sociopathic monster story.

The third story in *The Barrens and Others*, which completes a "triptych" set in the Incorporated Village of Monroe on Long Island, is a harrowing tale, which presents its homicidal monster and the policeman pursuing her as contrasted but fatally linked victims. "Topsy", a brief tale of uncontrollable obsession, is similarly cruel in its even-handedness, and the second of the two appended scripts, "Glim-Glim" is a parable warning against hasty stigmatization. Gahan Wilson is never so stoically analytical in his contemplation of the monstrousness of monsters, but he is equally intrigued by the problem involved in embracing viewpoints far removed from the stubbornly conventional. "It Twineth Round Thee in Joy" is a straightforward joke at the expense of pulp cliché, but "Best

Friends" is a much more vicious study of a distinctly modern sociopathic species, the eponymous character in "Yesterday's Witch" is closer in inclination, if not in ability, to a newly-emergent kind of curmudgeon, and "Come One, Come All" offers a cunning perversion of the calculated grossness of zombie movies.

There remain, of course, areas in the two collections that do not overlap. Paul Wilson includes two stories that are straightforward tales of ingenious criminality. "A Day in the Life" stars Repairman Jack, a fixer who moans about the bad example set by television vigilantes, whose popularity encourage his clients to think that he ought to be prepared to work for free. "Slasher" is a consummately nasty-minded account of a bereaved father whose illimitable and self-indulgent wrath is ripe for exploitation. Gahan Wilson's collection, on the other hand, includes several stories that are unashamedly quirky and whose sole *raison d'être* is their quirkiness. These include "The Sea Was Wet as Wet Could Be", "Traps", the story whose title is a blob of black ink, and the mock-allegorical title story. These are the tales that pull the two books back towards their very different directions of origin, and lend stress to their very different tonal qualities.

Even in these projecting ends of the spectra covered by the two books, however, there is a detectable similarity in the way that they deploy black comedy. Paul Wilson's tales would be very funny if their violence were not so hideously earnest, and Gahan Wilson's would be very dark were they not set up in such a conspicuously unserious manner. Both writers underline, in their very different ways, the brutal irony of our awareness of the inevitability of death, and of the many ignominious ways that we might ultimately meet it. That is, after all, the foundation on which all horror and much humor are built, the psychic bloodstream that binds so many different and seemingly unrelated writers together into a great fraternity.

Both these books are way out on the better side of average and neither has anything in it to disappoint an eclectic reader. If they fall short of award-winning brilliance, it is only because their competence keeps then well within the bounds of sanity—and that counts as an achievement, in horror fiction and comedy alike, where too many writers aim for excellence and extremism but only contrive to achieve eccentricity and embarrassment. There really are times when enough is as good as a feast.

"Burdens of the Past": *Fog Heart* **by Thomas Tessier (New York: St Martin's Press, February 1998. 319 p.) and** *Head Injuries* **by Conrad Williams (London: The Do-Not Press, October, 1998. 206 p.)**

Both of these novels focus on small group of individuals—two married couples in *Fog Heart*, three former school friends in Head Injuries—whose everyday lives are disturbed by enigmatic but increasingly troublesome reminders of long-buried and firmly repressed bad deeds. In each story there is a subset of characters positioned outside the group, whose members function as catalysts and active prompters, orchestrating the process by which the discarded burdens of the past are reshouldered in the present. In *Fog Heart* the subset consists of two half-sisters, one of whom is a medium with deep-rooted problems of her own, whereas in *Head Injuries* they are seemingly-independent *doppelgängers* of the lead characters; within each subset, though, the narrative spearhead is a young woman whose teasing sexuality serves as a lever to open up the wounds of a male protagonist. The horror element of each narrative consists of carefully-managed descriptions of the manner in which the residues of past sins swell and spread like metastasizing tumors, ultimately rupturing the shell of present normality.

Fog Heart is a meticulously contrived novel, measured out with great care. One plot strand describes the way in which wayward entrepreneur and apprentice psychopath Oliver Spence is gradually ensnared by supernatural warnings offered to his unsuspecting wife Carrie. The other describes how the restless academic Charley O'Donnell and his wife Jan are forced to come tom terms with the way in which their lost child died. The medium Oona Muir, who brings their two cases together, in order that they might inflame her own recalcitrant distress while she inflames theirs, provides the two relatively conventional subplots with a somewhat less conventional capstone, although the ultimate conclusion—which will surprise nobody—is that everybody is either a murderer or an accomplice.

Because *Head Injuries* is a first person narrative, attention is focused throughout on the predicament of David, who has been summoned to Morecambe by two of his old friends, Helen and Seamus. He is initially loath to admit that he has been suffering the same kind of supernatural intrusions into his life that have scared them half to death, and similarly reluctant to accept that the new acquaintances all three of them have recently made might serve no other function but to hasten their damnation. Driven by muted, but powerful, feelings of lust for Helen, and jealous hatred for Seamus, David struggles feebly against the net that has ensnared them all, but must in the end go with them to receive the judgment of fate—which is based on the unsurprising fact that the only one of them who has not committed actual murder feels just as guilty as the two who have.

Unlike Tessier, who carefully hoards his revelations, Williams deliberately includes a prologue that gives away the secret which David is trying to keep from himself, so the reader is always one step ahead of him as he progresses towards the inevitable revelation by slow and painful degrees. Although it is as meticulous in its way as *Fog Heart, Head Injuries* thus gives the impression of being less contrived, sternly declining the opportunity to set up narrative ambushes. Because Tessier's ambushes are so manifestly tokenistic, however, this difference in approach is merely formal.

Given that the psychological syndromes described are the same in both cases, and that the methods of extrapolation employed by the writers are not so very different, one might expect the two books to have much the same narrative texture. The fact that they actually offer very different reading experiences is only partly accountable in terms of the fact that one is by an American and the other a Briton. Tessier's book is unusually cosmopolitan for an American horror novel, reflecting the author's own experiences; he was at University in Dublin before living and working for some years in London. *Fog Heart* (which was initially published in the UK by Gollancz in 1997) makes use of British and Irish settings with ready competence; although its main characters are all US residents, none of the crimes that they have repressed were committed on American soil, and only one achieves a final reckoning there.

The keystone to the unfolding pattern of *Fog Heart*'s dark secrets—and, presumably, a significant element of the story's original inspiration—is a murder similar in all essential respects to those committed by the notorious English child murderess Mary Bell. Conrad Williams makes no reference to any similar case in his claustrophobically uncosmopolitan novel, but the narrative landscape of *Head Injuries* is one in which Mary Bell's murders could be easily accommodated. She was from north-east England, while all Williams' characters are from his native north-west, but, in this context, the similarities far outweigh the differences. The stark contrast between the two books derives from the fact that *Fog Heart* presents the world that encapsulates (and is encapsulated by) people like Mary Bell from a securely externalized narrative viewpoint, whereas *Head Injuries* adopts a narrative viewpoint that, albeit peripheral, is inextricably implicated in that world.

Although "class" is supposed to be an obsolete concept, it remains broadly true that unsuccessful Britons, in spite of the embourgeoisement of the Industrial Revolution, have never managed to escape the psychological oppression of fundamental class-divisions that go back to the Norman conquest, whereas successful Americans, despite several concerted attempts to devise a distinctive class culture, have never managed to convince themselves that the poor are different in any other respect than having less money. To put it more succinctly, there are many Britons who cannot conceive of themselves in any other terms than as terminally wretched born losers, while there are many Americans who cannot get their heads around the fact that sane people could possibly conceive of themselves in that way. It is entirely possible that neither Conrad Williams nor Thomas Tessier belongs to the relevant majority, but they certainly know people who do. This is presumably why the six major characters in *Fog Heart* all come across as ordinary folk, unluckily afflicted by capricious evil by virtue of avoidably bad childhoods, whereas the three major characters in *Head Injuries*—the *doppelgängers* remain conscientiously minor—all come across as poor sods who never had the slightest chance of ending up any other way.

Conrad Williams is not, of course, a "working class writer", for the simple reason that there is no such thing ("I was born working class," as Glen Baxter once lamented, "but the moment you pick up a pen and start to write, you're middle class") but he was born and raised in Warrington, which is the next best thing. He is far too accomplished a writer to be reckoned one of life's losers—although *Head Injuries*, issued by a small press, is certainly not going to make him rich—but he does understand perfectly well how and why his two male leads came to be the kind of people who have bootmarks ready-stamped into their doleful features. Thomas Tessier, on the other hand, is as solidly bourgeois as any hobbyist Bohemian; he might affect to despise the business canniness and shabby-genteel academicism that are supposed to contrast his two male leads, but he is of the same mock-aristocratic ilk as they. Where the Mary Bells of this world are concerned (and Williams is right to take it for granted that they are far less unusual than Tessier alleges), none of us is more than a voyeur, but some voyeurs can get much closer to her shoes than others.

The relative strength of the two books' effect will vary according to the reader's inclinations. Most readers will probably find the Tessier easier to get on with, because it contemplates the alien from afar. It does, of course, invite readers to wonder whether they too might have become monsters if they had been sufficiently ill-treated as children, but "there but for the grace of God...." has always been a consolatory formula. By assuming that nearly everyone comes out of childhood brutalized, if not actually mangled and maimed, Williams contrives to imply that being a guilt-ridden killer is merely par for the course, from which it follows that the only arbitrary horrors that afflict us are things like the desolate landscapes of out-of-season seaside resorts, and the fact that the people who live in them cannot quite comprehend that they are in Hell. One does not have to have seen Warrington and Morecambe, let alone have been born there, to get the point—if the testimony of horror fiction can be trusted, there are lots of American small towns in far worse condition—but one does have to be able to don the right kind of blood-tinted spectacles.

Personally, I found both books enjoyable in the perverted way that horror stories are supposed to be enjoyable, but I can't help feeling, presumably for reasons of perverse patriotism, that *Head Injuries* is the worthier work.

"NOW is the Winter of Our Discontent": *Satan Wants Me* by Robert Irwin (Sawtry, Cambs: Dedalus, April 1999. 320 p.)

So there we were, the British baby-boomers, just coming into adulthood. We had been born out of the hope to which VE day gave birth. We might have been taller had it not been for the persistence of food rationing throughout our earliest years. The worst burdens of citizenship did not lie heavily upon us; national service had been abolished just in time. The worst burdens of fifties austerity had recently been lifted; as Philip Larkin dutifully recorded, sexual intercourse had begun in 1963. Other nations were at war, but we were not. The winter of our adolescent discontent was about to be made glorious summer by the symbolic son/sun of....well, leave that blank for now.

Writers are supposed to do their quasi-autobiographical novels first and leave their masterpieces until later, but Robert Irwin has never been one for following convention. His first novel, *The Arabian Nightmare*, was such an obvious masterpiece that his subsequent works can easily seem like a set of mere doodles by comparison, albeit doodles of genius. Even his exquisite requiem for surrealism, *Exquisite Corpse*, edges its delicate melancholy with careful frivolity. *Satan Wants Me* is actually the second novel Irwin has based (very loosely) in personal experience, *The Limits of Vision* having been inspired by the time he spent as a non-earning house-husband while he toiled on *The Arabian Nightmare*. It is typical of his method that the earlier novel turns housework into a cosmic war against the evil wiles of Mucor, the spirit of uncleanliness, whose key weapon of defensive distraction against the ravages of boredom is the ability to construct elaborate fantasies. *Satan Wants Me* harks further back, to the rudderless life of a postgraduate student, cut adrift from almost all responsibility, for whom sex, drugs and rock-'n'-roll are not *quite* enough to fill the empty days. 1967 was the year in which Robert Irwin bought his copy of Aleister Crowley's *Magick in Theory and Practice*, and the rest is... well, not exactly history, but the sort of thing that a powerful and quirky imagination might be strongly tempted to substitute for history. Fortunately, Robert Irwin is no better than the average genius when it comes to resisting temptation.

The text of *Satan Wants Me* takes the form of a diary, which Peter Keswick is instructed to keep by Dr Felton, the Master supervising his instruction in the mysteries of the Black Book Lodge (a descendant organization of the Ordo Templi Orientis, which maintains its headquarters in Horapollo House). This diary is, of course, to be consulted on a regular basis by Dr Felton, and the alert reader will quickly catch on to the fact that, although there is much in it that strives mightily to give the impression of absolute honesty, there are also matters that will go surreptitiously unrecorded for diplomatic reasons. Only *very* alert readers will pick up all the clues that will allow them accurately to estimate the extent of this dissimulation, but this does not matter—one of the pleasures of reading is to be neatly surprised.

Peter's dissimulations are not the only ones relevant to the plot. Some of the mysteries of the Black Book Lodge are, indeed, mysteries, and some of them are far more mysterious than others. The reader might wonder why the early pages of the diary do not suggest to Dr Felton that Peter is a totally unsuitable recruit for a serious esoteric organization, but will quickly divine—although Peter is much slower on the uptake—that the Lodge has a particular interest in him, and that its careful interventions in his love life are aspects of a cunning plan. Although he is given *Moonchild* to read by way of homework (along with Aleister Crowley's other quasi-autobiographical novel, *Diary of a Drug-Fiend*) Peter is not sufficiently attentive to its plot to notice either the crucial similarities or the crucial differences between the scheme there outlined and the one that is enveloping him. He is, of course, distracted by his own hidden agenda—and by the time he is finally panicked into abandoning his own agenda, he is caught up far too intricately in the agendas of others to find easy release.

It may seem to be a slightly back-handed compliment to say that the greatest strength of *Satan Wants Me* is the quality of its bathos, but that is what the text intends. Writers who try to treat Crowleyesque magic with deadly earnest—like Dennis Wheatley, who was reaching the end of his best-selling career in 1967 and makes a cameo appearance in *Satan Wants Me*—only succeed in making it seem silly (a fact fully appreciated by Crowley, who included a reading list for would-be initiates in *Magick in Theory and Practice* which blithely recommends such puritan melodramas as comedies, while emphasizing that *Alice in Wonderland* is invaluable to those who truly understand the Kabbalah). It is actually far more effective to present that kind of magic dismissively and parodically, displaying its absurd pretensions *as* absurd pretensions, while granting it an insidious power nevertheless. Irwin's treatment of magic is sufficiently delicate to allow the interpretation that its effects might all be due to drug-distorted perceptions and the power of suggestion, but it is sufficiently disturbing to permit real horrors to creep into its action. The text continually moves from the high-flown rhetoric of Felton's instruction to the ham-fisted crudity of Peter's obedience, but the implicit irony of such bathetic moves gradually becomes infected with a genuine unease—and it is only when the plot makes its final precipitous descent from brief drug-assisted high to enduring brutal mundanity that the tragic dimension of the comedy is fully revealed.

As quasi-autobiographical novels go, *Satan Wants Me* is far from self-indulgent—much less so, in fact, than its predecessor. The heroine of *The Limits of Vision* might be barking mad, but she is an authentic heroine, and it would be difficult even for the most churlish reader not to take her side in all her struggles. Her fantasizing is bold and brilliant, recording a flamboyant triumph of the imagination over adversity. By contrast, even the most charitable reader would find Peter Keswick hard to like. Outside his uncontrolled bouts of chemically-assisted hallucination he is depressingly sane, and his sanity has a distinct yellow streak. His whole story, and especially its climax, is a cruel record of the triumph of adversity over imagination. The story whose protagonist he provides is, however, far cleverer and much subtler than he is. The only man over fifty who could look back at his twenty-one-year-old self—or any fictional analogue thereof—without contempt would be a fool or a hopeless victim of nostalgia, and Robert Irwin is neither; nor is he so unreasonable as to refuse to recognize the irony of that contempt or the accuracy of its measurement of his own intellectual progress.

Eric Lane, the heroic mastermind behind Dedalus, confessed to me the hope that *Satan Wants Me* might prove to be "Robert's most commercial book yet". Perhaps he is right. It is, after all, replete with sex, drugs, magic and the spirit of 1967, all of which are calculated to appeal to its target audience of 50-some-year-old baby boomers (who are the last people alive who still read books for fun and inspiration). There is a slight danger, though, that it might be just a little bit too close to their concerns for its own good. The diary's last entry is dated October 1997, and, if the mere mention of the present day were not enough to remind us of the difference between what we were and what we now are, that last chapter certainly hammers the message home. We might have thought at the time that adolescence was the winter of our discontent, but we know far better now. None of us expects to see the symbolic sun again, and we certainly wouldn't be inclined to seek hope in the son of.....well, anyone who hasn't guessed had better read the book. Anyone who has guessed ought to read it too; it's horrific, but it's the work of a truly remarkable writer.

PART FOUR

REVIEWS FROM *THE NEW YORK REVIEW OF SCIENCE FICTION*

King of Morning, Queen of Day by Ian McDonald (Bantam 1991, 390 p.)

In a delicately ironic afterword to *King of Morning, Queen of Day,* Ian McDonald quotes David Langford's sarcastic observation that "in Fantasy...all stories must run to three volumes and include a mention of the Wild Hunt". The reader, on reaching this afterword, will wryly recall that the story he or she has just finished was indeed distributed into three parts, albeit accumulated within a single weighty volume, and did indeed contain a mention of the Wild Hunt—but he or she will also be in no doubt that the casual insult has been utterly defused, because these things were done with the utmost propriety; there is absolutely nothing formularistic about *King of Morning, Queen of Day*.

A much shorter version of the first part of *King of Morning, Queen of Day* appeared under the same title in McDonald's collection *Empire Dreams*. The story in question compares and contrasts the experiences of a romantically-inclined teenage girl and her father; while the former discovers the Land of Faerie in close proximity to their home and sets out to photograph the fairies, the latter deduces that an apparent comet is actually an alien spaceship and sets out to communicate with its crew by means of powerful flashing lights. The girl produces something very like the infamous faked photographs of the Cottingley fairies, which fooled and beguiled Conan Doyle, but her father bankrupts himself trying unsuccessfully to prove his point in the face of public ridicule.

The short story revolves around its neat climactic twist, which overturns the expectations of rationally-minded science fiction readers, whose reflexive sympathies automatically enlist them to the cause of the astronomer. The stereotyped fairies are, indeed, delusions of a sort—it is the power of the girl's imagination, reaching out by way of a capricious wild talent, which has brought them into actual being—but so are the aliens, who have been produced by exactly the same means to a similarly seductive end. This de-science-fictionalizing move is, however, taken up very carefully as a premise for investigation in the longer version of the story and its two "sequels". This further exploration is conducted with the aid of a thoroughly scrupulous science-fictional conscience, but is no less bold for that, and the author provides an excellent exemplification of the way that a science-fictional method, when applied to the substance of fantasy, can make considerable adventurous headway into literary *terra incognita*.

The version of the original story contained in part one of the novel is much richer in detail, inquiring much more closely into the conscious and subconscious motives of the central character. It provides a little more information about the vengeful "seduction" that she unwittingly inflicts upon her father in order to punish him for his lack of sympathy for her girlish fantasies, and a good deal more about the dangerous seduction that she blithely shapes for herself. It is this self-seduction that becomes the prime mover of the unfolding plot of the novel. McDonald carefully lays down the metaphysics that permits it to happen, inventing a realm of potential energy called the mygmus which responds to the myth-making activities of humans in general, but can be manipulated much more dramatically by the particular (hereditary and sex-linked) talents of rare individuals. He is equally careful in developing accounts of how the two subsequent inheritors of the talent learn to cope with and choose to deploy their gift—a process made very much more complicated and hazardous by the continued otherwordly existence of their ancestor.

The spirit of the short story is maintained in one vital and productive respect: the modern mythologies that produce such icons as first contact with alien beings are treated in *King of Morning, Queen of Day* in exactly the same way as ancient Celtic mythology, and a central theme of the novel, as it progresses through the generations, is the way in which our nascent myths and our perception of the mythologies of the past are altered and renewed. This not only permits some spectacularly melodramatic plot-twisting—especially in the final section, when the up-to-the-minute-mythologies of teenage mutant ninja heroes, Space Invaders and slasher movies mingle and cross swords (literally) with Nimrod the Hunter & Co—but allows an extraordinarily intimate interweaving of the fantastic materials of the plot with the texture of everyday life. McDonald seizes these opportunities with avidity and panache, and makes such pyrotechnic use of them that this book establishes him in the very highest rank of modern fantasy writers. Just as John Crowley's *Little, Big*—which also appeared as a original paperback, thanks to the reluctance of publishers to invest heavily in anything truly innovative—was THE fantasy novel of the eighties, *King of Morning, Queen of Day* will surely prove to be THE fantasy novel of the nineties. It is a masterpiece, certain to attain the status of an acknowledged in time, although it might have to get there *via* the cumulative support of a cult following, if this paperback version proves to be as ephemeral as the majority of modern midlist paperbacks.

McDonald has already shown himself to be a stylish writer with a prolific imagination in the marvelously colorful *Desolation Road*, a work that did not suffer at all from being a sprawling patchwork of vignettes. His second novel, *Out on Blue Six*, was far less successful, mainly because the future society framework that was supposed to contain and constrain the elements of its plot was not up to the job. *King of Morning, Queen of Day* also has an abundance of fabulous freestanding vignettes—the first time we meet Tiresias and Gonzaga in part two is beautifully bizarre, and it will be a very clever reader who figures out there and then just who and what and why they are—but the ideative framework is sturdy enough to contain them all. Indeed, the true beauty of the exercise is that the ideative framework not only justifies but requires an elaborate array of stylized scenes and descriptions, in which the minutely naturalistic jogs elbows with the flagrantly exotic. McDonald has such a love of words and their rhythms, coupled with such careful control of the logic of extrapolation, that he is able to work wonders in meeting this requirement; no other contemporary writer could have risen to the challenge with such elegance, wit and charm.

King of Morning, Queen of Day is a novel that brings the very best out of the three-part structure that so much modern heroic fantasy employs simply as a pastiche device. Here, each of the three parts adds a new layer of complexity and a new dimension of revelation to the unfolding vision. To cap all this with a climax that is satisfactory without being trite, and properly conclusive without there being any hint of *deus ex machina* about it, is a considerable feat—and one entirely worthy of the flawed super-heroine who provides the culmination of the myth-sensitive line of descent.

It is difficult for a British writer—especially one who has remained curiously without honor even in his own divided country—to win awards whose voters and juries are predominantly American, but McDonald does have a following in the USA (*Desolation Road* topped the *Locus* poll for best first novel two years ago), so there is every reason to hope that *King of Morning, Queen of Day* will be widely read, and that it will in consequence reap its just reward sooner rather than later. No devotee of intelligent fantasy can afford to miss it.

The Norton Book of Science Fiction: North American Science Fiction, 1960-1990, edited by Ursula K. Le Guin and Brian Attebery (New York: Norton, 1993, 864 p.)

There is an easy way to edit a representative anthology of North American science fiction from 1960 to 1990. All one would need is a list of stories that won various awards and a pile of the various "Year's Best SF" collections, and a little time to figure out how to put together a set of stories in which the available total wordage were split into an appropriate number of smaller segments, with a reasonable spread of dates of publication and no author doubly represented. An editor who had never read a science fiction story in his life could certainly do it. A computer program could probably do it. Maybe even a trained pigeon could do it. The result would be an array of stories carrying a ready-made guarantee of literary quality, readability and popularity. The worst charge most reviewers would be able to level against such a book would probably be the over-familiarity of its contents—which might not matter a damn, given that the likely target audience of the book would probably not be restricted to regular readers of "Year's Best SF" collections.

Naturally enough, no one would ever give such a job to an editor who had never read a science fiction story in his life, let alone write a computer program or train a pigeon to do the job in his stead. Any publisher of good conscience would go to the best brains and most prestigious names in the field, and get them to work in collaboration to do the job *properly*—by which I mean sensitively, intelligently and, above all, conscientiously. Ironically, this *modus operandi* would inevitably transform an easy job into a very difficult one.

The task would become problematic even at a superficial level, because the expert editors would have to take it as axiomatic that they had to do something much cleverer than reprinting lots of

145

award-winning stories, and that they would have to devote a lot of methodical thought and reading-time to the awkward task of finding some top quality stories that had been overlooked or undervalued in their day. At a deeper level, it would be even more problematic, because the experts would be sharply aware of the fact that what they eventually came up with would be seen by its readers as a coherent whole as well as an assembly of parts—as a definitive statement about what "science fiction" had come to mean in the years 1960-1990, and what it ought to mean—and that they must be fully conscious of and fully responsible for their judgments. While a non-specialist editor, or a computer programmer, or a pigeon, could legitimately reply to critics "Hey guys, don't blame me—I just *found* the stuff ready-made, ready-tagged and ready-certified!" conscientious editors are bound to face up courageously to the accusation that they have *invented,* by careful selection, that which they are supposed to be representing and reflecting: the image, the identity and the evolutionary thrust of modern North American science fiction. Being the best brains in the business, they can hardly claim that they knew not what they did.

Given all this, the business of "reviewing" *The Norton Book of Science Fiction* can be quickly concluded. It is a book that contains sixty-seven fine sf stories selected with care and conscience by three of the best brains in the business (Karen Joy Fowler is credited along with the two senior editors as a "consultant" and seems to have been intimately involved in the selection process), who were careful and conscientious enough to ask for suggestions from a lot of other people too (including, I had better confess, me). I dare say that any reader will find a couple of stories herein that rub him or her up the wrong way, but the great majority of the material is excellent. My advice to would-be readers, therefore, is to buy the book and enjoy it; it is well worth the money.

To say all that is, however, pathetically easy—an ill-written computer program or half-trained pigeon could do as much. The conscientious reviewer, who is ambitious to pose as an expert, cannot possibly be content with such a swift paean of praise. He (or she, were someone else doing this in my place) is surely obliged to tackle the much more difficult and vexatious job of inquiring into the lesson that might be learned from the book, about the nature and the evolutionary dynamic of contemporary American science fiction.

Maybe this requires a better brain than mine, but I shall do my best.

* * * * * * *

Actually, the abovementioned task is made a little easier by the work that the editors have already put in. Because they have done their job so very conscientiously and self-consciously, many of the lessons to be learned from the book are made explicit and fully explained in Ms. Le Guin's excellent introduction, which is a fine essay on the nature and evolutionary dynamic of modern science fiction as well as an account of the range of the selected stories. I shall crib from this introduction shamelessly, adding elaborations of my own where I can. Should I appear at any point to be disagreeing with Ms. Le Guin, be assured that I do so respectfully; even the finest thesis tends to generate antitheses, at least some of which might be combined with it to provide a productive synthesis.

Ms. Le Guin obligingly beats around the bush of definition for a while before concluding that no very precise description of what "science fiction" is or ought to be is possible. Her argument is detailed, scrupulous and, in the end, unrepentant about the fact that a line between sf and fantasy has to be drawn *somewhere,* and that other rulers might have perfectly good arguments for drawing it somewhere else. She anticipates criticism from several directions, and mostly gets her retaliation in first. She is not sympathetic to "people suffering from nostalgia for an illusionary 'Golden Age' of 'hard' science fiction", and moves swiftly on to a broader and more welcoming concept of what can and does qualify as science fiction than the narrower notion which the hard men of the genre sometimes take up arms to defend.

As might be expected, Ms. Le Guin's characterization of sf draws upon the theoretical writings of her co-editor. There is no space here to do justice to the subtlety of their argument, but the core of it is that, although science is the framing "megatext" of sf, sf stories cannot and ought not to be "judged according to their actual scientific content". In this view, the decision as to whether or not a story qualifies as sf depends to some extent on its use of certain characteristic "icons"—some of which, like time-travel and faster-than-light travel, science finds difficult to tolerate—and, at a deeper level, on its acceptance of a *weltanschauung* in which phenomena are examined *"within the context of materialist cause and effect"* (her italics). Ms. Le Guin cleverly backs up her argument by citing the example of Bob Shaw's "Light of Other Days"—a story that many people (including me) have held up as a near-perfect example of what a good sf story can and ought to do—with a gentle reminder

147

that any competent physicist could easily think of three fatal reasons why slow glass could not possibly work. The point being made is that even hard sf entertains impossibilities, so what qualifies a story as sf has far more to do the *manner* in which the defining icons and other ideas are entertained—*i.e.*, with the *etiquette* of their deployment.

There are undoubtedly some critics who would disagree with this, but to my mind the point is incontrovertible. Where there does remain scope for further questions to be asked, though, is in the matter of the precise organization of the etiquette pertaining to qualification. To the extent that there is any widespread consensus among the writers, readers and critics of North American science fiction from 1960 to 1990 as to what might rightly be called "science fiction", Ms. Le Guin's summary must be deemed an admirable one; to the extent that there is legitimate disagreement, however, it must also be deemed a controversial one. Some people will think her idea of what constitutes sf is far too permissive if it includes such stories as Fritz Leiber's "The Winter Flies" and Orson Scott Card's "America" (both of which are conceded to be borderline cases by Ms. Le Guin); others might be rather more concerned about what has been excluded (without discussion) by a system of etiquette that—like all systems of etiquette—remains largely tacit and covert. The devil's advocate, confronted with this anthology, might even go so far as to argue that the terms under which science is admitted to the kind of science fiction that this anthology tolerates are so harshly restrictive as to constitute virtual banishment, and given that a conscientious reviewer might be said to have a duty to play devil's advocate....

I shall return to this point in due course.

* * * * * * *

Fully cognizant of the fact that it is a natural extension of her mission to explain, Ms. Le Guin extrapolates her discourse on matters of definition into a statistical analysis of the anthology's contents. She points out that fifty of the stories are set on Earth, four aboard spaceships, and thirteen on other planets, and that otherworldly settings are more commonly used in the earlier stories. She calculates that thirty-two of the stories are set mostly in the present or a not-much-changed near future, and thirty-three in a substantially changed future (the others being alternative history stories); again she notes that substantially-changed scenarios feature much more frequently in the earlier stories. She dutifully calls attention to the implication contained in these figures that, during the period in question, sf was becoming more concerned with the here-and-now, and that this is an important feature of the field's recent evolution.

Ms. Le Guin further observes that twenty-one of the stories feature aliens (although she acknowledges that difficulties of definition make the figure slightly uncertain), and that a higher proportion of stories featuring aliens are to be found in the work of female writers than that of male writers. She explains this by reference to the alienation of women in a male-dominated society, and cites James Tiptree Jr.'s "The Women Men Don't See" as a cardinal example of the way sf icons can be used to dramatize such issues in heartfelt fashion. (At some risk to my personal credibility I must confess that I had always thought of this story—like most of "Mr." Tiptree's work—as a sarcastic joke rather than a deeply-felt complaint, but I might be wrong.) Ms. Le Guin goes on to find that there are no monsters in the book, although she admits that difficulties of definition make this figure even more problematic than the last, and is perhaps too polite to mention that in all the stories in which women confront aliens, human males play the monstrous role with gusto. She is quite confident that there is only one robot, although she notes that intelligent and sometimes highly-articulate machinery that does not mimic human form is quite widely featured.

For the record, I will add a few statistical observations of my own.

Eleven of the stories come from *The Magazine of Fantasy & Science Fiction*, which published 372 issues in the relevant period. *Analog*, which published ten issues more because it went to a thirteen-times-a-year schedule in 1981, provides only two stories. *Isaac Asimov's Science Fiction Magazine* (164 issues) provides eight and *Galaxy* (139 issues) three. The magazine that has the highest ratio of inclusions to issues, surprisingly enough, is the British *Interzone* (three stories from forty-two issues)—a rather remarkable figure when one considers that ninety percent of *Interzone*'s contents were ineligible for consideration, by virtue of being written by non-North Americans. The highest-paying regular market for sf, *Omni*, contributes two stories from 147 issues. The most proportionately-successful single source of stories is, however, not a magazine at all; Terry Carr's anthology series *Universe* (fifteen issues) furnishes five stories. Other specialist sf/fantasy magazines contribute eleven stories, other original anthologies seventeen. The rest come from men's magazines and single-author collections (although the precise point of origin of the first story in the book, Damon Knight's "The Handler", remains stubbornly obscure).

What do these statistics tell us? To some extent, of course, they reflect the fact that the specialist magazines, which had dominated the field since its inception, suffered a dramatic loss of hegemony after 1960. Although they continued to be the primary market for short stories, in the sense that most short stories appeared there first, paperback books became the medium in which most short fiction—as well as the vast majority of novels—were most widely read. Inevitably, an increasing proportion of short fiction went directly into the paperback medium during the '60s and '70s. *Analog*, which—as *Astounding*—had been the main driving force in the evolution of the field in the '40s continued its retreat into a quiet and stagnant backwater, while *Galaxy*, which had been the main driving force in the '50s, went bust. The favor shown by the editors of the *NBSF* to sources on or beyond the fringe of the US magazine and series-anthology market is testimony to the extent to which the criteria of selection used by the magazine editors failed to cope with the broadening out of the field.

(Interestingly, although the *NBSF* reflects the fact only dimly, some of these trends went into reverse during the '80s, when the average sale of paperback books fell sharply as the marketplace became overcrowded, while the sales figures of the leading magazines held up fairly well.)

Now for some more contentious statistics.

While admitting that matters of definition are somewhat problematic, I calculate that the number of stories in the *NBSF* that contain some actual scientific discourse—in the sense that some sort of analysis in scientific terms, however superficial, is offered of the particular "icon" that the story contains, be it a natural phenomenon, a technology or an alien being—is twelve. (I have included in this number the one story calculatedly dealing with an "alternative science", exploring an intriguing corollary of the phlogiston theory; I have also included one very marginal case in order to ensure that the count should err, if it does err, on the side of generosity). By my count there are also twelve stories which contain no *internal* innovation at all, referring only to the contents of the world as we know them; these include, of course, stories with such "framing innovations" as alternative histories. Forty-one of the stories present their icons or other innovations purely and simply in terms of a set of given properties, without any attempt at analysis in physical or biological terms. The remaining two deal with parapsychological phenomena, unsupported by any jargon of apology.

Of the twelve stories that do include some scientific discourse, only six actually feature scientists involved in research. Three of these six are jokes; the other three (two of which are set in the past and feature actual historical figures) carefully juxtapose the scientific work of the characters with aspects of their personal lives, in such a way that the scientific discourse is transformed into a metaphor for something else.

The implication of all this is that there is precious little science in North American science fiction 1960-90, and what there is tends to be used for literary ends other than hypothetical extrapolation. It is not simply that the boundaries of sf have been extended from a hypothetical "hard core" to let in lots of "soft science fiction"; the fact is that, where any science at all is allowed to remain in the kind of science fiction exemplified by this anthology, it is made to work very hard indeed to earn its keep. It is not enough, in modern science fiction, for scientific discourse simply to be scientific discourse *per se*: it is usually included in a story in order to set up a joke, or a romantic tragedy, or to provide a curious kind of metaphor for some aspect of the dynamics of intimate human relationships. The science-fictional extrapolation of a premise, for the sake of trying to identify what consequences a new invention or discovery might have for society as a whole, actually seems to have become taboo in recent North American science fiction, on the grounds that such exercises lack human interest.

Speaking as the devil's advocate, I find this a trifle disappointing—and, in a way, rather sad.

It may be worth adding one further set of statistics, although it is one of which I am admittedly rather suspicious. There is a pervasive rumor—mostly spread by what Ms. Le Guin calls "people suffering from nostalgia for an illusionary 'Golden Age' of 'hard' science fiction"—that North American science fiction is "upbeat" by comparison with, say, European science fiction. It is true that this generalization is applied mainly to novels, but, as it is an unshakable item of faith for the editor of at least one leading American sf magazine, one might expect to find some trace of it in a representative anthology of North American sf. The reality is very different.

By my admittedly-problematic count, only twelve of the stories in this anthology could by any stretch of the imagination be said to have "happy endings". Twenty-two have frankly bleak or tragic endings; the remainder fall into a spectrum that ranges from the blackly comic through the satirically ironic to the perversely eccentric. Five of the twelve "happy endings" are contrived by means that are frankly miraculous, and only one is achieved by purposive and conscientious human endeavor—and that belongs to a story set in an alternative past, whose hero is executed by firing squad for his pains, thus compromising the upbeatness with a non-trivial measure of black irony.

The implication of this (as any devil's advocate would be duty-bound to point out) is that recent North American science fiction—at least so far as it stands any chance of being judged worthwhile by the best brains in the field—is in no way, shape or form "optimistic", and that such "optimism" as it does display usually takes the form of hoping that the day might be saved by some benign miracle. From the point of view of the average literary critic, who might have been deluded by ignorance into thinking that science fiction was primarily a vehicle for naïve technophilia and primitive wish-fulfillment, this is excellent news. Any sociological commentator who might have been deluded by naivety into thinking that science fiction was a good indicator of contemporary attitudes to the future would probably find it rather horrific.

* * * * * * *

There are, I suspect, some people who might interpret the figures cited above to mean that *The Norton Book of Science Fiction* presents a horribly distorted image of North American science fiction from 1960-1990. Such churlish individuals might argue that a truly representative anthology would have exhibited, alongside the softer stuff, far more of the "hard sf" that Ms. Le Guin relegates to the broader field's second or third division. The true sf, according to theorists of this stripe, is the sf of writers who are valiantly carrying forward the tradition of John W. Campbell Jr., Robert A. Heinlein, Isaac Asimov, and Larry Niven, who deserve to be given a place of honor in any representative anthology even if they have to rub shoulders with more bohemian types. (Asimov and Niven are, incidentally, omitted from the anthology although both of them published a reasonable amount of highly-praised short fiction in the relevant period, and David Brin is absent too—but Thomas M. Disch, John Sladek and Kit Reed are also omitted, so there seems little point in drawing up any indictment for prejudice along these lines.)

Personally, I do not think that dissent on these grounds is justified. I think that the contents of this book, as statistically analyzed above, really do give a true and accurate account of the phenomenon of North American science fiction from, 1960-1990. Although a trifle disappointed and saddened by the relative scarcity of actual scientific discourse, I do not think this could have been effectively remedied by adding more so-called "hard sf" because I am of the equally sad and disappointed opinion that so-called hard sf has been rotten to the core from the very beginning, eaten away from within by such cancers as Campbell's absurd fascination with parapsychology, Heinlein's paranoia and the fetishistic fascination with military hardware exhibited by many of its authors. Anyone who desires to speak for a "pure" kind of science fiction that always contains real science, and never contains anything but real science, seems to me to be fighting on behalf of a mirage that has never actually existed. If this book is correct in its analysis of the evolutionary dynamic of the field, it never will.

It is interesting, however, that when the stories included in this book have cause to refer to "science fiction", it is not to stories like themselves that they refer, but to an imaginary kind of story that is very different. Such a story is described in some detail in Eleanor Arnason's "The Warlord of Saturn's Moons", but a more sweeping and more general indictment can be found in the story that concludes the book: John Kessel's "Invaders". Ms. Le Guin, in her introduction, calls particular attention to this placement, which, although it was the product of a policy-decision to arrange the stories in order of their dates of publication, seems to her particularly apt. "I am glad that Kessel's 'Invaders' closes our book," she notes, "not only because it handles this urgent, difficult theme [what the post-Columbian conquest of America did to the native Americans] with wit and passion, but because its last words are the last words of all the words of all the stories in the book, and they are: 'and everyone lived happily ever after'."

This is an interesting observation, in that it seems superficially to pander to the idea that sf stories ought to be "upbeat", but it actually celebrates the undermining of that notion with a fierce and scalding irony. The "everybody" who lives happily ever after at the end of "Invaders" is the Incas, who—mercifully forewarned—have slaughtered the invading Spaniards, thus saving "the world" from "everything" that North America 1960-1990 (including, one presumes, its science fiction) stands for. The story juxtaposes its account of the devastation of Native American cultures by invaders with a similarly brutal account of the devastation of contemporary American culture by aliens, and argues forcibly that, if some such thing were to happen, contemporary America would fully deserve everything it got. Mr. Kessel adds a third narrative line to his story in which an authorial voice reflects upon the evils and follies of "science fiction", on the grounds that "science fiction" provides a kind of escapist fantasy that is both silly and morally dubious.

I feel slightly constrained in making this point because I have commented on this particular story before, in a review I wrote for *Foundation* of Mr. Kessel's collection *Meeting at Infinity*. That review prompted Mr. Kessel to write me a letter in which he complained bitterly about the tone and manner of my remarks. Shorn of a certain lurid ornamentation of wit (which Mr. Kessel thought neither funny nor clever) my argument suggested that Mr. Kessel's work was exemplary of a kind of science fiction that could be characterized by the title of an anthology Terry Carr once produced: *Science Fiction for People Who Hate Science Fiction*. What I meant by this was that, in attempting to obtain the respect and interest of the audience for "literary fiction", many editors and authors had begun actively to promote a kind of "user-friendly" science fiction in which the familiar motifs of science fiction—robots, aliens, spaceships, etc—are used not as premises for extrapolation but as quasi-allegorical figures in metaphorical accounts of the present-day human condition. Mr. Kessel's reply, in brief, was that most of what he wrote was not science fiction at all but "literary fantasy" and that the sort of sf he did occasionally write was perfectly legitimate. He was, of course, entirely right. Mr. Kessel disagreed with my suggestion that "Invaders" was an example of "Science Fiction for People Who Hate Science Fiction" on the grounds that the account of sf given in the third narrative thread of "Invaders" is actually rather generous, in that the authorial voice ultimately opines that the absurd and cowardly escapism of sf can be excused, because the world is such a horrid place that *any* attempt to escape deserves sympathy.

Perhaps I can make belated amends to Mr. Kessel now by admitting that, although his argument might be controversial as to matters of detail, its gist must be conceded. There can, of course, be no such thing as "Science Fiction for People Who Hate Science Fiction". In writing the kind of science fiction that dissented from the (false) image that earlier science fiction had somehow acquired, people like Mr. Kessel and Ms. Le Guin have clarified the matter of what science fiction is and ought to be—including its pet hates. We can now see, clearly, that science fiction, as represented and characterized by *The Norton Book of Science Fiction*, does not hate *itself* at all, although it does hate (mockingly, and with an occasional hint of back-handed generosity) lots of other things, including the kind of non-existent mirage-sf that is upbeat, escapist and hard.

According to *The Norton Book of Science Fiction*, what sf really hates is environmental pollution, xenophobia, corrupt political and sexual-political institutions, unfeeling people, cruelty, and various other entities too numerous to detail, but it does *not* hate anyone who has the courage and the determination to complain about these things, and it is always prepared to give aliens the benefit of the doubt, even when they aren't particularly cute to look at. Nor, according to the *NBSF*, does sf hate science, or technology, or the idea of progress—well, not exactly. Its feelings about science, technology and the idea of progress are, in fact, much more confused and much more embarrassed than frank hatred, not to the point that it refuses to let them in at all, but at least to the point where it only dares to entertain them if they can be excused by being likened to, or preferably converted into, something much more intimate and much more *worthy*.

Those of us who actually feel that there might be something to said for science, technology and all that stuff ought perhaps to be grateful for this small mercy. We are, after all, few in number and getting fewer all the time. I dare say that we will soon be extinct— and that, because we are, after all, devil's advocates rather than dinosaurs, no one will miss us. Not all the authors represented in the *NBSF* are collaborators in this process, but even those who are not recognize its force. By far the most imaginatively-adventurous story in the book, Frederik Pohl's marvel-filled "Day Million", constantly taunts and teases its readers with regard to their presumed tunnel-vision:

> I despair of telling you exactly what it was that Don did for a living—I don't mean for the sake of making money, I mean for the sake of giving purpose and meaning to his life, to keep him from going off his nut with boredom—except to say that it involved a lot of traveling. He traveled in interstellar space-ships. In order to make a spaceship go really fast about thirty-one male and seven genetically-female human beings had to do certain things, and Don was one of the thirty-one. Actually he contemplated options. This involved a lot of exposure to radiation

flux—not so much from his own station in the pro-
pulsion system as in the spillover from the next stage,
where a genetic female preferred selections and the
sub-nuclear particles making the selections she preferred demolished themselves in a shower of quanta.
Well, you don't give a rat's ass for that....

C'est la vie.

* * * * * * *

It is, of course, arguable that the label "science fiction" has become so ill-fitting as to be ludicrous, and that it only flourished in
the first place for eccentric historical reasons. Ms. Le Guin's Introduction to the present volume cites Samuel R. Delany's observation
that science fiction stories can meaningfully contain all the sentences of mundane fiction but that the reverse is not true, so that
mundane fiction ought really to be regarded as the subset. She does
not extend this observation—although she could—to note that all
the sentences that science fiction can meaningfully entertain can
also be entertained in fantasy, which can also entertain all the sentences (for instance, those dealing with gods, ghosts, fairies and
talking animals) that science fiction tends (not, alas, wholeheartedly)
to exclude.

Given that we can now identify a genre of "fantasy"—or, for
those concerned with matters of intellectual snobbery, "literary fantasy"—why should we bother with a subset of science fiction at all?
If aliens and robots and timeslips and psychotropic drugs are simply
to be reckoned parts of the standard vocabulary of modern allegory,
fable and satire, in what sense are they incompatible with gods,
ghosts, fairies and talking animals? Are not the anxieties that Ms. Le
Guin expresses as to whether "The Winter Flies" or "America" can
really qualify as sf, rather than fantasy, a little *passé*? Outside of a
few fannish dinosaurs, who really worries—or even wonders—
about such fine distinctions nowadays?

Were we to consult Hugo Gernsback (who, we recall, dismissed
all but one of the stories in the first *Hugo Winners* anthology as fantasies) he would certainly be hard pressed to find more than half a
dozen "scientifiction" stories in the present volume. (For what it
may be worth, my guess is that he would acknowledge six at the
very most, those six being "Day Million", Samuel R. Delany's
"High Weir", Poul Anderson's "Kyrie", Gregory Benford's "Expo-

sures", Greg Bear's "Schrödinger's Plague" and Michael Blumlein's "The Brains of Rats".) But this tells us nothing except that "science fiction" has changed out of all recognition since Hugo's day, not only in what it is but in what it pretends and aspires to be. That is the fact of the matter; it is pointless to deny it. It is pointless even to regret it, for it is difficult to imagine that things could be otherwise. All the other things that sf aspired or pretended to be, in the manifestos of its editors and critics, it manifestly failed to become—and its failure was so utter as to be ignominious.

This is not a puzzling phenomenon, and there is really no need to string this already-interminable essay out much further for the sake of explaining the obvious, but it so happens that there is a particularly eloquent statement of the case in another story in the book, which was published in the same year as "Day Million" (1966): James Blish's "How Beautiful With Banners". This would not be on Hugo's list of authentic sf stories, but it is certainly on mine. In the story, a scientist who is about to be quick-frozen to death is first forced to contemplate the icy wilderness that her life has (metaphorically) been, thus allowing the text to display the reasons why the tragic fate of its protagonist is so horribly and ironically appropriate:

"The life of science even in those days had been almost by definition the life of the eternal campus exile. There was so much to learn—or, at least, to show competence in—that people who wanted to be involved in the ordinary, vivid concerns of human beings could not stay in it long, indeed often could not be recruited. They turned aside from the prospect with a shudder or even a snort of scorn. To prepare for the sciences had become a career of infinitely protracted adolescence, from which one awakened fitfully to find one's adult self in the body of a stranger. It had given her no pride, no self-love, no defenses of any sort; only a queer kind of virgin numbness, highly dependent upon familiar surroundings and unvalued habits, and easily breached by any normally confident siege in print, in person, anywhere—and remaining just as numb as before when the spasm of fashion, politics or romanticism had swept by and left her stranded, too easy a recruit to have been allowed into the center of things or even considered for it."

It is no wonder that wise boys and girls—and wise sf writers too—stay as far away from pure science as possible; they know full well that it is likely to freeze their balls, their wombs and their very souls.

Well, perhaps.

157

It is no wonder, either, that mirage-sf never became anything more than mere escapism—but this does not mean that sf as an actual and evolving genre has failed. Its conspicuous success has been in becoming what it has become—what is represented by *The Norton Book of Science Fiction*—and there is evidence enough in these pages that its success has been at least a teensy-weensy bit glorious.

Here, I suppose, endeth the lesson—but at the risk of testing the reader's patience, I shall reproduce one last quote, this time from the publicity sheet that accompanied my review copy of the book. "Newcomers will delight," it says here, "in the sophisticated range of voices probing the nature of reality and the condition of the human spirit. Readers of all stripes will recognize in story after story the seriousness, imagination, passion, and wit that strike a resonant blow to the solar plexis [*sic*] and announce all truly great literature."

For myself, I cannot help but wonder whether the world might be a slightly better place if science were held in sufficiently high esteem that even a hyperbolically-inclined copy-writer would not only know how to spell "plexus" but might be enough of a pedant to speculate as to whether a plexus were really the kind of entity that could be expected to resonate when struck. At the end of the day, though, I know well enough that there's no earthly point in hankering after a world like that. It's pure fantasy, you see.

The Breath of Suspension by Alexander Jablokov (Sauk City, WI: Arkham House, 1994, 318 p.)

Arkham House continues to produce handsome illustrated editions of short story collections by outstanding new writers in the sf field, and deserves congratulation for so doing. This volume reprints ten stories by Alexander Jablokov with illustrations by J. K. Potter, and it is a book to dignify any shelf. All the stories in it first appeared in *Isaac Asimov's Science Fiction Magazine* between 1985 and 1992; they include two novellas, one of which is the title story and the other "A Deeper Sea", which formed the basis of Jablokov's second novel.

The earliest story here, "Beneath the Shadow of her Smile", is about a soldier condemned to fight eternally in a series of wars, apparently by virtue of a reckless prayer offered to an unnamed goddess in ancient times. Not content with conscripting him to the ranks in all the wars of actual history, the aforesaid goddess takes care to arrange that—for him at least—the wars will be interminable; *his* World War I did not end in 1918, nor his World War II in 1945. The story is entirely typical of Jablokov's *modus operandi*; it exemplifies his cavalier attitude to alternative histories, which he establishes in profligate confusion to serve relatively trivial narrative purposes, and it also exemplifies his fondness for wildly excessive *contes cruels*. He gives the impression of being a man who might readily use a sledgehammer to crack a nut, and then make reparation of a sort by constructing a lachrymose sob story reflecting ironically upon the suffering of the shell-shocked kernel.

"At the Cross-Time Jaunters' Ball" and "Many Mansions" offer further demonstrations of Jablokov's flamboyant way the time travel and its science-fictional correlates. Both are melodramatic comedies. The first features a critic of alternative realities, created for art's sake, whose precious few psychological havens from the confusing riot of false reality are casually stripped away. The second offers a charmingly straight-faced extrapolation of Karl Marx's proposition that religion is "the opium of the masses", presenting a fast-moving account of time-hopping gangsters, who buy up dogmas from the peasants to sell at a vast profit elsewhere in a strangely sensation-starved universe. "The Ring of Memory" is another convoluted tale of hectic time-tripping, in which the eventual Gordian knot of repeated histories is offered as tragedy rather than farce.

"Deathbinder" is the cruelest of the collection's *contes cruels*. It adopts the premise that, although death has been final until the recent past, new medical technologies have now permitted ghosts to come into being. Through no fault of their own, the resultant disinherited spirits blight everything with which they come into contact, and must be literally nailed down if their malaise is to be confined. The story describes the troubled mission of the one man sensitive enough to see and secure the ghosts, carefully hoarding its nastiest revelation for use as a brutal punch line. Two other stories in the collection are similarly ingenious in their bleak morbidity: "Living Will", in which an attempt to use technology in compensating for the erosions of senility inevitably goes awry; and "The Death Artist", in which yet another justifiably-paranoid central character contrives to decode the complex subconscious motives controlling his relentless fascination with suicide.

"The Breath of Suspension" and "Above Ancient Seas" are the most delicate stories in the collection, forsaking the excesses that crowd and hurry most of the other items in favor of contemplative reflection. What they reflect upon (if I might be permitted to oversimplify in the interests of economy) is the question of what drives people to transform and transcend their limited circumstances; both tales call attention to the significant role played in such achievements by stubbornly symbolic gestures. These stories carry a far more intimate and desolate sense of psychological imprisonment than the author's calculatedly excessive exercises, and this sensibility is carried over into "A Deeper Sea", which is certainly the most ambitious and perhaps the most effective story in the collection. It covers vast tracts of narrative ground in its forty-odd pages but relegates its violent events to the background of the central character's conscience-stricken ruminations on the cruel ironies of fate. "A Deeper Sea" is one of the few sf stories about intelligent dolphins that suggests that, were they able to talk, they would probably prove to be almost as nasty as we are, but it compensates by suggesting that the margin of culpability might still be sufficient to require a magnificently melodramatic gesture of reparation.

As with most contemporary science fiction, *The Breath of Suspension* is determinedly introspective. It answers the modern editorial demand that fiction should be "character-driven" by setting forth tortured protagonists, and then torturing them a lot more, so that any victories over circumstance they might win over cruel circumstance will seem tremendous, and any failure on their part simply becomes further evidence of the vicious nasty-mindedness of fate. Science-fictional motifs are recruited with contemptuous abandon to decorate the plights of such characters, and to escalate the scale of their conflicts with destiny; the logic of the devices involved is never brought into question, nor are the implicit premises ever extrapolated so as to examine their effect on the world external to the characters' emotional orgies. This is, essentially, fiction for self-obsessed readers, which panders to self-obsession by placing, not merely the universe of space and time we know and don't particularly love, but all conceivable universes of space and time at the beck and call of private sensation. It is romantic fiction without the object of desire, crime fiction in which the murderer is always the mirror-image of the detective, futuristic fiction in which there isn't even a secure present or past from which to look out upon the eternal vistas of oblivion. It is a distinctively modern kind of art for art's sake.

According to the back flap, Alexander Jablokov is an ardent environmentalist and hiker. These interests may help to explain his apparent conviction that, whenever we run out of places to get lost in, it becomes impossible to avoid finding ourselves. His arguments to the effect that this will not be a comforting experience are so gaudily presented as to be not very convincing, even when they try to be, but that doesn't necessarily make the conclusion untrue.

Days of Cain by J. R. Dunn (New York: Avon, August 1997, 328 p.)

In one of Oscar Wilde's fables a company of nymphs visit the pool where the tragedy of Echo and Narcissus had been acted out, eager to obtain first-hand testimony regarding the quality of the beauty that so entranced Narcissus as he gazed at his own reflection. Alas, the pool cannot tell them, for, while Narcissus gazed at his reflection in its surface, the pool had been utterly entranced by its own reflection in the youth's staring eyes.

This parable stands in a neat relationship with one of the most famous aphorisms of Nietzsche, which proposes that, when you look long into an abyss, the abyss also looks into you. Nietzsche, of course, does not specify what there is to be seen in the abyss, but he was a philosopher, routinely over-optimistic regarding the ambition of the human mind. Wilde was an artist, and one of *his* most famous aphorisms was that life imitates art far more than art imitates life.

Cosmology is, by definition, a sustained attempt to look long and hard into the deepest abyss of all. The appreciation of the true size and age of the universe that has emerged by slow degrees over the last hundred and fifty years has been a rather sobering experience, insofar as it has informed us of our utter insignificance in a scheme so vast as to be hardly imaginable. Most of us, staring into this abyss, have been unable to muster the least conviction that the abyss, in looking back at us, could see anything at all—and the same majority has accepted that, even if it could, we could have no more significance than mere bacteria seething in a speck of slime. To suppose that all of us might see things that way is, however, to reckon without the awesome power of human narcissism.

When the so-called anthropic cosmological principle was first mooted by Brandon Carter in 1973, the first response of many philosophers must have been to invoke the customary cliché: that it was either trivial or false, depending on the strength of its assertion. Few could have imagined that, after a gestation period of two decades, it would have given birth to the most spectacular scholarly fantasy ever produced within the physical sciences: Frank Tipler's *The Physics of Immortality* (1994). Once that scholarly fantasy had been produced, however, it required only a tiny imaginative step to real-

ize that writers of science fiction would seize upon this gift with un-
paralleled avidity.

By the end of the century, Tipler's version of the Omega Point
will be one of the central myths of our ailing genre, for the very
good reason that it allows us to look into the furthest abyss and believe, not only that the furthest abyss is looking into us, but *that it
likes what it sees*! It does not necessarily love us, but it cares about
us; it is fascinated by us; we matter to it. Near-infinite and near-
eternal as it may be, like Wilde's version of the pool of Narcissus it
needs our eyes to see itself, in order that it too might practice the
fine art of narcissism and transmute that art into the substance of life
itself.

Exuberant and essentially *nice* versions of this myth of universal reconstruction have been produced by Robert Reed (*A Exaltation
of Larks*) and Charles Sheffield ("At the Eschaton"/*Tomorrow and
Tomorrow*)—and such works have allowed us to appreciate for the
first time how far-sighted James Blish's *A Clash of Cymbals* was—
but it is not at all surprising that more cynical versions are already
snapping at their heels.

The Prophet Tipler promises us that the godlike intelligence that
will invest the entire universe, as it reaches the limits of its expansion, will recreate us all in order to understand itself, thus giving us
the afterlife of which we have always dreamed but for which we
have never *really* dared to hope. Here is a veritable Heaven, super-
vised by a Star Maker which will help to engineer the universe's
collapse in such a way that the next Big Bang produces a better universe—by which we mean, of course, a universe that human eyes
could look upon more gladly than the awful abyss presently to hand.
We are glad to be offered the possibility, of course, but we cannot
help asking the hard questions. If this is our Heaven, what of Hell?
How will the ultimate intelligence understand the nastier bits of its
own history? How, for instance, will it understand Auschwitz?

In J. R. Dunn's *Days of Cain,* the ultimate universal intelligence
is called the Moiety. From the lofty viewpoint of the Omega Point it
uses time-travel, not merely as a means of understanding its own
origins and nature, but as a means of ensuring its own existence and
identity. Unlike all us zombies, it knows exactly where it came
from, although it is still trying to figure out exactly where it is going, and why. In order to make sure that it never loses its grip on
reality, it recruits hirelings from every era of its history, and from
every significant location therein, whose function it is to prevent
"continuity breaks". Not unnaturally, however, this police force con-

tinually produces renegade groups, who decide that the people whose history they are policing are of more urgent moral concern than the invisible and incomprehensible Moiety.

These heretics, doubting the omnipotence, omniscience and omnibenevolence of their effective creator, set out valiantly on missions of salvation—pursued, of course, by the faithful whose cause they have deserted. Such pursuits are difficult in purely tactical terms because of a certain waywardness affecting the technology of time-travel, but they are also difficult in moral terms. The transparently good intentions of the renegades cannot help but pose a problem for their pursuers; the motive force that might impel a company of saints to prevent or subvert Auschwitz is obvious and clear, but what motive force can possibly justify those who seek to preserve and sustain it?

Dunn does not bother to put the reader into the mind of his heretic saint, Anna Lewin. We see her only through the eyes of others: the Moiety dropout Lisette Mirbeau, who sympathizes with her; the loyal operative Gaspar James, whose job it is to stop her; the Auschwitz inmate Rebeka Motzin, who learns from her brief acquaintance how to cultivate the will to survive. All of them see her as a charismatic and uncannily forceful figure, but all of them know from the very beginning what she can never admit: that she cannot in the end prevail; that sainthood is ultimately impotent in the face of reality. Dunn's interest is focused, as it should be, on the inflexibility of that reality; it is Rebeka's world-view and Gaspar's conscience that are sectioned, stained and set beneath the object-lens of his literary microscope—and the conscience of Gerd Reber, the "good German", who never becomes fully aware of Anna Lewin's existence, but feels the blast of her righteous contempt nevertheless.

Days of Cain is a powerful book. It has the advantage of dealing with powerful materials, but authors who can deploy such potentially-explosive materials with this degree of care and control are rare. The passages describing events within Auschwitz are brilliantly done, walking the tightrope that stretches from analysis to outrage with minute care. Those chapters that use Reber's viewpoint rather than Rebeka's are a *tour de force*, intensely claustrophobic and intimately discomfiting. The political infighting of the time police seems slightly hysterical by comparison, and Gaspar's inner turmoil never rings true in juxtaposition with Reber's—but that is partly the point, as the story graphically illustrates when the time comes for the Moiety to pin its good conduct medal on Gaspar, while Reber lies dying of a stroke.

Insofar as *Days of Cain* has a conclusion, it recalls the oft-told and horribly bittersweet tale of the learned Jews confined in a concentration camp who put God on trial for permitting their plight, duly found Him guilty on all counts, and then commenced to pray. Dunn refrains from explicit sermonizing, so the reader is free to read this as ironic black comedy rather than an earnest reiteration of the gloomy message of *Ecclesiastes*, but the end is just as open, just as ambivalent and just as brutal whichever way it is conceived. The truly significant element of the novel's denouement, however, is not what the Moiety actually *says* to Gaspar in its quaintly ungrammatical fashion, nor even whether what is says to him makes any sense, once its meaning has been deciphered, but the mere fact that it bothers to speak to him at all.

During his day-trips to Auschwitz, Gaspar has looked into the abyss, and has rightly been appalled by the awareness that the abyss in question is within him as well as without, not simply because he is temporarily complicit in its evil, but because he is heir to and parent of its infection. How else is he to cope with this but to embrace the awareness that beyond *that* abyss is another, and that the abyss beyond the abyss reflects a far lovelier image, a far gentler echo? How else, after all, are *we* to cope with it?

It's all a pack of lies, of course—but if we only wrote the truth in our journals, what on earth would we read on the down-bound train?

The Fantasy Hall of Fame edited by Robert Silverberg (New York: HarperPrism, March 1998, xii + 562 p.)

Three hundred years have passed since Charles Perrault issued the anonymous collection of short stories that helped Antoine Galland's translation of the Arabian Nights to inspire the first fashionable wave of modern fantasy, whose "Hall of Fame" featured Madame d'Aulnoy, Jean de Bibiena, Pierre Crébillon fils, Jacques Cazotte, Thomas Gueulette, Alain-René Lesage and Voltaire. Unfortunately, save for William Beckford's *Vathek*, the fashion never made much headway outside France and the last traces of its produce had all but vanished a century later, when the tradition of German Romanticism launched by the *märchen* of Johann Musäus, J. W. Goethe, Ludwig Tieck, Wilhelm Hauff, Friedrich de la Motte Fouqué, Adalbert von Chamisso and the Brothers Grimm gave birth to a rather different species of fantasy, whose "Hall of Fame" eventually expanded beyond the borders of Germany to encompass Hans Christian Andersen, John Sterling, George MacDonald, Théophile Gautier, Anatole France, Nikolai Gogol, Ivan Turgenev and Jonas Lie.

It was this second wave of modern fantasy that first reached the American shore, being carried forward—magnificently, if not very far—by Nathaniel Hawthorne, Edgar Allan Poe and Washington Irving, but it too failed to stay the full distance. Although it never died away completely, it had lost most of its impetus by the end of the nineteenth century.

The key theme of the first fashionable flurry of modern fantasy genre was *civilization*—which, in Perrault's usage, referred to the process by which children and savages might be fitted for adult society. Many of the fantasies produced within that genre were designed for the moral and sentimental education of individuals who stood in need of such education; the remainder were self-congratulatory satires that served to illustrate to those already educated the fragile thinness and polished brightness of the relevant veneer.

The key theme of the second wave of modern fantasy was *volksgeist*—which, in Jakob Grimm's usage, referred to the way in which the folklore of a people preserved and refined its cultural heritage. Many of the fantasies produced within that genre were designed to search out and interrogate the roots of collective identity; the remainder consisted of attempts to strengthen and redirect the currents of moral thought that would form the key element of the cultural heritage of the future. This literary movement became international because the nascent German nation-state was not the only region whose inhabitants felt that they needed to restore better contact with their roots, and certainly not the only one whose inhabitants felt the need to build a better cultural heritage for future generations.

The second kind of fantasy never became extinct, even in America. It had certainly become etiolated by the end of the nineteenth century, when it had fallen into the custody of such minor writers as Frank R. Stockton and Eugene Field, but it never vanished. Nor was there any settlement of a central controversy imported into it by its pioneers, who wondered whether the roots and dynamics of American culture ought to be sought in the unique aspects of American history (as most of Hawthorne's work and some of Irving's implied) or whether they ought to be traced back to the European cultures from which successive waves of American immigrants had come (as most of Poe's work and the rest of Irving's implied).

As the twentieth century built up a head of steam the tradition of American fantasy was continually, if rather eccentrically, renewed. Influences from French Decadent Romanticism were imported by Robert W. Chambers, James Huneker, James Branch Cabell and the West Coast "Bohemians" associated with Ambrose Bierce. The tradition of fantastic Americana devised by Washington Irving and continued by Mark Twain was further extended by Stephen Vincent Benét. A distinctive species of sentimental fantasy was invented by Robert Nathan. American children's fiction was gifted with its own pick-and-mix fantasy parallel, by courtesy of L. Frank Baum. Comic fantasy of the kind popularized in Britain by F. Anstey also became popular in the US by courtesy of Thorne Smith, who employed anarchic humor to subvert the pretensions of Prohibition much as Anstey had used them to poke fun at Victorian rectitude. Pulp fiction generated a new species of unfettered literary daydreams by courtesy of odysseys in exotica penned by Edgar Rice Burroughs and A. Merritt.

This long and fairly noble history receives remarkably short shrift in the introduction to *The Fantasy Hall of Fame* established by a ballot of the membership of the recently-renamed Science Fiction and Fantasy Writers of America. The first phase of that ballot established *a priori* that American genre fantasy was born in 1939, when John W. Campbell Jr. founded *Unknown*, and became moribund in 1942, when that magazine folded. Not until the late 1960s, we are assured by Silverberg's introduction, did genre fantasy get into gear again, when the huge success of US paperback reprints created the market space for Lin Carter to launch the Ballantine "Adult Fantasy" series (although it is admitted that this series mostly consisted of older "classics").

Silverberg has nothing much to say about what happened to the newly-identified marketing category thereafter, the rest being assumed to be perfectly familiar to the audience of this anthology—and hence, one presumes, the audience of this review. As with the first assumption, this one serves to cover up the fact that virtually everything that ordinary readers might consider to be "fantasy" has been ruthlessly excluded from the dark and narrow corridor of this particular "Hall of Fame". Indeed, its relationship to post-1970 genre fantasy is even more peculiar and more remote than its relationship to pre-1939 fantasy.

* * * * * * *

Lin Carter's Adult Fantasy series was, of course, a concerted attempt to re-connect those fugitive traditions of American fantasy that, in the wake of *Unknown,* had maintained a precarious existence on the periphery of genre science fiction, with the older traditions. The "history" that Carter constructed—he, of course, saw it as a matter of *re*construction—was essentially an instrument for connoisseurs, which would allow them to see how the works of such early pulp writers as A. Merritt, Robert E. Howard and Clark Ashton Smith were connected, oddly but intricately, with the esoteric works of Lord Dunsany, William Morris, George Meredith, Anatole France and many others—works that had also exercised a considerable influence upon such contemporary writers of upmarket fantasy as C. S. Lewis and J. R. R. Tolkien. Carter also sought to replace and rehabilitate within that solidified tradition such "literary orphans" as Eric Rucker Eddison, Hope Mirrlees and Evangeline Walton. It was intrinsic to the theoretical basis of this history that fantasy, as a genre—including its eccentric extensions into pulp fiction—was important, profound *and esoteric*.

The introductions to the series of *Year's Best Fantasy* anthologies that Carter began editing for DAW in 1975 commented approvingly on the way that contemporary writers like Richard Adams and Patricia A. McKillip had succeeded in selling books written for children to an adult audience. He also rejoiced in the revitalization of sword and sorcery fiction by the endeavors of such writers as Michael Moorcock, who had, at last, taken up where Robert E. Howard had left off in the 1930s. In his 1978 anthology, however—surveying the produce of 1977—Carter introduced a new category into its summary appendix in order to warn readers against "The Worst Book Ever": *The Sword of Shannara* by Terry Brooks. Although Carter took the trouble to berate everyone involved in the publication of Brooks' "war crime of a novel", he did not even deign to mention Stephen R. Donaldson's *Chronicles of Thomas Covenant,* all three volumes of which had also been published in 1977— after having been rejected by every single editor in America because every single one of them (until Ballantine hired Lester del Rey to replace Lin Carter) *knew* that it was unsaleable.

It was, therefore, in frank defiance even of the self-appointed champion of the newly-rehatched fantasy genre that Brooks and Donaldson demonstrated how much commercial potential genre fantasy had, and in what directions its future lay. They paved the way for genre fantasy to spawn a whole series of best-selling endeavors, including series of books by Marion Zimmer Bradley, Piers Anthony, David Eddings, Raymond Feist, Guy Gavriel Key, and the collaborators Margaret Weis and Tracy Hickman. (The only Carter "discovery" who needs to be added to the list is Katherine Kurtz.)

In the eyes of American readers *circa* 1990—the cut-off date for the ballots that determined the contents of *The Fantasy Hall of Fame*—these best-selling writers not only constituted genre fantasy's "Hall of Fame" but actually *were* the contemporary fantasy genre. Not one of them is, however, included—or even mentioned—in *The Fantasy Hall of Fame*. Nor is Adams, nor McKillip, nor Moorcock—nor, for that matter, are numerous writers whose works attained considerable sales collectively, if not individually, including Andre Norton, John Jakes, Jane Yolen and Terry Pratchett. The members of the SFWA, in voting for the stories to be included in this showcase anthology, have contrived the remarkable feat of omitting almost every writer (the sole exception is Ursula K. Le Guin) who might sensibly have been said in 1990 to have made a significant contribution to the establishment of fantasy as a marketing category, and hence as a thriving popular genre.

The principal reason for this peculiar state of affairs is, of course, that popular genre fantasy mostly consists of very long works, most of which extend through several volumes. Because this anthology had an upper word-limit of 15,000 words (although whoever counted the words in Anthony Boucher's "The Compleat Werewolf" must have used a dodgy calculator) most of the fantasy best-sellers had produced little or no qualifying work, and those items that did qualify were of little significance within their oeuvres. That might have been regarded as a sensible reason for using a different methodology to construct a fantasy "Hall of Fame", but the members of the SFWA have their own idea of what constitutes fantasy, and where excellence can be found therein. It is not entirely surprising that they should have clung hard to the notion that in constructing their own "Hall of Fame"—in which they cast votes for one another with relentless fervor, admitting only a few favored outsiders—they were doing something worthwhile. Perhaps they were—but, given the slightness of the introduction, it might be as difficult for a disinterested observer to discern what they were trying to achieve as it is to analyze and evaluate what they have actually contrived.

There are thirty stories in *The Fantasy Hall of Fame*. They are supposed to include the fifteen individual stories that proved most popular in the SFWA ballot, plus fifteen runners-up—including stories by those authors who obtained a high collective score from two or more nominees without any individual story placing in the top fifteen. No explanation is given for the fact that, although James Tiptree Jr.'s "Her Smoke Rose Up Forever" placed equal tenth, neither that story nor any other by Tiptree—who placed ninth in the authors' list—is included. This omission reduces the number of contributions by female writers to five, one of whom (Tanith Lee) is also one of the three contributors from outside the USA.

The fact that a ballot of the members of the Science Fiction and Fantasy Writers of America produced a Hall of Fame ninety percent of whose inclusions hail from the USA is not particularly unusual; American culture has always had stubbornly centripetal tendencies. Nor need we be surprised, given that SFWA once stood for the Science Fiction Writers of America, that the proportion of writers included who are better known for their science fiction than their fantasy is only slightly less (86.67% by my count). This latter prejudice has at least as profound an influence on the kinds of fantasy that are foregrounded by the anthology as the former; the book might have been more accurately advertised as a collection of the favorite fantasy stories of and by famous science fiction writers. The voters did try hard enough to overcome their ghetto mentality to grant first place in the poll for one of only two stories to bear the by-line of a non-genre writer—Shirley Jackson's "The Lottery"—but the token gesture recognizes an authentic kinship between that particular story and their own produce. It does not serve to alleviate the comfortable parochiality of the collection—and thus, alas, merely adds to the shallowness of its *civilization* and the narrowness of its *volksgeist*.

In saying this, I do not mean to imply that the stories in *The Fantasy Hall of Fame* are bad; they are consistently excellent, and half a dozen might be rated as literary works of the very highest quality—but their excellence is confined to a few distinct lines within the vast spectrum of fantasy, and those are mostly black lines formed by the calculated extinction of the kinds of color that most exponents of the lost fantasy genres of the eighteenth and nineteenth centuries considered to be its quintessential qualities.

* * * * * * *

"The Lottery" is set in an anonymous American small town; it describes the enactment there, a few days after the summer solstice, of an almost-forgotten ritual of human sacrifice, which has already been abandoned in neighboring villages. The whole point of the story is the manifest absurdity of the allegedly ancient ritual; the underlying assumption is that America is the last place on Earth where such echoes of the distant past can have any meaning. The implication is that the ultimate horror available for contemplation by the American mind is that there are still people in the backwoods who have not yet shed the burden of their origins and committed themselves to the past-free future.

The significance of the fact that the SFWA members chose to co-opt "The Lottery" is further emphasized by their second *ad hoc* adoption: "Tlön, Uqbar, Orbis Tertius" by Jorge Luis Borges. This story deals with a phantom of the scholarly imagination: a nonexistent nation in a non-existent world that can be glimpsed only in the pages of aberrant copies of reference books, and where people *do not think as we do*! This, to, is an archetypal fantasy of *disconnection*, whose fantasy element is quintessentially arbitrary, devoid of any conceivable relevance to the *civilization* of actual children or the *volksgeist* of actual people. (Not all of Borges' work is like that, of course.)

The brutal disconnection of fantasy motifs from their origins provides the opening moves of the first two stories in the book: "Trouble with Water" by H. L. Gold and "Nothing in the Rules" by L. Sprague de Camp. The point of both stories is that, whatever significance water gnomes and mermaids might have had in the past, their American manifestations are merely problems to be solved, or opportunities to be seized by individuals engaged in competition with their fellows. Similar processes of preliminary de-historicization followed by re-accommodation to American pragmatism can be seen in Boucher's "The Complete Werewolf", Robert A. Heinlein's "Our Fair City" and James Blish's "There Shall be no Darkness". Ray Bradbury's "The Small Assassin" is a similar adjustment-of-perspective story within an even-more-intimate context. All these stories do include an educative element comparable to Perraultian *civilization*, but its key element is admirably summed up by de Camp's title, and relentlessly repeated within his story: the point is to win, and anything within the rules is acceptable. The story might be offered as a useful parable to any Briton puzzled by the fact that the Americans contrived to turn rugby into American football, or rounders into baseball.

The only pre-1950 story in *The Fantasy Hall of Fame* entirely alien to this pattern is C. L. Moore's remarkable "Fruit of Knowledge", a *conte philosophique* that was presumably inspired by John Erskine's satire *Adam and Eve* (which had presumably been inspired in its turn by Rémy de Gourmont's *Lilith*). It is significant that the only other story in the anthology carefully and conscientiously rooted in a mythological tradition assumed by the story to be still alive and kicking is Gene Wolfe's "The Detective of Dreams"—a tale of which the best and the worst that can be said is that G. K. Chesterton would have *loved* to have written it. The one ancient tradition to which America has clung hard is, of course, the Christian tradition, sanitized (if not actually sterilized) by Fundamentalism. Philip K. Dick's calculatedly heretical "Faith of our Fathers" and Robert Silverberg's "Basileus"—of which the worst and the best that can be said is that G. K. Chesterton would have loathed them—similarly thrive on that recognition. The second Pentateuch-based fantasy in the book—Ted Chiang's "Tower of Babylon"—is not a *conte philosophique* at all, but an idea-as-hero story even more thoroughly science-fictional in its method and outlook than Silverberg's tale of computer-nerd insanity.

(It might be as well to further this digression by observing that, apart from Biblical mythology, the only authentic mythology to which any stories in the book refer at all is Native American mythology. R. A. Lafferty's "Narrow Valley" is far less reverent than Ursula K. le Guin's "Buffalo Gals, Won't You Come Out Tonight", but no less sympathetic; both tales, however, take care to provide eloquent symbolism of the fact that the Amerindian world-view is something that has relevance only to the remotest periphery of contemporary American culture. Lucius Shepard's "The Jaguar Hunter" also invests itself with earnest pseudo-anthropological mysticism, but might be regarded as a fearful celebration of the extent to which the rest of the world has come to seem awfully alien to Americans abroad.)

The pattern established by the stories of the 1940s is further extrapolated, albeit sarcastically, in such 1950s tales as Avram Davidson's "The Golem", Poul Anderson's "Operation Afreet" and Robert Bloch's "That Hell-Bound Train". Like F. Anstey and Thorne Smith, these writers were perfectly conscious of the absurdity of the pretensions their stories set out to undermine—but, like F. Anstey and Thorne Smith, they also preserved a careful sentimental regard for those pretensions. The pattern is absent from such *contes cruels* as Jack Vance's "The Loom of Darkness" and Margaret St. Clair's "The Man Who Sold Rope to the Gnoles", but it is part of their bedrock nevertheless. In these carefully-mannered exercises in exotica, the attempted pragmatism of the central characters is mocked and penalized—but the apparatus invoked for that purpose is wholly invented and entirely arbitrary. The disconnection of the stories from

171

any actual tradition of *civilization* or *volksgeist* is an essential component of their charm. "The Silken-Swift" by Theodore Sturgeon stands somewhat aside from the other stories of its period in being a conscientiously-formed parable, but its fabular element is as carefully disconnected from its roots as any. The first of the 1960s stories—"The Bazaar of the Bizarre" by Fritz Leiber—is a gleeful celebration of the distance that American sword and sorcery fiction had travelled since the days when Fafhrd and the Gray Mouser (in the long-unsold "Adept's Gambit") had been part of our past rather than the world of "Nehwon".

The most "European" of all the stories in the book is "Come Lady Death" by Peter S. Beagle, which is set in London and is reminiscent of the folktale that had provided the basis of Selma Lagerlöf's *Körkarlen* (1912). It contrasts sharply, and interestingly, with the two stories written by *bona fide* Europeans: J. G. Ballard's "The Drowned Giant" and Tanith Lee's "The Demoness". The former is an ironic hymn to the forces of dispassionate disconnection and pragmatic commercialism, whose dispassionate satire probably seems a little less scathing to Americans than it does to everyone else. The latter takes the all-purpose gaudy Fantasyland developed (in the wake of Clark Ashton Smith) by Jack Vance and Fritz Leiber to an unusual extreme, echoing Moore's proto-feminist rhetoric in a harrowing fable of remarkable richness and complexity. It is, perhaps, this tale, more than any other, that demonstrates the utilitarian flexibility of the disconnecting moves made by this kind of American fantasy—but, like the Ballard story, it has a chilly objectivity that ought to make it feel far less comfortable to its readers than the authentically American inclusions.

An opposite extreme of narrative temperature is represented by the torrid sickliness of the two stories that bracket Lee's: "The Ghost of a Model T" by Clifford D. Simak and "Jeffty Is Five" by Harlan Ellison, the latter being the story that placed second to "The Lottery" in the ballot. Both are tales of nostalgia run riot, taken into realms of sickly sentimentality to which few literary travelers have ever penetrated—but the past that is recalled with such amazing fervor is made up entirely of the products of American commercial enterprise. That these stories are sincerely heartfelt, no one can doubt, but they represent a degree of commodity fetishism so obsessive that they are bound to seem utterly bizarre and irredeemably perverse to the un-American eye. They attack the values of the present with merciless force, but their base-referent in so doing is the prices of the day before yesterday. The lost "heritage" for which they weep is the (presumably fictitious) America in which mass-produced cars and candy bars gave full value for money; the implication is that there was nothing before the miraculous regime of primal consumerism but a void; Ray Bradbury's "small assassin" would presumably have agreed wholeheartedly.

The story that came third in the SFWA poll, Roger Zelazny's "Unicorn Variations", is a straightforward extrapolation and modernization of the outlook of the two stories from 1939 issues of *Unknown*, which captures their essence beautifully and adapts it to a modern eco-political context as cleverly as any survivalist manual. The story that tied with Bloch for fourth place, Terry Bisson's much-lauded "Bears Discover Fire", is a straightforward exercise in whimsical Americana—whose fantasy element, according to rumor, was added purely in order to enable the story to be published in a science fiction magazine. Like the slightly older stories by Simak and Ellison, these two items are thoroughly escapist, but the strategies of escape that they espouse reproduce with awesome exactitude the tunnel-vision of the attitudes from which escape is allegedly necessary. Within this particular Hall of Fame they do indeed represent the contemporary State of the Art.

* * * * * * *

It may be worth noting that not all fantasy produced by American authors between 1939 and 1990 was of the determinedly parochial, conscientiously disconnected and eupsychically pragmatic kind that fills this particular Hall of Fame. One writer conspicuous by his absence is Thomas Burnett Swann, whose early short stories were re-imported to the USA during the early days of the fantasy boom, having initially seen the light in the British magazine *Science-Fantasy*. There is, however, no doubt that *The Fantasy Hall of Fame* does skim a substantial quota of cream from its own particular subspecies of American fantasy—and that this kind of fantasy has come to be seen by some of its adherents as the freshly-rooted but sturdy stem that eventually flourished into the contemporary marketing category. By this reckoning, the big best-sellers are to be seen merely as cheap popular extensions of something much worthier.

A rough theoretical basis for this kind of fantasy has been sketched out in an interesting essay by Michael Swanwick, which was published in the November 1994 issue of *Asimov's Science Fiction*. Swanwick set off therein in search of something which could plausibly be held to unite a considerable number of the best contemporary fantasy texts, linking them in such a way that they might form the fundamental organizing structure of the genre in the way that "hard science fiction" is sometimes held to form the fundamental organizing structure of genre sf.

The long subtitle of Swanwick's essay begins by advertising it as "A Cruise through the Hard Fantasy Archipelago in Search of the Lonely and the Rum". The essay's central argument is that if it is to be judged by its best examples rather than it worst, genre fantasy is more like an archipelago of islands than a literary continent, because the primary acts of differentiation performed by its writers disconnect their texts from one another as well as from the familiar world. According to Swanwick, because fantasy texts—virtually by definition—refuse to accept the logical bonds that tie hard science fiction texts together, they resist being gathered into the kind of common enterprise that unites hard sf texts in their celebration of the glorious mechanics of progress.

Swanwick declares:

> I'm going to write about what Tove Jansson called 'the lonely and the rum', the unschoolable and ungroupable, those strange and shaggy literary creatures that have no ilk or kin and that mathematically can be contained in no set smaller than the set of all sets contained in no other sets. For ease of argument, I'm going to call this congeries of works *hard fantasy*, because I honestly believe that it holds a central place in its genre analogous to a place hard science fiction holds in SF.
>
> Our voyage will be treacherous, for the waters are uncharted and by the very nature of our quest many an important work will be ignored entirely. It is possible, too, that we shall occasionally land on what only appears to be an island. There are Faerie isles, after all, and some that seem solid now may turn to whales or mist in the morning. But the danger is justified not only by the beauty and wonder of our destinations, but because these are the works that drive fantasy, the source and justification for the entire genre, the engine that burns at the heart of its star.

This approach makes disconnection, isolation and unashamed idiosyncrasy the fundamental virtues as well as the fundamental

properties of genre fantasy—and no one commissioned to summa-
rize and weigh the contents of *The Fantasy Hall of Fame* could deny
that Swanwick certainly has a point. It is, of course, perfectly obvious that J. R. R. Tolkien was not trying to achieve any such disconnection when he embarked on the lifelong obsession that produced
The Lord of the Rings—indeed, his specific purpose was to provide
a mythology tailor-made for the purpose of reassembling and recon-
necting the fugitive threads of Anglo-Saxon myth that had been
snapped and scattered by the Norman conquest—but it is equally
obvious that this had nothing to do with the book's phenomenal success in America. Indeed, the subsequent success of *The Sword of
Shannara* and its countless analogues demonstrates, with appalling
clarity, that what American readers valued in *The Lord of the Rings*
was the exact opposite of what Tolkien valued in it: its apparent
self-enclosure and seeming removal from anything they recognized
as belonging to the actual present or the actual past. What had been
intended as a bridge between islands became, in the eyes of its most
devoted admirers, an island in itself—albeit one that was fated to
become the key exemplar of a rapidly-expanding and hectically
crowded archipelago.

If Swanwick's thesis really does provide an ideological basis
for modern fantasy, and a tentative explanation of some of its perversities, then *The Fantasy Hall of Fame* becomes much easier to
understand. On the tiny but once-populous island of Tana in Vanu-
atu there is a tiny cult of Pilipantists, who have revered the Duke of
Edinburgh as a god ever since the now-defunct royal yacht Britannia
paid a flying visit to the island in the 1950s. When performance artist and long-time sf fan Ken Campbell embarked upon a pilgrimage
to this remarkable spot in the 1980s he took with him a photograph
of buck-toothed scouse comedian Ken Dodd, which he presented to
the chief of the Pilipantists—who was, of course, delighted to add it
to his own sacred Hall of Fame. Had F. Scott Fitzgerald and Ernest
Hemingway been present, the former might well have commented
that there was a world of difference between Tana and the USA.
"Yes," Ken Campbell would surely have put in, knowing exactly
what was to come. "The Americans have more money." They also
live in a much larger, but somewhat narrower, fantasy archipelago.

King Rat (London: Macmillan, 1998, 333 p.) and *Perdido Street Station* (London: Macmillan, March 2000, 717 p.), both by China Miéville.

According to the thesis set out in Desmond Morris's cult classic of yesteryear, *The Human Zoo,* we are not well-equipped by nature for living in cities. Morris's long service at Regent's Park Zoo in London gave him abundant opportunities to study the various forms of neurotic behavior to which animals in cages are unfortunately prone, and it required only the tiniest leap of the imagination to see the same manifestations of dissatisfaction, madness and self-abuse carbon-copied in the quotidian patterns of human city life. It seems tragically probable that the animals in the zoo cannot even take refuge in dreams of escape, because they lack the necessary mental gift. We humans—most of us, at any rate—do not lack power of imagination, but the same faculty that allows us to embark on flights of fancy to the land of Cokaygne also allows us to understand, as the animals in the zoo presumably do not, that we shall never truly escape the human zoo, because we have never really wanted to. We are far too heavily addicted to the comforts provided by our keepers; even those of us who have never tried living as hunter-gatherers for as much as half a day know full well that it is a fate far worse than incarceration and institutionalization.

There are, however, creatures which enjoy the best of both worlds. The elephant house at Regent's Park Zoo is infested by mice (of which the elephants, contrary to rumor, are not in the least afraid). The greater city that surrounds it, like all great human cities, is infested by rats. The city that is our zoo, with all the disadvantages as well as all the advantages of zoo life, is rat Cokaygne: an expansive realm of marvelous generosity and ease, flowing with the superabundant milk and honey of human litter and waste. O to be a rat, now that the winter of rodent discontent is made glorious summer by the sons of Yorick!

The protagonist of China Miéville's *King Rat,* Saul Garamond, is a disaffected city-dweller who arrives home one night to discover—somewhat belatedly—that his sole remaining parent has been defenestrated and that he, by virtue of being found at the scene, is the chief suspect. No sooner has he been hurled into a cage beneath the local police station, however, than he is visited by King Rat, the monarch of London's underworld. King Rat tells him that his is a mixed heritage, and that it is time for the ratty part of his soul to emerge, so that all the Cokaygnian gifts of rat-kind will be his for the taking. It is a offer he cannot refuse, even though he suspects—as any imaginative person would—that there will be a downside to the deal and a hefty price to pay.

Although the alien blood that courses in Saul's heart is royal rather than common rat blood, but the privileges of rat royalty have been somewhat confused by history. King Rat is the victim of meek rebellion, not exactly deposed but definitely despised. His subjects no longer recognize his majesty, because of an unfortunate incident in Hamelin—which was, in rat eyes, a kind of Utopia, or perhaps a kind of Jerusalem, until the Pied Piper came along. King Rat was the sole survivor of the Hamelin holocaust; no other rat has forgiven him for it, and he cannot forgive himself. Now, the Pied Piper is in London—a prospect that terrifies the king of the birds and the king of the spiders every bit as much as it terrifies King Rat—and a second reckoning is due. Saul is King Rat's not-so-secret weapon in that coming conflict: a hybrid creature whose second self will always be able to remain aloof from whichever species-specific music the piper uses to beguile him.

That, at least, is the theory. In fact, the demonic Piper has advantages other than his music. He is exceedingly strong—defenestrating heavy human beings is a mere bagatelle to him—and exceedingly cunning. His attempts to locate and destroy King Rat's secret weapon cut a broad swathe through the ranks of Saul's friends, and introduce him to a new kind of music, which has long been Saul's passion: Jungle. The masterwork of the obsessive Natasha, mistress and manipulator of drum'n'bass, becomes the Piper's ace in the hole, carefully designed for deployment against King Rat's last trump. Nor are the Piper's depredations the only blight cast upon Saul's new life as a rat; Saul learns secrets that estrange him from the King, then experiences misadventures that turn the king of the birds against him. He is tempted to become King Rat himself by the tentative allegiance that the rats of London offer to his royal blood, but is not entirely certain that he is prepared to forsake his human privileges. All these issues have to be settled in the climactic battle, when all the Junglists in London gather at the Elephant and Castle, and the contending rhythms of city life must reach some kind of resolution.

King Rat is a good book by any standards, all the more impressive for being the first published novel of a young writer still engaged in studying for a PhD at the London School of Economics. It is awesomely quirky in its design, fabulously vivid in its imagery, and bumptiously zestful in its execution. The plot glides along like a skater on a slope, but there are depths beneath the transparent surface into which the narrative viewpoint continually glances, supplementing the flow of entertainment with a healthy intellectual satisfaction. It has the suggestion of being the work of a writer capable of breaking new ground in literary fantasy, one who might in time do great things. It is not unknown for works of this appearance to flatter merely to deceive, but more than adequate proof of the promise of *King Rat* is contained in Miéville's second novel, the prodigious *Perdido Street Station. Perdido Street Station* is the most impressive work of imaginative fiction produced in Britain since Robert Irwin's epochal account of *The Arabian Nightmare* (a novel that receives a passing nod of acknowledgement in *King Rat*).

The setting of Miéville's second opus is removed from the actual city of London to the hypothetical city of New Crobuzon, which is elaborately characterized in the opening pages as a landscape replete with "squat churches like troglodytic things", "sewers ridding the earth like secular sepulchres" and "libraries fat with forgotten volumes" and summed up a few pages later as "a huge plague pit, a morbific city". The narrative eases the reader into this archetypal urban wasteland with a brief description of a journey from its periphery to its core undertaken by one of the story's main protagonists, Yagharek.

Yagharek is a garuda, one of numerous exotic species sharing the world whose metropolis New Crobuzon is. Although there are representatives of most of these species within the city, they live in the margins of what is, in essence, human civilization. Some are exploited workers, some constitute ghetto-dwelling social microcosms. The garuda are one of the tinier minorities within New Crobuzon, because they are winged creatures whose native realm is the sky. Most of them live far away from the city, but Yagharek is an exile in more than one sense. Having been convicted of a horrid crime (whose exact nature we are not told until the final stages of the story) he has been literally stripped of his wings; his only hope of ever being able to fly again is to seek assistance from the scientists of New Crobuzon, who have yet to master the art of artificial flight, but have imagination and technology enough to be within sight of some such discovery.

The man commissioned by Yagharek to restore his lost ability to fly is Isaac Dan der Grimnebulin, a researcher estranged from the local university, to which he still maintains an umbilical but largely tokenistic attachment. His estrangement is partly due to his disapproval of his old department's involvement in the politically and commercially guided practices of biothaumaturgy, whose spin-off includes a host of "reshaped" citizens. Many, but not all, of the reshaped are victims of a savagely punitive legal system; all but a few are harmless, if utterly wretched, but the few—including the mysterious crime lord Motley—are viciously vengeful. The reshaped are more grotesque by far than the natural half-human species sharing the city with orthodox humankind, although some of these also tend to the bizarre. Isaac's credentials as an unusually tolerant man are established by the fact that his lover, Lin, is a khepri: an insect-headed sculptress whose medium is her own spittle.

Isaac throws himself into the challenge offered by Yagharek, collecting all manner of flying creatures so that he may study the fundamental mechanics of flight. Unfortunately, one of the many petty thieves and fences to whom he subcontracts this preliminary work contrives to land him with a remarkable larva, which seems extraordinarily reluctant to grow, let alone to metamorphose; it is only by a fluke that he discovers that the only food capable of sustaining it is a popular street drug ineloquently called "dreamshit". When he begins to make progress in his work, the recalcitrant larva is sidelined, almost forgotten by the time it finally condescends to pupate—an error of omission that leads to disaster.

When an imago eventually emerges from the pupa it immediately goes in search of others of its kind, and liberates captive specimens kept to provide a secret supply of the ultimate hallucinogen (whose carefully-degraded derivative is dreamshit). Once free, these creatures—predators upon the stuff of dreams, mind itself—pose a menace so terrible that the denizens of Hell, to whom the city's government maintain a hotline, turn coward in its face. (Even demons are mindful, and imaginative; they have as much to lose in confrontation with these predators as mere men.)

With the government effectively powerless—and, indeed, bent on wreaking vengeance upon the people responsible for the city's peril—it is left to Isaac and his associates to undo the damage. Among the allies solicited by the governors, only the enigmatic Weaver—a spider king far more powerful than the one in *King Rat*, whose spinnerets bind space and time into multidimensional webs and knots—is ready and willing to play a part, but Isaac finds another ally almost as powerful, and almost as dangerous, in the Construct Council, a godlike intelligence in the process of being born out of the linkage of all the city's mechanical servitors. Aided by the Weaver and the Council, Isaac and Yagharek gather a small army to do battle against the predators. An initial attack launched against their nest is only partly successful, requiring a second battle to be fought in the environs of New Crobuzon's most imposing edifice: the phantasmagoric extrapolation of King's Cross, Paddington, Victoria and Waterloo all rolled into one that is Perdido Street Station. It is a battle fought in the knowledge that it must be won, even though the consequences of victory might prove to be merely the lesser of two evils.

As with the climactic battle in *King Rat*, to which the police detectives investigating the death of Saul's father were not invited, the climactic conflict of *Perdido Street Station* is fought by and for the city's outsiders: individualists who have renounced the burden of civilization, at least to the extent of slipping through the bars of the cages in the human zoo. There is something of the animal in them, but also something of divine right. They do not aspire to the rodent condition as such, but to an alchemical fusion of ratty facility and the ambition of expert dreamers. Yagharek has lost his entitlement to fly, but Isaac is yet to claim his, and *Perdido Street Station* ends in the only way that a morally and intellectually responsible fantasy can: with the forces of imminent evil defeated and the hopes of immanent good on the brink of pupation, but with a fair way to go before the kind of metamorphosis becomes possible that might one day transform the ugly heart of New Crobuzon into a Utopia fit for human beings.

China Miéville's depiction of New Crobuzon is a phantasmagoria as prolific and as potentially disturbing as a monster-crowded painting by Bosch or Brueghel, but it is no more a nightmare pure and simple than the vision of London's underworld contained in *King Rat*. It contains a great deal that is ugly, and its masters are fully entitled to their hotline to Hell, but it is a modern Garden of Earthly Delights rather than a purgatory—which, by virtue of being modern, is in the throes of progress. It is because the nasty sprawl of New Crobuzon holds the potential of something better, and more munificent, that it can play host to real heroes, whose victories are more than sport and whose potential rewards are more than Heaven. Unlike *King Rat*, which stops one step shorter, *Perdido Street Station* informs us that although we shall never escape the human zoo, because we have never really wanted to, we might yet remake it in such a way that our cages will not drive us mad.

INDEX

"Above Ancient Seas" 159
Abraham 27
Ace 113
Adam 27, 51
Adam and Eve 170
Adams, Richard 167-168
Addams, Charles 131
The Adding Machine 37
"Adept's Gambit" 111, 172
The Adventures of King Pausole 32
The Adventures of Meng & Ecker 28-29
Aegypt 58
"Again" 65
Aitken, Maria 112
"The Alchemy of the Throat" 91
Alice in Wonderland 140
Aliens 60
All the Bells on Earth 113, 117
"America" 148, 156
Analog 149-150
Ancient Images 51-53
Andersen, Hans Christian 164-165
Anderson, Poul 156, 171
Anderton, James 27-28
"Androgyne" 17
"...And the Horses Hiss at Midnight" 91
"...And the Sun Shone By Night" 65
Angel Heart 84
The Angel of the West Window 57-60
Anno Dracula 128, 130
Anstey, F. 40, 166, 171
Anthony, Piers 167-168
Anticipations 93
Apel, Johann 67
Aphrodite 32
Aquinas, Thomas 124
The Arabian Nightmare 138-139, 178
The Arabian Nights, aka *The Thousand-and-One-Nights* 32, 125, 164

"Area, The" 81
À rebours 15, 23, 25, 64
Argento, Dario 128
Arkham House 99, 158
Arnason, Eleanor 153
"Arria Marcella" 32
"The Ash of Memory, the Dust of Desire" 16
Ash-Tree Press 118, 122
Asimov, Isaac 152
Asimov's Science Fiction 173-174
Astounding 150
Asylum 110-112
Ataraxia 24
Atlas 25
Attebery, Brian 145
"At the Cross-Time Jaunters' Ball" 159
"At the Eschaton" 162
Aubrey, John 30
Auerbach, Nina 95-98
Augustus 123
Aulnoy, Madame d' 164
Avon 161
Avillion 120
Back to the USSA 130
Badley, Linda 102-107
Bailey, Hilary 30
Balcombe, Florence 97
Ballantine 166
Ballard, J. G. 172
Balzac, Honoré de 25
Bantam 142
Barbey d'Aurevilly, Jules-Amadée 36
Bardot, Brigitte 44-45
Barker, Clive 23, 102-107, 114
The Barrens and Others 131-134
Basile, Giambattista 69
"Basileus" 171
Bats and Red Velvet (later *BRV*) 11
Batsford, B. T. 24
Baudelaire, Charles 32, 36, 70, 99-100
Baum, L. Frank 166
Baxter, Glen 137
Bava, Mario 128
"The Bazaar of the Bizarre" 172
Beagle, Peter S. 172
Bear, Greg 157
Beardsley, Aubrey 21
"Bears Discover Fire" 173
Beckford, William 24, 33, 164
The Beetle 120
Beeton, Mrs, 36

Behrends, Steve 99
Bell, Mary 136-137
"Beneath the Shadow of Her Smile" 158
Benét, Stephen Vincent 166
Benford, Gregory 156-157
Bergson, Henri 80-81
Bergstrom, Elaine 17
Berkley 113
"Best Friends" 133-134
Bibiena, Jean de 164
Bierce, Ambrose 99, 166
Bisson, Terry 173
The Black Book 64
"Black Cocktail" 108-109
Black Mask 42
Blackwood's Magazine 120
Blake, William 15, 17, 23, 27
Blameless in Abaddon 27
Blaylock, James P. 113-117
Bleiler, Everett F. 58
Blish, James 157, 162, 170
Bloch, Robert 132, 171, 173
Blood and Roses 66
Blood Kiss: Vampire Erotica 88-92
"The Blood of the Wälsungs" 17
The Bloody Red Baron 128, 130
The Blue Dahlia 44
"Blue Monday" 28
Blumlein, Michael 157
"Bob Dylan, Troy Jonson and the Speed Queen" 132
Boccaccio, Giovanni 69
Bogart, Humphrey 54
Il Boia scarlatto 129
"The Book" 132-133
A Book of Bargains 21
The Book of Hyperborea 99-102
Borges, Jorge Luis 170
Borgo Press 12
Bosch, Hieronymus 180
Boucher, Anthony 168, 170
"Bouvard" 71
"The Bowmen" 78
Bradbury, Ray 170, 173
Bradley, Marion Zimmer 167
"The Brains of Rats" 157
The Breath of Suspension 158-161
"The Breath of Suspension" 159
The Bride of Frankenstein 130
Brillat-Savarin, Anthelme 36
Brin, David 152
Brite, Poppy Z. 16, 88-92

The British Science Fiction Association 10
Britton, David 27-28
Brooke, Rupert 77
Brooks, Terry 167
Brueghel, Pieter 180
Brummell, George "Beau" 36
Bruno, Giordano 58
"Buffalo Gals, Won't You Come Out Tonight" 171
"The Burgomaster in the Bottle" 70
Burroughs, Edgar Rice 166
Busson, Paul 58
Butler, Samuel 37
Byrne, Eugene 130
Byron, Lord 15, 26, 31, 34-35, 67, 125
Cabell, James Branch 99, 166
Cadigan, Pat 10
"Cadillac Ranch" 28
"Café Endless: Spring Rain" 91
"Calcutta, Lord of Nerves" 16
Califia, Pat 17
Campbell, John W. Jr. 152-153, 166
Campbell, Ken 175
Campbell, Ramsey 51-53, 65
Candlenight 60-62
Caprichos 23
"Captain Gubart's Fortune" 70
Card, Orson Scott 148
Carlyle, Thomas 67
 "Carmilla" 17
Carr, Terry 154
Carradine, John 55
Carroll, John 107-110
Carroll & Graf 127
Carter, Angela 49-51
Carter, Brandon 161
Carter, Lin 166-167
Cartland, Barbara 91
"The Casino Mirago" 133
The Castle of Otranto 33
"Catalepsy #1" 65
Cazotte, Jacques 164
Chambers, Robert W. 99, 132, 166
Chamisso, Adalbert von 69-70, 164
Chandler, Raymond 42-44
Charles, René 90
Chatto & Windus 19
Chesterton, G. K. 171
Chiang, Ted 171
The Chronicles of Thomas Covenant 167
Clash of Cymbals, A 162
The Cleft and Other Odd Tales 131-134

"Cherry" 91
"Cinnamon Roses" 90
Circlet Press 88
Clairmont, Claire 67
"Clarimonde" 32
Cleis, 17
Collingwood, R. C. 123
Collins, Nancy 91
Collins, Robert A. 10
"The Color of Her Eyes" 90
"Come, Lady Death" 172
"Come One, Come All" 134
"The Coming of the White Worm" 100
"The Compleat Werewolf" 168, 170
Conjure Wife 111
Constantine, Storm 20-21, 25
Conway, David 66
Cordell, Cleo 25
Corpus Delicti 24-25
The Correct Sadist 65
Cosmopolitan 37
Craik, Mrs. 120, 122
Crawford, Ann (Baroness von Rabe) 96
Creation Books/Creation Press 25, 32, 63-66
Creation Records 25
Crébillon, Pierre *fils* 164
Creed 20
Crowley, Aleister 139-140
Crowley, John 58, 144
Dalby, Richard 118-119, 122
Dalton, James 122
The Damnation Game 106
A Dance in Blood Velvet 21
Dances with Wolves 75
"Dancing Nightly" 91
The Dark Blood of Poppies 21
The Dark Domain 79-82
"The Dark Eidolon" 101
Darker Angels 34-35, 123-127
Dark Feasts 65
"Dark Seduction" 90
Datlow, Ellen 132
Daughter of the Night 17
Daughters of Darkness: Lesbian Vampire Stories 17
Davidson, Avram 171
DAW Books 167
Day, Doris 45-46
"A Day in the Life" 134
"Day Million" 155-157
Days of Cain 161-164
"The Dead Love You" 108

"A Dead Man's Bone" 70
The Dealings of Daniel Kesserich 110-112
"The Death Artist" 159
"Deathbinder" 159
"The Death-Bride" 67-68
"The Death's Head" 67
de Camp, L. Sprague 170
"The Decay of Lying" 121
Dedalus 17-18, 25, 32, 57, 59, 63, 79, 138, 141
The Dedalus Book of German Decadence 17
The Dedalus Book of Polish Fantasy 81
Dee, John 57-60
Dee, Ron 91
"A Deeper Sea" 158, 160
"Definitive Therapy" 133
Delacorte Press 82
Delany, Samuel R. 156
De Lint, Charles 91
Deliver Us from Evil 30-31
Del Rey, Lester 167
"The Demoness" 172
De Mille, Cecil B. 51
Derleth, August 120
Des Esseintes, Jean 15, 19, 36
"Desolation" 17
Desolation Road 144-145
"The Detective of Dreams" 171
Devereaux, Robert 89
Devil, The 19, 26, 30
Diary of a Drug-Fiend 139
Dick, Philip K. 171
Different Seasons 72
The Digging Leviathan 113
Dionysus 31
Disch, Thomas M. 152
"The Discovery of the Future" 93
Dodd, Ken 175
La Dolce Vita 128
Donaldson, Stephen R. 167
Do-Not Press 135
Donovan, Dick 119, 122
Dover Books 58
Dowson, Ernest 21
Doyle, Sir Arthur Conan 85-87, 142
Dracula 15, 23, 30-31
"Dracula Cha Cha Cha" 129
Dracula, Count 26, 30, 97-98, 128-129
The Dracula Tape 30
Dracula the Undead 29-30
Drawing Blood 16
"The Drowned Giant" 172

Dublin University Magazine 120
Duckworth 60
Duke of Edinburgh 175
"Dumb Love" 67
D'un pays lointain 99
Dunn, J. R. 161-164
Dunsany, Lord 167
Durtro Press 25
Duryea, Dan 54
Dvorkin, David 90
"Dying in Bangkok" 75
Dziemianowicz, Stefan 12
Earthquake Weather 31
Ecclesiastes 164
Eddings, David 168
Eddison, Eric Rucker 167
The Edge of Running Water 110
"Elixir" 91
Elizabeth I 69
Ellis, Havelock 23
Ellison, Harlan 172-173
"Eloise" 66
Empire Dreams 142
"The Empire of the Necromancers" 101
Engstrom. Elizabeth 91
Enoch, Book of 20
"Entropy's Bed at Midnight" 74-75
Erckmann-Chatrian 69-70
Erewhon 37
Erskine, John 170
An Essay on Population 23
Etkind, Mark 34
Eureka 121
Eve 27, 49-51
An Exaltation of Larks 162
Expiration Date 31
"Exposures" 156-157
Exquisite Corpse 139
"Faith of Our Fathers" 171
Falling Angel 84-85
The Fall of the House of Usher 50
"The Family Portraits" 67
Fantasmagoriana 67-68
Fantastic Tales 69-71
The Fantasy Hall of Fame 164-175
Fantasy Review 10
Fanthorpe, R. Lionel 119
"The Fated" 71
"The Fated Hour" 67-68
Faust 50
Faust, Christa 91

"Feelings" 133
Feist, Raymond 168
Fellini, Frederico 128
Ferris, Henry 118-123
Field, Eugene 165
Field, W. C. 87
The Fields of the Nephilim 24
"The Final Fête of Abba Ali" 92
Finney, Jack 47-49
"Fireside Horrors for Christmas" 122
Fitzgerald, F. Scott 175
"Flashback" 75-76
Fogazzaro, Antonio 69
Fog Heart 135-138
Forge 131
Foundation 9-10, 12, 154
Fouqué, Friedrich de la Motte 164
Fowler, Christopher (author) 18
Fowler, Christopher (editor) 10
Fowler, Karen Joy 146
France, Anatole 18, 165, 167
Frankenstein 67-68
Frankenstein's Bride 30
Freud, Sigmund 80-81, 103, 106
"Friend's Best Man" 108-109
"The Frog Prince" 132-133
"From Hunger" 92
From Ritual to Record 113
From the Teeth of Angels 107
"Fruit of Knowledge" 170
Fry, Stephen 36
"Fumes" 80-81
G, Amelia 90
Galaxy 149-150
Galland, Antoine 164
The Garden of Delight 24
Garelick, Rhonda K. 36
Gather, Darkness! 111
Gautier, Théophile 32, 69-71, 99, 165
Genesis 25
"Geraldine" 91
"German Ghosts and Ghost-Seers" 121-122
Gernsback, Hugo 156
Gespensterbuch 67
Ghosts and Scholars 118
"The Ghost of a Model T" 172
The Ghost Story Society 118
"The Gift of Neptune" 92
"A Gift of the Gods" 133
Gilbert, William 96
Gilles de Rais 63-64

Girodias, Maurice 32
Gladwell, Adele Olive 66
"The Glance" 80
Glasby, John 119
"The Glass of Blood" 17
"Glim-Glim" 133
Glyndwr, Owain 61
God 18-19, 26, 29
Goethe, J. W. 184
Gogol, Nikolai 165
Gold, H. L. 170
"Der Golden Topf" 58
The Golem 57-58, 60
"The Golem" 171
Gollancz 34, 49, 136
Gothic Rock 24
The Gothic Society 67
Gourmont, Rémy de 99, 170
Goya 23
Grabinski, Stefan 79-82
Graves, Robert 123-124
Gray, Dorian 15
"The Great Lover" (Brooke) 77-78
"The Great Lover" (Simmons) 73-74, 77-79
The Green Face 59
Greenwood Press 102
Griffith, D. W. 51
Grimm, Brothers 164-165
The Grotesque 111
Gueulette, Thomas 164
Guidio, Kris 28
Hale, Terry 67
"The Handler" 150
"Hansel and Grettel" 132
Harcourt Brace 27
Harlequin 91
HarperCollins 102
HarperPrism 88, 164
Harris, Thomas 66
Hartwell, David, 12-13
Hauff, Wilhelm 164
The Haunted Chair and Other Stories 118-123
Havoc, James 63-65
Hawthorne, Nathaniel 165
Head Injuries 135-138
Heidegger, Martin 82, 84
Heinlein, Robert A. 152-153, 170
Hemingway, Ernest 175
Herbert, A. P. 77
Heron, Liz 18
"Her Smoke Rose Up Forever" 169

The Hex Files: The Goth Bible 24-25
Hickman, Tracy 168
Highsmith, Patricia 129
"High Weir" 156
Hippocrene 17
"His Mouth Will Taste of Wormwood" 16
Hjortsberg, William 84-88
Hodge, Brian 91
Hoffmann, E. T. A. 58, 69, 121, 129
Holder, Nancy 91
Holland, Tom 26, 30-31, 128
Holmes, Sherlock 26, 86
Homunculus 113, 117
Houdini, Harry 85-87
Houghton Mifflin 42
Howard, Robert E. 167
"How Beautiful With Banners" 157
"The Human Tragedy" 18
The Human Zoo 176
The 100 Best Detectives 12
The 100 Best Fantasy Novels 12
The 100 Best Hollywood Novels 12
The 100 Best Horror Novels 12
The 100 Best Science Fiction Novels 12
Huneker, James 166
Hunter, Jack 63
Hutzulak, Clint 65
Huysmans, Joris-Karl 15, 19, 23, 25-26, 63-64
I, Claudius 123
The Idea of History 123
Interview with the Vampire 30
Interzone 149
"In the Compartment" 80
"In the Greenhouse" 91
"In This Soul of a Woman" 91
"Invaders" 153-154
The Invisible Man 111
Irving, Washington 165
Irwin, Robert 32-33, 138-141, 178
Isaac 27
Isaac Asimov's Science Fiction Magazine 149, 158
"It Twineth Round Thee in Joy" 133
I, Vampire 17
Jablokov, Alexander 158-161
Jackson, Shirley 169
"The Jaguar Hunter" 171
Jakes, John 168
Jakubowski, Max 12
James, M. R. 52
"The Jane Fonda Room" 107-108
"Jeffty Is Five" 172

Jenkins, Herbert 39
Jeter, K. W. 113
Jettatura 71
Joan of Arc 63
Job 26
Johnson, Madeleine 81
Jones, Stephen 12
Joshi, S. T. 118, 120, 122
Judgment of Tears 127-131
Juliette 15, 23
Justine 15, 23
The Kabbalah 140
Kaldera, Raven 90
Karloff, Boris 51
Kasak, Richard 32, 88
Kast, Pierre 30
Kay, Guy Gavriel 168
Keaton, Buster 87
Keats, John 35
Kelley, Edward 59
Kessel, John 11, 153-154
Khnopff, Fernand 32
Kilpatrick, Nancy 90
King, Stephen 72, 102-103, 114
King of Morning, Queen of Day 142-145
King Rat 176-180
Knight, Amarantha 88-92
Knight, Damon 150
Knopf 102
Koja, Kathe 82-84, 91
Körkarlen 172
Kurtz, Katherine 168
"Kyrie" 156
Là-Bas 64
The Lady in the Lake 42
Lafferty, R. A. 171
Lagerlöf, Selma 172
Laidlaw, Marc 93-95
"The Lake of the Three Lampreys" 70
Land of Dreams 113, 117
The Land of Laughs 107
Lane, Eric 141
Langford, David 142
Larkin, Philip 138
Last Call 31
The Last Coin 113
"The Last Lords of Gardonal" 96
Last of the Vampires 96
The Last Supper 50
Laughing Gas 39-42
Laveau, Marie 35, 126

"A Leaf from the Berlin Chronicles" 120
Leavis, F. R. 98
Leconte de Lisle, Charles 99
Lee, Tanith 169, 172
Le Fanu, Joseph Sheridan 17, 31
Legend 51
"Legends of the Black Castle" 70
Le Guin, Ursula K. 145, 147-149, 151-154, 156, 168, 171
Leiber, Fritz 110-112, 148, 172
Leonardo da Vinci 50
Lesage, Alain-René 164
"The Letter U" 70
Lewis, C. S. 167
Lewis. D. F. 23, 65
Lewis, Matthew Gregory 15, 23
Lie, Jonas 165
"The Life of My Crime" 108
"Light of Other Days" 147
Ligotti, Thomas 16, 23
Lilith 170
Lilith 21, 26, 50
The Limits of Vision 139-140
Lincoln, Abraham 35
Lipinski, Miroslaw 79
Little, Big 144
The Little Sister 42-44
Littlewood, Joan 130
"Living Will" 159
Livy 123-124
Li Yu 32
London After Midnight 24-25
The Lone Ranger 95
The Long Goodbye 44
"The Loom of Darkness" 171
Lord Horror 28
Lord Kelvin's Machine 117
The Lord of the Rings 175
Loren, Sophia 44
Lorrain, Jean 17
Lost Souls 16
"The Lottery" 169-170, 172
Louÿs, Pierre 32
Love Bites 88-92
"Love Comes in Fragments" 65
Lovecraft. H. P. 20, 94-95, 100, 132
Lovedeath 72-79
"Loved to Death" 90
Love in Vein: Twenty Original Tales of Vampiric Erotica 88-92
Löw, Rabbi Judah 59
Lugosi, Bela 51
MacDonald, George 165

Machen, Arthur 78
Macmillan 176
MacNish, Robert 39-40, 122
Mademoiselle de Maupin 32
The Magazine of Fantasy & Science Fiction 149
Magick in Theory and Practice 139-140
Mallarmé, Stéphane 36
Malthus, T. R. 23
Malzberg, Barry 44-46, 91
Mann, Thomas 17
"The Man Who Sold Rope to the Gnoles" 171
The Man Who Was Born Again 58, 60
"Many Mansions" 159
"The Marble Boy" 133
Marianne Dreams 81
Marion's Wall 47-49
Marks, Paul 65
Marlowe, Christopher 30
Marquise de Sade 18
Marsh, Richard 118-123
Marx, Karl 159
Master of Fallen Years 21
Mastroianni, Marcello 129
McDonald, Ian 142-145
McDowell, Ian 91
McGrath, Patrick 110-112
McKillip, Patricia A. 167-168
Meeting at Infinity 154
Memnoch the Devil 19, 104
Meng & Ecker 28-29
Mengele, Dr. 28
Mercer, Mick 24-25
Mercury House 69
Meredith, George 167
Merritt, A. 166-167
The Merry Thoughts 24
"Mesmerism" 121
Metal Angel 18-19
"Metamorphoses of the Vampire" 32
"A Metempsychosis" 40
Meyrink, Gustave 57-60
Michaud, Marc 12
Michelet, Jules 124
Miéville, Chine 176-180
Milton, John 17, 30
Mirrlees, Hope 167
The Mission 24
"Mister Ice Cold" 133
The Monk 15, 23
"The Monkey and Basil Holderness" 21
"Monsters" 65

Monteleone, Thomas F. 92
Moonchild 139
Moon Dance 35, 125-126
Moorcock, Michael 12, 167-168
Moore, C. L. 170, 172
Moore, James A. 90
Moreau, Gustave 32
Morlan, A. R. 91
Morris Desmond 176
Morris, William 167
Morrow, James 27
"The Mortal Immortal" 69
Motherfuckers 28
"The Motion Demon" 80
"Mr. Fiddlehead" 109
"Mrs. Rinaldi's Angel" 16
Muddock, Joyce 119
Mudford, William 120, 122
"The Mummy's Foot" 70
Murray, Will 99
Musäus, Johann 67, 164
"The Mysterious Compact" 121
"Narrow Valley" 171
Nathan, Robert 166
Necrofile 12
"Necromancy in Naat" 100-101
Necronomicon Press 12, 20, 99-102
Nevermore 84-88
Newman, Kim 12, 54-56, 98, 127-131
New Order 28
The New York Review of Science Fiction 12-13
Nietzsche, Friedrich 26, 29, 161
"A Night at the Bell Inn" 120
"A Night in a Haunted House" 120
The Night Mayor 54-56
The Night of the Living Dead 36
Night Relics 113-117
A Night with Mephistopheles 118-123
"A Night with Mephistopheles" 120
Niven, Larry 152
Noctuary 15
Norton 145
Norton, Andre 168
The Norton Book of Science Fiction 145-158
Nosferatu 97
"The Nostalgia for Desire" 65
"Nothing in the Rules" 170
Oh What a Lovely War 130
Olympia Press 32, 44
Omni 149
"One of Cleopatra's Nights" 32

"On the Nightmare" 122
"The Onyx Ring" 120
"Operation Afreet" 171
...*Or Not To Be: A Collection of Suicide Notes* 33-34
Orridge, Genesis P. 64-65
O'Sullivan, Vincent 21
"The Other Side" 25
"Our Fair City" 170
Our Vampires, Ourselves 95-98
Out of Space and Time 99
Out on Blue Six 144
Outside the Human Aquarium 100
Owen, Wilfred 77
Paglia, Camille 96-97
Pan 31
The Panic Hand 107-110
Paper Grail, The 113
Pardoe, Rosemary 118
The Passion of New Eve 49-51
Pathétique 23
Pearson, Jim 71
"Pelts" 133
Penguin 29
Perdido Street Station 176-180
"The Perfect Form" 90
Perrault, Charles 164-165, 170
Peter, Michael Paul 64
"Peter Schlemihl" 70
Philbin, Mike 64
The Physics of Immortality 161-162
Playback 42, 44
"Pleasure Domes" 90
Poe, Edgar Allan 35-36, 66, 69-70, 86-87, 99, 121, 125, 130, 165
Pohl, Frederik 155-156
Polidori, John 31, 34, 36, 67-68
The Polish Jew 70
Pollio 123, 127
Pollock, Walter Herries 122
"Postgraduate" 108
Potter, J. K. 158
"The Power of the Mandarin" 132
Powers, Tim 31, 98, 113
Pratchett, Terry 168
Prayer Cushions of the Flesh 32-33
"Predator" 90
Priest, Christopher 9-10
Princeton University Press 36
Pringle, David 12
Proby, P. J. 28
Przybyszewski, Stanislaus 17
Ptacek, Kathryn 90

Pupillo, Massimo 129
"A Quarter Past You" 108
Rachilde 16, 18
Raism 63-64
Random House 110
"Rath Krespel" 121
Red Hedz 64
Red Stains 63-66
Reed, Kit 152
Reed, Jeremy 66
Reed, Robert 162
Reed, Tony 64-65
"Reign of Blood" 90
Rice, Anne 19, 23, 30, 102-107
Rice, Elmer 37-39
Richard, Cliff 130
Richtofen, Manfred von 128
Rickman, Phil 60-62
"The Ring of Memory" 159
Rising Star: Dandyism, Gender and Performance in the Fin-de-Siècle 36
Ritter, Thelma 54
Riverside 34
Robinson, Edward G. 54
Roc 18
Rochester, Earl of 30
"Rockabilly" 133
Rohmer, Sax 132
Rossetti, Dante Gabriel 32
Runyon, Damon 86
Russell, Eric Frank 94
Rymer, James Malcolm 96
Saberhagen, Fred 30
Sabrina 44
Sacrament 102-107
Sade, Marquis de 15, 18, 23, 64, 66
"The Sadness of Detail" 108
Salah, Pat 90
Sallee, Wayne Allen 92
Salmonson, Jessica Amanda 91-92
"The Sandman" 129
The Saragossa Manuscript 125
Sassoon, Siegfried 77
Satan 18-19
Satanskin 63-65
Satan Wants Me 138-141
"Saturnin Sektor" 80-81
Savoy 28
The Savoy Hitler Youth Band 28
Savoy Records 28
Savoy Wars 28
Scenting Hallowed Blood 25

Scheherazade 127
"Schrödinger's Plague" 157
Schulze, Friedrich 67
The Science Fiction and Fantasy Writers of America 166
Science Fiction Chronicle 34
Science Fiction for People Who Hate Science Fiction 154
Scott, Jody 17
Screem 11
Screen 44-46
"Sea Gulls" 133
"The Sea Was Wet as Wet Could Be" 134
Sellers, Terrence 65
Servant of the Bones 102-107
"The Seven Geases" 100-101
Shaw, Bob 147
The She-Devils 32
Sheffield, Charles 162
Shelley, Percy Bysshe 27, 35, 67, 123
Shelley, Mary 67-69, 71
Shepard, Lucius 171
Signet Books 20
The Silence of the Lambs 66
"The Silken Swift" 172
Silverberg, Robert 164, 166, 171
Simak, Clifford D. 172-173
Simmons, Dan 72-79
Simon & Schuster 47, 54
Simplicissimus 57
Sinister Barrier 94
The Sisters of Mercy 24
Sladek, John 152
"Slasher" 134
Slaves of the Death Spiders 12
Sleeping in Flame 107
"Sleeping with Teeth Women" 75
Sloane, William 110
"A Slow Red Whisper of Sand" 89, 92
"The Small Assassin" 170
Smeds, Dave 90
"Smiling Eyes and Haunted Face" 90
Smith, Clark Ashton 20-21, 65, 99-102, 167, 172
Smith, Thorne 166, 171
Soft and Others 131
Somtow, S. P. 34-36, 123-127
Sopor Aeternus and the Ensemble of Shadows 24
La Sorcière 124
Sorley, Charles 77
"Soulmates" 91
Spanky 18
Speculation 9-10
Spencer, John 119

Spider 111
"The Spirit Barber" 67
"A Spirit in a Raspberry" 70
Springer, Nancy 18
Springsteen, Bruce 28
Stalking Tender Prey 20, 25
St. Clair, Margaret 171
Stenbock, Count Stanislaus Eric 24-25
Sterling, John 120, 122, 165
The St. James Guide to Horror, Ghost and Gothic Writers 118
St. Martin's Press 93, 107, 135
Stockton, Frank R. 165
Stoker, Bram 15, 23, 26, 29, 31, 97
"The Storm" 67
Storr, Catherine 81
"Strabismus" 80-81
Strange Angels 82-84
Straparola, Gianfrancesco 69
The Stress of Her Regard 31
Studies in Death 25
Studies in the Psychology of Sex 23
Sturgeon, Theodore 172
Supernatural Stories 119
Supping with Panthers 26, 30
Swamp Fetus 16
Swann, Thomas Burnett 173
Swanwick, Michael 173-175
The Sword of Shannara 167, 175
Symonds, Arthur 25
"Szamota's Mistress" 80
"A Tale of the Gravedigger" 80
Tales of the Dead: The Ghost Stories of the Villa Deodati 67-69
Tales of Zothique 20-21, 99-102
Tan, Cecilia 88-92
Tarchetti, I. U. 69-71
Tartarus Press 118, 122
A Taste of Blood Wine 21
Taylor, Elizabeth 44
Tchaikovsky, Pyotr Ilyich 23
Teach Yourself Books 34
The Temple Press 64-65
"Tenants" 133
"The Tenth Toe" 132-133
Tessier, Thomas 135-138
"The Testament of Athammaus" 101
"That Hell-Bound Train" 171
"Them Bleaks" 132
"There Shall Be No Darkness" 170
The 37th Mandala 93-95
Tiberius, Roman Emperor 123
Tibet, David 25

Tieck, Ludwig 164
Time and Again 47
The Time Machine 111
Tipler, Frank 161-162
Tiptree, James Jr. 149, 169
"Tlön, Uqbar, Orbis Tertius" 170
"Tobias Guarnerius" 121
Tolkien, J. R. R. 167, 175
Tomorrow and Tomorrow 162
Tonto 95-96, 98
"Topsy" 133
Tor Books 110, 123, 131
"Tourniquet" 65
To Walk the Night 110
"Tower of Babylon" 171
Tower of Fear 51-53
Towing Jehovah 27
Trakl, George 17
"Traps" 134
Trois filles et sa mère 32
"Trouble with Water" 170
"The True Story of a Vampire" 25
"The Tsalal" 16
Turgenev, Ivan 165
Twilight Zone 65
"Ubbo-Sathla" 100
"Uh-Oh City" 108-109
"Unicorn Variations" 173
Universe 149
University of Chicago Press 95
Unknown 166-167
Upton, Smyth 96
Utterson, Sarah 67
"The Vampire" 17
Vampire Junction 125
The Vampire Lestat 106
The Vampires of Alfama 30, 97
Vampyr 97
The Vampyre (Holland) 26, 30-31
The Vampyre (Polidori) 67-68
Vance, Jack 171-172
Vathek 33, 164
Vector 10
"The Vengeance of the Elementals" 80-81
Venuti, Laurence 69, 71
Verga, Giovanni 69
"Verschoyle's House" 21
Vice Versa 40
Victoria, Queen 128
"Viol d'Amor" 25
Voice of our Shadow 107

Voltaire 33, 164
"The Voyage of King Euvoran" 100
A Voyage to Purilia 37-39
Wagner, Richard 73, 76, 79
Walpole, Horace 24, 33
Walton, Evangeline 167
"The Wandering Train" 80
"Wanting" 90
Ward Lock 70
"The Warlord of Saturn's Moons" 153
Warner 72
Warrington, Freda 21, 25, 29-30
Watts, G. F. 77-78
Weis, Margaret 168
The Wellesley Index to Victorian Periodicals 120, 122
The Well of Saint Clare 18
Wells, H. G. 93, 110-111
West, A. G. 77
Weston, Jessie 113
Weston, Peter 9
Wheatley, Dennis 140
"A Wheel in the Desert, the Moon on Some Swings" 107, 109
The White Goddess 124
Whitman, Walt 35, 125
Wilde, Oscar 21, 23-24, 28, 36, 97, 121, 161-162
"Will" 21
Williams, Conrad 135-138
Williamson, Aaron 65
Willis, Danielle 92
Wilson, David Niall 90
Wilson, F. Paul 131-134
Wilson, Gahan 131-134
Windling, Terri 132
"The Winter Flies" 148, 156
Winter Tides 113-117
Wodehouse, P. G. 39-42
Wolfe, Gene 92, 171
"The Women Men Don't See" 149
The Woodrow Wilson Dime 47
Writing Fantasy and Science Fiction 34
Writing Horror and the Body 102-107
Wuthering Heights 50
Xanadu 12
"Xeethra" 101
Yarbro, Chelsea Quinn 128
Yates, Frances 58
"Yesterday's Witch" 134
Yolen, Jane 168
Zelazny, Roger 173
Zeus 31

ABOUT THE AUTHOR

BRIAN STABLEFORD was born in Yorkshire in 1948. He taught at the University of Reading for several years, but is now a full-time writer. He has written many science fiction and fantasy novels, including: *The Empire of Fear, The Werewolves of London, Year Zero, The Curse of the Coral Bride*, and *The Stones of Camelot*. Collections of his short stories include: *Sexual Chemistry: Sardonic Tales of the Genetic Revolution, Designer Genes: Tales of the Biotech Revolution*, and *Sheena and Other Gothic Tales*. He has written numerous nonfiction books, including *Scientific Romance in Britain, 1890-1950, Glorious Perversity: The Decline and Fall of Literary Decadence*, and *Science Fact and Science Fiction: An Encyclopedia*. He has contributed hundreds of biographical and critical entries to reference books, including both editions of *The Encyclopedia of Science Fiction* and several editions of the library guide, *Anatomy of Wonder*. He has also translated numerous novels from the French language, including several by the feuilletonist Paul Féval.

Lightning Source UK Ltd.
Milton Keynes UK
05 August 2010

157977UK00001B/33/P